"Matthew Soule has written a terrific cutting edge book. If you care about health and happiness and developing your potential in ANY aspect of life, start reading!"

Brother John N Beall
Martial Artist, Author, Inventor, Musician

"In Fight Freeze Fast F^ck Breathe, Mastering the Stress Response, Matt Soule has articulated a set of exercises and approaches for positively disrupting chronic stress. His approach is centered on the conscious use of primal stressors - like conflict, cold, hunger, sex - stresses that our bodies and minds have been genetically prepared to recognize. Practicing even a couple of his stress tools has already created a big positive impact on my mental and physical health: better sleep, better decision making under stress, a stronger defense against what had been pretty regular bouts of depression. Most important, I feel I have concrete strategies for tackling stress in my life in whatever form it may take, now and in the future - and that's powerful stuff indeed."

Alex MacLeod
Carpenter, Grappler, Outdoor Adventurer

"Profound, cutting-edge ... Matt Soule is a modern day Magellan who sets out to explore the depths of what the human body is capable of doing. Always pushing the boundaries of what is possible. His self-discovery and documentation of mastering the stress response puts into context the personal experience and the science behind expanding comfort zones and stress coping mechanisms. He walks the talk and after reading this book he has me convinced that I NEED to master the stress response. Must read if you are a high altitude alpinist."

Brad LaMar
Mountaineer, Nature Photographer

"This book captures in clear and powerful detail the critical elements to harness our human potential. Each of us is capable of living lives filled with happiness, love, personal success, and meaning; we're hard wired for it. Mastering the stress response as explained in *Fight, Fast, Freeze, Fuck, Breathe* is the gateway to the full expression of ourselves."

Jake Levine
Entrepreneur, Engineer, Artist, Father

Fight | Freeze | Fast | F^ck | Breathe

FIGHT | FREEZE | FAST |F^CK | BREATHE

Mastering the Stress Response

MATT SOULE

⌘

DARK WELL MEDIA

Seattle

DISCLAIMERS

This book is for informational purposes only and is not intended to diagnose, treat, cure, or prevent any condition or disease. You understand that this book is not intended as a substitute for consultation with a licensed practitioner. Further, the publisher and the author strongly recommend that you consult with your physician before beginning any exercise program. You should be in good physical condition and be able to participate in the exercise. The author is not a licensed healthcare provider and represents that he has no expertise in diagnosing, examining, or treating medical conditions of any kind, or in determining the effect of any specific exercise on a medical condition.The use of this book implies your acceptance of this disclaimer. Additionally, the publisher and the author make no guarantees concerning the level of success you may experience by following the advice and strategies contained in this book. You accept the risk that results will differ for each individual. The testimonials and examples provided in this book show exceptional results, which may not apply to the average reader, and are not intended to represent or guarantee that you will achieve the same or similar results. The publisher and the author advise you to take full responsibility for your safety and know your limits. Before practicing the skills described in this book, be sure that your equipment is well maintained and do not take risks beyond your level of experience, aptitude, training, and comfort level.

The views and opinions expressed herein are those of the author and do not seek to represent the Wim Hof Method or Innerfire organization in any official capacity. For direct resources on the Wim Hof Method, please visit wimhofmethod.com.

Printed in the United States of America
First Printing, 2021
ISBN 978-1-7362969-0-5

Dark Well Media | Seattle,WA

The following are registered trademarks used in this book:
Tsun Jo®, TrainingMask 2.0®, Vibram®, LEGO®, Tonka®, Black Hole®, Ford®, Brain Research through Advancing Innovative Neurotechnologies®, Volkswagen®

Dedicated to
the great teachers of my life
who have challenged me
to think differently.

TABLE OF CONTENTS

BOOK I
KILIQUEST TO DISCOVER BREATH
1

BOOK II
WHAT IS THE STRESS RESPONSE
AND WHY DO WE WANT TO MASTER IT?
51

BOOK III
SURVIVAL STRESS TOOLS: THE TRAINING GUIDE
137

FOREWORD

IN THE FIFTH century B.C.E., in ancient Greece, Hippocrates, the father of medicine, based his therapeutic approach on the healing power of nature. According to his doctrine, the body contains a natural way, an intrinsic power, to heal and take care of itself. In essence, Hippocratic therapy focused on facilitating this natural process through rest, proper diet, fresh air, and cleansing of the body: very simple treatments that gave the body time to identify the problem, activate the immune system, and do what was necessary to repair it, all in the midst of a favorable environment.

In order for a human to regain stability, one must be capable of adaptation, have adequate nutrition, and exhibit patience. The rewards are health, cellular memory, and learned knowledge. We are complex entities; we need to learn how to listen to ourselves in order to treat illnesses better. Hippocrates's insight, that it "Is far more important to know what person the disease has than what disease the person has," contains great wisdom.

More than two millennia later, at the beginning of the twentieth century C.E., Hans Selye, the "father of stress research," was conducting studies focusing on the signs and symptoms observable in animals used for endocrinology research when he observed significant changes in his subjects. The wide variety of reactions initially led him to describe these changes as the "nonspecific response of the body to any demand." Through additional studies and observations, such responses eventually became known as Selye's syndrome, or "general adaptation syndrome."

Dr. Selye presented the stress response as occurring in three phases: the alarm reaction, the stage of resistance, and finally exhaustion, culminating in death. When a person is exposed to a stressor—such as a real or perceived threat, extreme temperature changes, a physical injury, or even trying to get the best tan—he or she is going to seek balance, or homeostasis, by adapting to that stressor. However, if a person resists or is incapable of change, making balance an impossibility, sooner or later, that person will move to stage three. Stress is a choreographed series of events, not a mere psychological term, and all individuals are subject to the effects of these events.

In this work, the author uses both personal experiences and in-depth research to explain phenomena in a way that is simple yet true to the importance of the subject.

In a quest to master the stress response, the reader will discover the anatomy, physiology, and purpose of five survival stress tools, marshalling exercises to generate readiness, understanding, and commitment along the way. This work is definitely an art in self-knowledge. Being able to apply what you will learn can help you develop a stronger, healthier, more adaptive lifestyle. A life without stressors may be easier than one with them, but the fact is that adverse conditions and stressors will never completely disappear. However, our understanding of their function and how we perceive them can change, making this new life easier.

There is no doubt that the human being is a restless creature and is always looking for more knowledge. We make efforts to know the depths of the sea, we invest years and resources in creating new technologies, we want to go to places never seen before.

We want more understanding and within each of us is a universe ready to be explored. Though I say this in a romantic way, the fact is that the early twenty-first century is proving to be a great time for neurosciences around the world. Our exploration of the human mind is proving to be one of the longest, most challenging, and most beautiful trips ever attempted by our species. And though we still do not have everything resolved, current initiatives such as The Brain Research through Advancing Innovative Neurotechnologies® (BRAIN) aim to promote neurosciences to develop a better understanding of how the brain works on all levels. But you don't need to be a neuroscientist to want to know more about what drives, motivates, and excites us as humans; this book addresses precisely such questions.

The path of this knowledge is no doubt long, but we have come a great distance from Hippocrates' theory of the four humours. Today, not only do we know that the brain communicates through synapses using neurotransmitters, we have named them, we know what they do and we have even found a way to influence them.

"Men ought to know that from the brain, and from the brain only, arise our pleasures, joys, laughter and jests, as well as our sorrows, pains, griefs and tears, through it, in particular we think, see, hear, and distinguish the ugly from the beautiful, the bad from the good, the pleasant from the unpleasant, in some cases using custom as a test, in others perceiving them from their utility. It is the same thing which makes us mad or delirious, inspires us with dread or fear, whether by night or by day, brings sleeplessness, and acts that are contrary to habit." - Hippocrates

Dr. Ariadna Uriarte, MD
Neuropsychologist, Sexologist

INTRODUCTION

Dear Reader,

Thank you for picking up a copy of this book. If you've read my bio and the blurb on the back of this book, you may be wondering what are survival stress tools and why would I want to use them? This brief introduction will help answer those questions and hopefully, prompt you to read and understand the rest of this book. The information herein will let you understand and implement your ability to not only handle life's stressors, but to thrive amidst them. So let's get to it…

What are survival stress tools?

These are specific, high-threshold training tools that tap into the deepest parts of our survival instincts and offer the fastest means of adapting to confront the widest variety of stressors we experience as modern humans. These specific tools work well because **we are evolutionarily wired for such tools.** The underlying mechanisms have been developed and refined over the course of our history as a species. As such, survival stress tools offer unique access to the deepest and oldest parts of our brains and bodies that guide and dictate so much of our behavior, especially as we confront stress in our lives. Training that specifically taps into our evolutionary makeup has the potential to help us not only recalibrate our stress, but to combat all types of stress. By training at the highest threshold of stress we experience, we can redefine our base stress levels to vastly improve our relationship to the increasingly wide range of stressors we face.

What are the unique aspects of the five survival stress tools?

Each survival stress tool offers a wide range of physical, mental, and emotional benefits, when trained and applied correctly.

When properly trained, **Fight** (meaning specific martial arts training) is a relational acute stress tool that lets us develop an incredible array of both gross and refined motor skills. It helps us discern the difference between competition and cooperation and trains us to identify both situations better. This tool improves creativity, as well as the speed and quality of the decision-making process. It is unique in helping us practice when and how to fight while confronting fears around personal safety and the security of those we care about. This tool taps into and helps us overcome fear of conflict, fear of pain or injury, fear of helplessness, fear of harm to both self and others, and fear of death. Fight teaches us critical facets of adaptability and how to find peace in chaos.

When appropriately trained, **Freeze** (meaning specific temperature training) is an environmental acute stress tool that vastly improves our cardiovascular and immune systems. It also directly supports cellular repair and recovery. Mentally and emotionally, it allows us to practice full acceptance of the things we cannot change, thereby contributing greatly to significant emotional resolution. Freeze can help us confront known difficulties—, such as loss, grief, past or current traumas, depression, or feelings of being overwhelmed by life circumstances—but it can also help us tap into our fear of the unknown—such as anxieties and death. This tool lets us learn to reinterpret physical and emotional pain, adapt, and find acceptance.

When we train with **Fast** (meaning to go without food for specific time periods) in the correct manner, it becomes an environmental acute stress tool that physically helps us optimize our bodies through hormone and gene expression, improves our senses, and contributes to our longevity. We also confront the stress of scarcity and learn to overcome the fear of having to go without. This not only helps us confront the fear of death, it lets us better discern between want and need while simultaneously engendering gratitude for abundance and simplicity alike. Fast can also help to mitigate economic anxieties by teaching us how to adapt and do more with less.

Training with **Fuck** (meaning sex, sexual eroticism, and intimacy) appropriately allows us to use it as a relational acute stress tool that improves immune function, strengthens us physically, and refines coordination. It improves cooperation and communication between individuals, and it helps us confront the fears of loneliness, inadequacy, acceptance, and death and legacy. It can help us learn patience, come to terms with emotional vulnerability, and learn to trust and accept ourselves and others. This tool can help us understand the value of expressing our authentic selves, learn to nurture and harness desire and passion, and cultivate and discern what we really want.

The **Breathe** tool, when used correctly, is a stress tool modulator that allows us to purposefully induce acute stress for health benefits and harness it for improved performance. At the same time, this tool can improve immune function, optimize hormones, develop and refine nervous system messaging, strengthen respiratory operation and cardiovascular health, improve blood flow, clear metabolic waste, and vastly improve recovery times for everything from injury to fatigue. Mentally and psychologically, it helps to confront fear of death, resolve traumas, improve focus, and heighten potential. Breath is the physical, mental, and emotional rudder that steers the nervous system for peak human performance.

Independently, each of the five survival stress tools—Fight, Freeze, Fast, Fuck, and Breathe—offers unique benefits to the practitioner who intentionally engages in them for health and well-being. However, when combined, or stacked, the sum of the parts is far greater than the individual components. The result is a synergistic effect that promotes the fastest degree of adaptability and fosters comfort, peace, and resilience in a challenging world. Together, these tools can help us confidently and securely face the unknown with calm, resolve, and determination.

Can survival stress tools effectively deal with chronic stress? It seems they would more likely lead to burnout. How can I better understand the counterintuitive nature of using high-threshold acute stress tools to combat chronic stress?

In the simplest terms, chronic stress is the enemy while acute stress, or stress that is short in duration, is the ally. Survival stress tools, when trained under a short-term stress model, redefines what is possible and increases our fitness to handle any situation.

Today, the average human's nervous system often exists in a chronically elevated stress state, one that it is difficult or even impossible to de-escalate using lower-threshold exercises and activities. When we train through a lens of survival, it forces us to confront some of the highest possible degrees of stress. By modulating tumultuous activities with periods of calm, our ability to handle stressors—up to and including those at the threshold of survival—is vastly improved. Through careful preparation, we can train in a way that optimizes risk without getting burned out, injured, or worse. The key to mastering stress lies within not only the survival stress tools, but also in how we use them to improve our relationship to stress.

If I gave you a toolkit to maximize your ability to thrive in any situation, but you didn't know how to use the tools in that kit, it would be useless. Therefore, an instruction manual is also necessary, one that discusses each tool, when to switch from one to another, and the training needed to develop the tools for optimal functioning.

Creating and understanding the toolkit starts with a deeper understanding of ourselves; we must learn how to elicit various responses from our nervous systems under the variety of conditions that we may encounter. With such an ability, implementing and practicing useful tactics becomes possible. Making smarter decisions with open eyes becomes feasible. Understanding and implementing proactive—rather than reactive—steps becomes actionable. And over time, with proper practice, it all becomes effortless.

In modern society, we are under near-constant stress punctuated by moments of extremity that often turn out to be debilitating for the unprepared. Human biology contributes to this response. For example, when released, the neurochemical norepinephrine reroutes blood flow to prepare us for particular types of actions. In sufficient but reasonable doses, it is helpful for action-oriented behavior, memory, attention, focus, and learning. But in chronically high doses, it strips us of our ability to reason and recover. Spending too long in a high-action state makes us reactive and prevents rest, recovery, and effective immune function. Furthermore, the amygdala, which is involved in mediating emotion and memory, increases its activity to support perceived external demands. . As the amygdala rapidly fires, and as the body prioritizes increased norepinephrine, blood flow is increasingly restricted from the reasoning part of the brain: the neocortex.

We may ask, why would Mother Nature set it up that way? The simple answer is that not all operations of the human body can be prioritized at once. When we exist in an action state, we need norepinephrine and other neurochemicals to do their important work. The problem is, there must be balance. Humans are incredibly complex organisms: the most sophisticated beings of which we are currently aware. Furthermore, from an evolutionary perspective, modern life has come upon our species very suddenly. We have changed our world too fast for many aspects of our evolution to keep pace. And perhaps more importantly, how we generally live is not helping to speed up our adaptation to this new world.

Life is and always has been a narrow window of existence. To recognize this precarious state that we, and all other life as we know it, confront daily is simply to describe reality in direct terms. Therefore, where to focus our efforts in order to maximize this existence, both in duration and in experience, is of primary concern. Yet, we often find ourselves at odds with our own nature.

All life attempts to defy death only to succumb to its inescapable grip, and instinctually, we know that. No wonder our survival brain and its emotional circuitry tries to hijack our actions in an attempt to ward off death. But as self-aware entities, we know it will not work.

So, take a deep breath. Let it go. You have more control than you realize. Not over death, but over your reactions and experiences leading up to it. We must learn to harness our nervous system, mediate and integrate our emotional state, and approach the problems facing us with qualitative skills.

We must unleash our warrior spirits to ensure life's quality, not just to endure life's survival.

Stress is the number one thing we must learn to manage if we are to have better outcomes, improved decisions, and optimized health *regardless of our individual starting profiles*. When it comes to any of the above, there are many environmental and genetic factors that can play a role. But if we desire improvement, we must start with *managing* the stress response. If we wish to maximize ourselves in this world, we must strive to *master* the stress response. To do so will allow us to harness the best of what our individual bodies and brains can be and express. We must train our nervous systems to have an hormetic response to stress under a variety of high-threshold conditions. We must strive to eliminate chronic stress, which impairs our decision-making abilities, progressively degrades our systems leading to anxiety, depression, and other mental and emotional disorders, eventually devastates the immune system, and spurs wasteful panic and paralysis.

To master the stress response is to have a profound impact on our physiology, survivability, and ability to thrive now and in the future, whatever may come.

How to read this book

This book is divided into three large main parts: Book I, Book II and Book III. Book I describes my story of discovery as I sought answers to questions on breathing fundamentals under the high-stress conditions of a rapid ascent into high altitude. My experiences provided answers to those questions and informed a complex personal landscape of training preparation, goal setting, and adaptability.

Book II delves into what the stress response is, what mastery is, and why it is important—especially in relation to mastering the stress response. I discuss what makes humans unique and how we can intentionally tailor our choices to lead to unknown heights of potential. This section contains some concrete concepts, as well as some insights into the complicated language often used to describe our complex brains and bodies. It also explores some of the philosophical underpinnings of why I have chosen survival stress tools and the training modalities surrounding them; this topic includes a very brief but deep dive into the concept of consciousness. For some of us, a discussion around consciousness may be initially hard to digest. If you decide that reading this section is too much, I encourage you to move on to Book III and begin your training. Then, once you have some experience with these survival stress tools, periodically return to Book II and the discussion around consciousness will continue to become much clearer.

Book III is a guide to using specific tools, applications, and regimens to master the stress response. Fight, Freeze, Fast, Fuck, and Breathe offer unique access to the deepest parts of ourselves; moreover, they do so at a speed found nowhere else without unnecessarily increasing the risk curve. In a world of ever-increasing demands, optimized risk training that provides both depth and speed is essential for success.

In all three books, as well as throughout the many subsections contained in each, I offer as much personal story as I do technical knowledge. My goal as a teacher is to present the broader principles anchored by stories, anecdotes, experts, and cited resources. Through this combination, the complex information herein will become clearer and actionable in your life.

In many ways, you could read Book I, Book II, and Book III in any order. So, if you find yourself needing or wanting to skip around, please do so.

I hope reading this book has as much impact on your life as writing it has changed and improved my own.

With gratitude,
Matt

BOOK I

KILIQUEST TO DISCOVER BREATH

I N LATE JANUARY 2019, less than four weeks before a team of twelve members was scheduled to arrive in Tanzania from destinations all over the world, I made the decision that I would join them as lucky number thirteen. The goal, an unacclimatized forty-eight-hour ascent of Mt. Kilimanjaro, has become a formidable, ambitious standard in an international organization to which I belong: the Wim Hof Method (WHM). Wim Hof, creator of the method, set a world record of forty-eight hours back in 2014 with the largest group ever to ascend Kilimanjaro.

The forty-eight-hour ascent of Mt. Kilimanjaro is emerging as one of the most desirable challenges of the rapidly growing WHM community, and for good reason. Kilimanjaro is not a technical climb; you don't need ropes, harnesses and crampons. Yet, it is not a feat to be attempted without proper caution. You may not need the skills required to ascend a mountain like Denali or Everest, but you must be able to handle the physical stress of climbing 19,341 ft. Moreover, you need the ability to adapt to an environment that produces potentially deadly challenges to life's basic necessities, among them eating, sleeping and breathing.

At the apex of Mt. Kilimanjaro, there is 50 percent less oxygen available than there is at sea level. The forty-eight-hour challenge combines the physical stress of climbing more than 19,000 feet with the pressures of reduced oxygen and severely reduced time to adapt: not a combination to be taken lightly. WHM, a tool that touts fast adaptation and increased energy production, is put to the test by such a challenge. This is what makes it attractive.

My reluctance to commit to the team at an earlier date was not a matter of interest but of competing time demands. I had spent the previous year touring with Wim Hof throughout the United States and Canada, conducting events with hundreds of people. And the previous fall, I had begun teaching for the WHM Academy, training the incoming instructors from both North and South America as well as Australia. These commitments, as well as being a full-time single father and the head of a sizable martial arts school, made it difficult to commit to flying to the opposite side of the world even for only eight days.

Such a challenge was deeply alluring in its own right. More important though, and what ultimately decided me to commit to the trip, was my desire to perform a series of experiments. A growing number of questions had been emerging from my trials with WHM and various other breathing methods from around the world. I had been exploring a variety of applications inspired by protocols from the WHM, everything from sports performance and recovery to self-defense to sex and intimacy. Noticing where certain breathing protocols worked best, where they could be augmented, or where they impaired optimal functionality was revealing deeper fundamentals and how they impacted the nervous system. This discovery had prompted continued experimentation with breathing variations and integrating them with principles from martial arts and other stress-response tools already in my repertoire. I was getting consistent results, and it was like finding a skeleton key that could open innumerable doors: the potential was huge. However, I still had a few outstanding questions that were either unanswered or unclear:

Under what exact conditions should I be trying to breathe slowly and / or lightly?

What is the true story behind nasal and mouth breathing? Where and how do each excel and under what conditions?

Is nasal breathing superior most of the time? Or, what is the optimal balance between nasal and mouth breathing?

Could I mostly focus on mouth breathing and still mediate my fight or flight response? Or would that approach impair functionality under imposed high stress?

Does rapid breathing undermine performance capability?

How important are rhythm and mindset to controlling tension under high stress?

To what extent could I control blood and muscle oxygenation utilizing various muscular contractions and vocalizations while primarily using mouth breathing?

Does rapid breathing really reduce or cut off oxygen distribution to the tissues?

What is the true story behind nasal and mouth breathing? Where and how would each excel and under what conditions?

How fast could I, a man of forty-plus years, recover from completing this feat?

How successful would my lifestyle approach of combining multiple stress-response tools be in completing a high-stress event for which I had little specific preparation? Would my principle-based approach prepare me for any high stress endeavor, extreme altitude climbing included?

Many of these underlying questions had also arisen in the larger breathing community. Various breathing methods made different claims in the areas of health, wellness, and performance, and the information just was not adding up.

I had performed a number of high-threshold tests, but I was at a point where I needed a final test—one that would use specific equipment to yield data. A rapid ascent of Mt. Kilimanjaro with instruments to measure different types of oxygen levels would ideally round out the experiments I had been working on. So on January 24, 2019, I committed. I bought my plane ticket and the equipment needed, confirmed my reservation with the guide company, and let the team know that I was in.

When I first told people I was going to climb Kilimanjaro, their reaction was typically one of two responses. The first was along the lines of, "Wow, you are bold. That is crazy. I could never do that," while the second response was, "My uncle/grandmother/friend/ whole family did that." Both reactions seemed extreme, and neither did much to help me mentally prepare for the challenge I was going to undertake.

It is true that the vast majority of climbing routes on Mt. Kilimanjaro are nontechnical. However, the mountain's sheer size and height create difficulties and clear dangers, altitude being the foremost. To emphasize, the WHM challenge is to climb to the 19,341-ft summit in fewer than forty-eight hours *and without prior acclimatization.* To put a few things into perspective, let's look at the statistics.

According to figures published by Kilimanjaro National Park, approximately 35,000 people attempt the summit each year. Success rates₁ are as follows:

- For climbers who take eight or more days to ascend and descend, the success rate is about 85 percent.

- For climbers on seven-day routes, the success rate drops to 64 percent.

- For climbers on six-day routes, the success rate continues its downward trend to 44 percent.

- Finally, for climbers on five-day routes (meaning they typically climb for approximately four days and descent for one to two), the success rate is only 27 percent.

And one more statistic: Estimated deaths per year are between three and seven.

Deaths? On a nontechnical mountain? Yes. The deaths result from both high-altitude pulmonary edema (HAPE) and high-altitude cerebral (HACE) mountain sickness, as well as falls and hypothermia.

What the stats reveal is that it is all about time on the mountain: giving the body time to properly adapt to the reduced density of available oxygen in the environment. Having more days for the body to make more red blood cells leads to better oxygen carrying, capture, and delivery. Plus, depending on genetics, more efficient oxygen use may begin to take place. But time was one thing we would not be giving ourselves. At forty-eight hours, our goal was at least 33 to 50 percent faster than the fastest climbs.

If conversations got this far, people in the relative know would ask about athletes like Killian Jornet and Karl Egloff, who did the climb in a handful of hours. However, there are two important facts to remember about such individuals: One, both these men and others who attempt the individual world record for fastest ascent of Mt. Kilimanjaro live or spend significant time at high altitude; and two, they train on Kilimanjaro for several days to acclimatize before attempting the record.

These facts do not to lessen their extraordinary feats, nor negate their elite physical natures. Rather, they simply illustrate that the challenges are fundamentally different in nature, and indeed, should not be compared to each other. The key thing to understand is that at the fundamental level, everybody needs time to adapt to high altitude. What my team and I were trying to determine was, could we substantially shorten the typical adaptation time to yield high-level results?

To adapt to high altitude, the body produces more red blood cells that can carry oxygen, a process that usually takes several days. By attempting to bypass this time factor, we would be asking our bodies to adapt at a much faster pace. Additionally, a faster summit would mean using more oxygen, because of the extra muscle strain and reduced time for recovery. This was to be a tremendously taxing load on the body and taking the challenge very seriously was in order.

The Team

It took me a while to get my head wrapped around all of this and really understand the challenge. When I was finally able to articulate it clearly to others, friends and family often asked, "Is

Wim going?" In other words, would we be guided by a strong experienced leader? When a group has a strong leader, he or she can help them find and bring forth the best inside themselves. Over the years, Wim has led a number of groups on challenges similar to the forty-eight-hour Mt. Kilimanjaro climb, helping them to drastically reduce ascent times. It is as if he, as a leader, can crack a shell, giving individuals access to a secret power they didn't know they had.

However, as I explained to my friends, Wim would not be going. This was an independently planned endeavor, admittedly with strangers from around the world who I had never met and only communicated with briefly through online chats. On the surface, this admittedly sounded a little crazy. No formal organization was behind this thing and the risks were high: not necessarily a recipe for a guaranteed outcome.

I learned later—and by later I mean when I showed up in Africa—that most of the team members already knew each other. They had bonded deeply on a shared trip to Poland where, by happenstance, they had gotten shacked together at Wim's cabin at the annual Poland Experience, during which students train in WHM.

Each year, the Poland Experience has grown in popularity. Scott Carney, author of *What Doesn't Kill Us*, also participated in this experience in 2014 to prepare for his own Mt. Kilimanjaro excursion with Wim and company. At that time, only twenty individuals were in attendance. By the time my future team members attended their Poland Experience in 2018, attendance had ballooned to eighty per week. The local hotel was completely full, and Wim's cabin was the only other available space.

The two Rauls—Raul R. and Raul H. —both from Florida, Marcin from Poland, Sergio from Italy, Steven from Spain, Pi from New York, Bart from the Netherlands, Raphael from Germany, and Josef from Thailand were among the team members who first met in Poland. Their connectedness had by no means been guaranteed. Virtually all were from different countries and had different backgrounds, though most were entrepreneurs, managers, or CEOs. All were highly independent, and most were leaders among leaders: not exactly the type of people likely to bond with each other, yet bond they did.

In truth, their resumés and personality portraits are rather intimidating. Pi is deeply analytic. As a business leader managing a global team for a Fortune 100 company, he is a critical thinker and sharp decision maker. He has a background in nuclear physics and has authored two technical books on the subject. Raul R. is a successful entrepreneur, father of five children, loving husband, police officer, and volunteer SWAT team member. Raul H. is a highly talented pharmaceutical sales rep and founder of his own consulting firm. In addition, he is a father of two, devoted family man, and excellent spear fisherman. Jozef, by contrast, is more of a rebel. Blunt, ostentatious and a bold risk taker, he is an entrepreneur and a jokester. Bart is a professional break dancer, instructor, and choreographer. He is also an entrepreneur who runs an arts education facility. Rafael (Rafa) is a former professional athlete and current businessman. A naturally strong leader and organizer, he is also incredibly bright and direct. Steven, a startup collaborator, is another talented leader. He is also analytical, compassionate, and a devoted family man. Sergio is an easygoing world traveler, a happy and carefree man who approaches the world like a playground. He is quick to laugh and smile. Marcin meanwhile works in international finance. He is extremely well read, insightful, and a quiet observer most of the time.

This motley of men had endured challenges, told jokes, and laughed together, but they also recognized a strong kinship that they shared but could not fully explain. Significant connections at WHM retreats are not uncommon, but the bonds these guys had forged were of a unique nature.

The team members who had not been part of the Poland group were Dustin; his partner, Natalie; Mark; and me. Dustin and Natalie were from the San Francisco area, where Dustin was a WHM Instructor. He had been tapped early on because the group felt like it would be a good idea to have an instructor along to help inform the training. He ended up playing a pivotal role in the pre-climb leadership and instruction. Natalie was quiet but very determined for reasons she didn't share. Mark was on a quest to reaffirm his strength in the world. He had battled hard against personal demons and having triumphed, he was hungry to set and accomplish goals.

In the late summer of 2018, Sergio contacted me. He introduced himself as a fellow Hofer (having done the Poland Experience in 2017) who would be passing through Seattle on his way to Vancouver, BC, and he asked if he could drop in on a local WHM workshop I would be holding. I told him sure, it would be nice to meet him. He didn't end up making it to Seattle, but our brief digital interaction led to him pitching to the existing group that I be included in their plans to do a rapid ascent of Mt. Kilimanjaro.

When the members formed the WhatsApp group that would serve as the primary communication tool, they added me. One of the members, Steven, really advocated on my behalf, urging the group to keep me on even though I couldn't initially commit in full. Being on the group chat gave me a window to observe the types of personalities that were taking part.

At first, watching the chats, I was totally unsure if I wanted to join these people. When one of the group organizers, Steven, asked us to send him money to hold our reservations, it briefly crossed my mind that this was some kind of scam. It also occurred to me that they might not be entirely serious about the climb. The jokes and pictures of flexed biceps posted to the group seemed out of place. Again, I thought we were all strangers to each other more or less. Anyone who has ever tried to land a joke over a group text to strangers and fallen flat should be able to relate to my confusion. But over the course of a few months, watching and reading the WhatsApp group chat, I got a better sense of the members.

The group also formed a shared Trello board, where I got to see the many preparation details each member had contributed. It was really through this medium that I could see they were serious and organized. Finally, in late January 2019 just a little more than a month before the scheduled departure, I simply took the risk and said yes.

My final commitment caused a stir within the group. Steven, for reasons still unclear to me, continued to advocate on my behalf, for which I am grateful. I then had to make sure that I had all the equipment needed, both to actually climb the mountain and to perform my experiments.

I went through the suggested list of trekking poles, water bottles, drinking tablets, rain gear and the like. I made a short list of what I didn't have already and ordered it. That left the outstanding equipment I would need for my tests, which would primarily involve two different blood oximeters. The first was a standard model most of us have worn during any doctor visit; partially encloses your finger to read oxygen in the blood, also known as SpO2. The other oximeter was a new device on the market called a Humon Hex (HH). Dustin had made arrangements for team members who were interested to purchase one of these devices. I ordered mine right away. Rather than reading blood oxygen, the HH reads oxygen saturation in muscle tissue: a very important distinction to get to the bottom of my questions.

The HH was developed out of research that started at M.I.T. (Massachusetts Institute of Technology). It is touted as the first clinically validated muscle oxygen tracker. Tested through Harvard Medical School, it has demonstrated 96 percent accuracy compared to the gold Standard ISS metaOX. Using a light spectroscopy along the near-infrared spectrum, the HH captures color variation in the tissue to determine oxygen saturation in the muscle tissue, or SmO2. It tracks muscle oxygen usage in real time uploading the data to the app on your phone as you use the device. Two other helpful features of the HH are its ability to read a lactate threshold, which is useful in measuring workload intensity of the muscle, and infer V02 max, which is the maximum rate of oxygen consumption during high-intensity exercise.

The HH and the standard blood oximeter would prove highly informative as I carried out various experiments both on and off the mountain. The information each of these devices would yield was part of the data necessary to clarify many of the questions growing more and more prevalent in the breathing community. Starting from the beginning of the route, I began to experiment with utilizing breath techniques to determine how breathing different ways affected blood and muscle oxygen saturation as we ascended in elevation. Next, I had to orient myself around the challenge I was about to take on. The first thing I did after committing to the trip was meditate, playing over what was known, what was unknown, what was significant, and what gaps should be filled in. I was knowledgeable about performance. I was aware of how important training and preparation are when attempting anything difficult, especially for the first time. And I knew that I had never been to such a high elevation. Furthermore, the mountains in my region that don't require a guide or technical mountaineering skills are generally lower than 10,000 ft, so I wouldn't have an opportunity to practice going to moderately high altitudes, never mind extreme altitudes. Moreover, this was to be an unacclimatized attempt, so any alternative travel or training arrangements were out. I had to rely on what was available in my gym and surrounding area while I continued to work full-time and take care of my daughter.

Replaying past instances of success and failure in my head, almost all had been predictable from the extent of my preparations. This makes sense, of course. Nothing is certain, but if you want to succeed, the better prepared you are, the more likely it is you will achieve the desired outcome. There were perhaps a few things I could do, but mostly I would be relying on my lifestyle approach of stacking several tools together, what I have come to call survival stress tools. This would serve as my methodology for this high stress endeavor. Using this knowledge as the foundation, I strategically laid out the rest of my training and preparation.

People often view a challenge as impossible until someone does it; then, that accomplishment simply sets the new standard. The most obvious and often-cited example is the one-mile race. For years, breaking a four-minute mile was deemed impossible; no one seemed capable of doing it. Then in 1954, Roger Bannister ran one mile in 3:59.4. The flood gates opened and new possibilities inundated the human consciousness. Ten years later, male high school athletes began to join the ranks of those capable of a sub-four minute mile. Today, it is the standard for all professional middle-distance runners. The current record stands at 3:43.13, nearly seventeen seconds less than the four-minute mark.

There is little doubt that improved running techniques have aided many of these men in achieving what was once thought to be impossible. Consider Roger Banister for a moment. He was a medical student, studying neurology, who had minimal training in running. What separated him were two facts: One, his mindset was fully committed through extreme resolve and determination, and two, his training methods were modern and superior. Indeed, he had been influenced by two of the most progressive and best running coaches of the day, Franz Stampfl and Arthur Lydiard, the latter of who is regarded by many as the best running coach of all time.

Banister adopted the advanced techniques championed by these coaches in the development of his running. He used interval training, periodization, and hill running, all of which developed his capacity and gave him confidence that he could do what nobody else had done. Races in 1952 and 1953 gave him a glimpse that the barrier to be broken, as runners managed times as little as 4:02. And then, on May 6, 1954, Roger Banister broke the record at 3:59.4. He retired from running later that year.[1]

The advanced methods developed by Lydiard and Stampfl were Bannister's toolkit. With such a toolkit, it becomes feasible to shrink the time needed to train while still progressing to the point of success. This is the true value of a high-quality method.

While on the actual climb, I would be relying on WHM to complete the Kilimanjaro challenge. Wim's proven track record of high-altitude climbing and my extensive experience utilizing this method gave me confidence in its efficacy. By using certain protocols, practitioners of WHM are able to exert a greater degree of control over their bodies. The principles that underlie WHM can be summarized as using stress tools to harness the nervous system for improved health, well-being, and performance. Furthermore, the method has a demonstrated ability to adapt the body rapidly to high altitude.

However, there was still the question that confronts anyone who sets themselves a challenge of this magnitude. The basic query that drives many of us to take on challenges or to avoid truly investigating life's possibilities: Could I actually do it?

How many of us let things get in the way of our goals? How many of us have made excuses, allowing the subtle increase of resistance to prevent accomplishment? How many of us convince ourselves that we simply can't take the risk? Perhaps we have a deep desire, but all too often, we never take the actionable steps to realize the outcome. We suffer because of it.

There is little escape from suffering in this world. Choosing to accept suffering, to turn it into fuel, not only makes it tolerable, it expands your comfort zone far beyond what luxuries could ever manage to do.

When I searched inside myself, I found uncertainty and a gnawing feeling of unease. When I later asked the other team members, many of them admitted to the same feelings. But the thirteen of us who finally committed to the climb were willing to accept the suffering required to answer the question that burned in each one of us: *Could we do it?*

There is something very real—as well as exciting and terrifying—about orienting one's life around a truly difficult goal. You know that you will, in all likelihood, have to push yourself to your limits, and that if you succumb to hesitation or make a misstep, it may mean failure. Figuring out a goal that is difficult enough to fulfill this requirement, yet not so difficult as to be impossible, is a tricky business. To flirt with the line of what is possible is exhilarating, fulfilling, and thus extremely rewarding—especially when the stakes are high. This creates some of the magic of a forty-eight-hour unacclimatized climb using breathing protocols, grit, and determination amidst strong acceptance of suffering.

We had to make special arrangements in order to make this attempt. Forty-eight hours is *significantly less* than the minimum ascent time typically allowed by climbing expedition companies for Mt. Kilimanjaro. Some of the top companies refuse to offer a five-day option at all, because of the low success rate and increased dangers posed by reduced time to acclimate. Every company I have come across that so much as mentions a five-day option strongly recommends six days minimum to allow for acclimatization. Well prepared, yet unacclimatized, we knew this challenge would be formidable, but we also knew it was possible.

With just weeks to go, I ordered the final pieces of equipment I would need, scheduled my vaccines, and bought a plane ticket for my mother to come up to Seattle and care for my daughter while I was away. When I got those details set, I turned my focus to my training. What could I do in the weeks before departure to efficiently prepare me to best the extent possible?

In the end, I only did four things: I used a restrictive training mask, I was very disciplined with my diet and fasting routines, I did extra rounds of breathing and cold protocols of WHM—both for prep and recovery on every training session I did—and I scheduled two challenging hikes in the mountains.

The Mask

EPO is protein that signals the human body to produce more red blood cells for better oxygen-carrying capacity. Research at the University of Wisconsin has demonstrated that the elevation TrainingMask 2.0, which I used, doesn't likely trigger the body to produce EPO in high quantities. However, the mask did seem to improve the subjects' respiratory muscle strength. Since I knew that the Mt. Kilimanjaro challenge would require various breathing WHM protocols for high altitude, I used this mask extensively in my training sessions. I needed my diaphragm and auxiliary respiratory muscles to be as strong as possible. So for six to seven days of every week leading up to departure, I wore the mask in various settings.

I wore the mask during the fifteen-minute high intensity bag work that accompanies virtually every martial arts class I teach. I got plenty of double takes from my students, not to mention comments that I looked "like the villain, Bane, from *The Dark Knight Rises*." We all had a good laugh.

I wore the mask while hiking nine miles in the mountains in shorts on a winter day carrying a load of about 20 lbs on my back. A storm hit that day, and cotton ball-sized snowflakes littering the air made the experience feel magical. My goal was to hike to a mountaintop lake in a beautiful area in the North Cascades of Washington, and take a dip in the frigid water at the end of the trail. When I got to the top, the lake was frozen solid; I hadn't brought an axe, so I turned around and headed back down. On the return trip, only about a mile from the trailhead, I found a waterfall and pool just right for my training purposes. The water, which must have been right around freezing temperature, soothed my aching muscles and sent a jolt of energy into my body, making me feel rejuvenated. I went back to training the next day, recovered and ready for more.

I tried to wear the mask anywhere I reasonably could. The exception to my mask training was the second hike, which took place on a trail called Mailbox Peak. It is called that because the top of the trail boasts an actual mailbox from which you can send letters. The panoramic views at the top of the hike are breathtaking; as you rotate, you see the city of Seattle, a swath of the Cascade Mountains, Glacier Peak, and the 14,411-ft Mt. Rainier stratovolcano peak rising from its base at near sea level. But I didn't choose this particular hike because of the stunning views—I chose the nearly 9.5-mile loop because of its rapid ascent difficulty. The highest point of Mailbox Peak is only 4,822 ft, but it gains 4,000 feet of elevation and fast. The tight switchbacks on the climb require deep lunge steps to gain footing on tree roots and two-foot-high steps. It is a steep and brutal hike.

I wore my hiking boots that day. I love those boots. They have Vibram soles and excellent support. The only drawback is that they are a bit heavy. I left the training mask at home because that day's hike was about speed, and I wanted to make sure I could at least try to keep up with my hiking partner, Dustin for that day.

Dustin is a world-class competitive ultra-marathoner. When I told him that I would be climbing Kilimanjaro, he suggested that I do this Mailbox Peak as a prep. I took his advice and he agreed to come with me. As we set that day, I noticed that he was wearing trail shoes, even though it was winter and there was significant snow and ice on the trail. He had brought a set of mini-spikes, called clats, that could be attached to his shoes easily in case he needed extra traction. He looked at my boots. "Heavy, huh?" I nodded but told him I liked the grip and support. We pressed on and summited the trail in about two hours. I smiled when I saw the funny-looking mailbox at the top.

We took in the view, snapped a few pictures, and jogged down the long way. My heavy boots made it challenging. Dustin had no trouble with the snow and ice we encountered. I was surprised, so I asked him about his shoes. He raved about them. "They're called Speedgoats. If I were you, I would order a pair for Kili." I ordered a pair as soon as I got home that day.

The rest of the month, I wore the restrictive mask in all of my martial arts training sessions and maintained consistent practice of WHM. For diet, I continued with my typical routine, which primarily consisted of time-restricted eating inside of roughly six hours and consuming high-protein, low-carb foods with quality fats during the times I did eat. I did one twenty-four-hour fast in the three weeks leading up to the Kilimanjaro climb. Fasts can be a useful survival stress tool, since they induce hormetic stress and clean out the body, making it more efficient.

It was nearly time to leave and I was still waiting for equipment that I had ordered to arrive. My HH oximeter finally arrived on February 21, with just one week to spare. I immediately unpackaged it, put on my new Speedgoats, and headed for the small gym on the ground floor of my condo complex. I hooked up the HH to my body and selected the threshold test feature. I ran for forty-three minutes before I had to stop the test early to go pick up my daughter. That six-mile run on the treadmill was my last difficult training session before departure.

I had the right equipment, the right shoes, and a clear idea of the experiments I wanted to conduct. Prepared as I felt though, not all challenges can be accounted for in advance.

Moshi Town

It is an accumulated twenty-one hours of flight time to get from my home of Seattle to Moshi Town of Tanzania, Africa: five hours to JFK in New York, another twelve-and-a-half hours to DOH in Qatar, and six-and-a-half hours to JRO Kilimanjaro airport. On March 1, 2019, I landed at 3:40 p.m. local Tanzanian time, the equivalent of 4:40 a.m. in Seattle. After landing, it was still an hour's drive to Moshi Town.

The trip is enough to give you jet lag for a week. The time zone shift is effectively eleven hours, making your biological clock do close to a one-eighty. To say this disrupts your circadian rhythm is an understatement. Fortunately, breathing protocols and cold training allowed me to combat the problem. While not a formally studied mechanism as of this writing, certain breathing techniques likely engage a part of the brain called the suprachiasmatic nucleus located in the hypothalamus, which is the primary governor of circadian rhythm. So using my personal routines helped me rapidly get rid of my jet lag, and I was *very* grateful. We only had one day for the entire team to be together before we would depart for Kilimanjaro National Park. I was the last one to arrive in Africa, and I needed to be focused, not jet lagged.

When I showed up at our hotel, only a few of the group were there; most spent the day on a local tour. But the plan was for us all to meet early the next morning for a group session. I decided to rest as much as I could that evening.

The following morning, March 2, we were up at seven o'clock local time. We gathered in a common area on the hotel grounds, to which the innkeepers allowed us sole access for roughly an hour. They seemed to be highly intrigued by our mission of a rapid ascent. They treated us a little like you might treat a crazy person you give deference to simply because you can't relate to what they are saying or doing.

Inspired by Wim Hof, this group of individuals from all over the world was now at a little hotel in Moshi Town, armed with determination but not without nerves. Since I hardly knew anything about any of these people, I was eager to bond as much as we could in the short time we had together.

When I had originally purchased my ticket back in January, I had planned to arrive on March 2. However, this had caused some backlash within the group. Due to my late commitment, I had missed out on the decision that March 2 would be a mandatory group training day. My arrival on the mandatory training day was unacceptable. After some heated discussions, I scrambled and managed to rebook my ticket for one day earlier. All had been resolved, but there was residual tension. Now that we were finally sitting together for the first time, it was important to be able to break the proverbial ice and address any leftover resentments or reservations before we tackled the climb.

One thing I would learn to value about this group was the level of honesty and straightforwardness that they all possessed. They were of a unique breed: strong, compassionate, direct, and intense. They were vocal but not unforgiving.

There is a type of conscious breathing, a protocol that we use in WHM that can be an extremely powerful tool for group bonding. It is also highly useful to fend off jetlag and reset your body's proper balance. A common name for it is power breathing.

Lying in a circle, we did a power breathing session together, connecting deeply to ourselves while allowing the exercise to serve as a bonding mechanism to create group cohesion. The session immediately sent all participants into a deep, connected trance. We lay there, connecting as a single unit.

When we finished, we were at once open, trusting, forthright, honest, and unflinching with each other. We sat in a circle to briefly outline why we were there. Rafa, the team member from Germany, gave me a sharp look. He had unfinished business he wanted to share. With full directness, he asked why it had taken me so long to commit to the team. An outside observer might have noted a tinge of hostility in his manner. For him, to ensure both group cohesion and individual safety, it was important that every individual have the same level of commitment. We would all be relying on one another. He needed a clear answer to make certain that no one person was going to compromise another's safety, well-being, or ability to accomplish the goal.

So I gave my reasons as clearly as I could. I assured the group that I was indeed ready to climb. And just like that, Rafa and I got past that initial confrontation. The group said they understood where I was coming from. The barriers, there moments before, came down quickly thanks to Rafa's directness.

One of the beautiful aspects of conscious breathing, and of WHM, is that it primes your brain to connect to yourself and others. It removes the blocks that we find so often in life when trying to communicate with one another. Accessing the right words in a clear, thoughtful manner becomes possible. Emotions are both present and in check.

The dialogue that morning was open. We were able to converse with open hearts without sacrificing our strong natural personalities (which virtually everyone on the trip had). Each of these people was strong and passionate. The vast majority possessed intelligence across a wide spectrum: emotionally, logically, physically, and conversationally. As I said before—this group was of a unique breed.

Dustin, for his part, had gotten Wim to record a speech, which he played for us on speaker. We all left the breathing session closer and inspired. Steven had made arrangements with the hotel staff to have ice delivered for cold training later that afternoon. This was to be the final training exercise of the day. Gathering in Mark's room, we stripped to our underwear—a few opted for swimsuits—and took turns in the ice bath for two-minute rounds. Each of us was able to get the reset we needed, and we even managed not to use all the ice. Rejuvenated and jet lag free, we laughed with pleasure in the hot African sun. We were prepared to take on the next step of the process. In fewer than twelve hours, it would be time to depart for the base of the park entrance.

The morning of March 3, our first climbing day, I was up at four thirty. I gathered all my gear and took it to the front office on my way to the on-site cafe. The buffet that awaited us was extensive. Typically, I eat a great deal of protein, fast regularly, and limit my carb intake. That morning though, I piled food on my plate: thin pancakes topped with dollops of peanut butter, an omelet with local Tanzanian chilies, roasted mushrooms, potatoes, veggies slathered in butter, several cups of avocado juice, and coffee. I ate close to three thousand calories and felt ready for the day.

We got our gear loaded into the truck, grinning at one another. Our team was accompanied by four guides and six porters, all of who would be instrumental in our climb. Our lead guide called for a quick picture before we headed out. We smiled in the dim morning light. Time to go.

We had to leave early that morning due to a local race that was taking place throughout Moshi Town. There were to be roadblocks prioritizing runners. In the early morning light, we mostly made our way down roads of red dirt; thin black asphalt covered the busier of them, their edges unhewn. We drove past shanties and local businesses that could have been open or abandoned—it was hard to tell.

After twisting through the backstreets, we finally emerged into more rural surroundings. Banana trees the size of upright Volkswagen buses littered every plot of land. Green foliage of varying densities haphazardly covered the terrain, as if a landscaper's work had been undone during the night. The warm, red earth, rich with nutrients, was unable to be constrained in any real fashion. After an hour, the white glacier cap of the mountain's peak became visible. A chill of excitement filled the truck. We were close.

The facilities near the park entrance consist of no more than a medium-sized parking lot, two sets of stairs up to the registration office, a covered area with a few park benches, bathrooms, and a gift shop. We checked in and grabbed our lunches, which had been prepared by the porters. We all did a final equipment check.

I strapped the HH oximeter around my leg to read my quadricep oxygen saturation. Walking past the park rules sign, I smiled as I read rule six: *Allow plenty of time for the body to acclimatize by ascending slowly.*

At an elevation of about 5,300 ft, the trail began with low-density, jungle-like foliage lining both sides of the dirt path, which was sparsely patterned with stones. As I filmed our entry on my phone, I tripped while relaying the morning's affairs. Raul H. re-enacted my fumble to general laughter, myself included. All of us were in good spirits.

At 8:40 a.m., we officially entered the park and commenced the Marangu Route.

Experimentalism

First Experiment

At rest, saturated oxygen levels in the blood (again, referred to as SpO2) tend to be at 95 percent or higher in healthy people. Oxygen saturation in the thigh muscle tissues (SmO2) is quite a bit lower, commonly around 50 to 70 percent at rest. This is important so that the directional flows of oxygen and carbon dioxide are maintained. Oxygen moves from the higher-concentration environment in the blood to the lower-concentration environment in the tissues. Conversely, carbon dioxide, which is at a relatively higher concentration in the tissues, moves to the blood.

As you begin to exercise, oxygen is pulled from the atmosphere into the lungs, and from the lungs it is transferred to the blood. Once in the blood, it travels through the vascular system to be distributed to the muscle tissues, as well as the many other vital organs and tissues throughout the body. Initially, as your metabolic activity increases and blood circulation quickens, oxygen levels in the blood temporarily decrease, as the oxygen is rapidly pulled out of the faster-moving blood to feed the tissues that need it. Respiration increases as a result, helping to replenish the oxygen in the blood until things stabilize. Once stabilized, blood oxygen levels will increase back to 95 percent or more, even as muscle tissues oxygen levels increase to 75 to 80 percent. This situation holds until the activity output exceeds your ability to replenish the oxygen used, at which point you hit your threshold.

At the start of the route, I checked in to get a reading of my SpO2 and SmO2: blood oxygen 92 percent, muscle tissue oxygen 59 percent. My heart rate was steady at between 113 and 118 beats per minute.

Within the first twenty minutes I started to do my first experiment. Readings on the HH showed my muscles were warming up: SmO2 had risen to 68 percent while SpO2 was holding steady in the low- to mid-90s. While walking, I tried using my mouth to breathe, adding a slight restriction of air with my tongue placement. If I pulled in deep breaths back-to-back, about ten or so, the HH reading would spike to 75 percent in muscle tissue oxygen saturation. Simultaneously, my blood oxygen simultaneously rose steadily to the high 90s.

Bart Test 1

One of my team members, Bart, also had an HH and a standard blood oximeter. When I had talked to him about what I planned to do on the climb, he had been eager to participate as well. I asked him to perform different experiments while I filmed him. He started with normal breathing, as I had on the initial part of the climb. When I asked him to show me the readings, his SmO2 was 69 percent and his SpO2 was 91 percent—both very similar to mine. His next assignment was to do a breath hold while walking on a gentle uphill grade, then to try to reload the oxygen saturation using slow nasal inhales.

He exhaled through his nose, then held his breath while he continued walking. The reading on his HH began to drop rapidly and steadily: 68, 64, 63—down to 61 percent in just thirty-four seconds. Then, using just his nose, he began taking breaths to replenish the oxygen. Slowly, the saturation increased in his muscles. SpO2 kept dropping all the way to 75 percent as SmO2 slowly rose. After ten nasal breaths over the course of thirty-three seconds, his SpO2 was 75 percent and his SmO2 was 65 percent.

Then he switched his breathing style, rapidly pulling strong inhalations through the mouth (slight restriction of air by the tongue) while continuing to walk. Within thirty seconds he had readings of 96 percent SpO2 and 71 percent SmO2: a marked change from the nasal inhales.

As we climbed, the greenery began to change slightly, the montane forest vegetation giving way to denser jungle; the red earth path cutting its way through the foliage continued to mark our route. After three hours of climbing, we arrived at Mandara Hut at an elevation of almost 9,000 ft.

Mandara Hut offers overnight cabin stays, a lunch hall, and bathroom amenities, but our ascent plan did not afford us the opportunity to remain there for long. We stopped briefly to regroup, took a short rest, and grabbed a bite to eat.

The group had split, a few members trailing some distance behind. We ate our lunch by a sign that announced the distance to each station along the route. Horombo Hut, our destination for the day, was still another seven miles ahead.

While waiting for the last of our party to join us, we took pictures of our shirtless selves in silly poses to pass the time. After forty-five minutes, the others caught up. While they ate their own lunches, Bart spotted two white-tailed monkeys in the trees, so we watched them for a quarter hour. After that, hydrated and fed, we were all eager to hit the trail once more.

As we re-entered the thick green trees, Pi remarked, "We look like Vikings from the future." He had a point. Gators covered our legs and wrapped our shoes. Bare skin peeked out between the tops of the gators and our shorts. Our bare chests were exposed to the forest air. We did indeed look like ancient warriors in futuristic clothes.

On this second leg of our journey, the environs changed rather suddenly. In a matter of 400 feet of elevation, we transitioned from montane forest to moorland composed of rolling hills, grey-green grasses, sages, and small deciduous trees. The landscape was now visible for thousands of feet all around us. Elephant-grey clouds hung in the air like a thick sheet of skin covering the sky. I looked at my SpO2: steady at 91%.

Bart Test 2

Bart's blood oxygen, however, was down in the 80s, and his muscle oxygen had dropped to 64 percent, so we decided to do another round of the breath-hold walk. He exhaled nasally then held his breath for as long as he could climbing the gradual slope. Within twenty-eight seconds, his muscle oxygen had dropped dramatically to 56 percent. This time however, upon breathing regularly again to restore the oxygen, he used only his mouth. Within ten seconds, his muscle oxygen had jumped back to 60 percent; within thirty seconds, it was back up to 64 percent. After one minute of breathing through his mouth as he walked, Bart's muscle saturation was 68 percent and his blood oxygen was 91 percent.

We walked on, looking at the tans and grey-greens that made up our surroundings. At just over 10,100 ft, the nine of us who had pulled ahead, including two of our guides, stopped to do some quick altitude mountain sickness (AMS) testing. This involves a brief survey to gauge declined motor capability, headaches, or other issues that are common symptoms of AMS. By the time most of the trailing members had caught up with us, we were ready to continue. Everyone had passed the AMS testing without issue.

The gray sky that had been following us suddenly turned dark, and the wind began to blow harder. Within thirty minutes, the first raindrops began to come down. This initially caused us to don our rain jackets. The human body, even in shorts and at altitude, can often handle and still conserve heat in snowy conditions. Rain on the other hand, especially cold rain, saps heat and energy quickly. After just a few minutes, however, our initial vigilance subsided and our light raincoats came off. We felt good, and we were generating sufficient heat energy to manage easily. By 11,000 feet the rain was forming puddles on the trail, and our pace had slowed considerably.

Just before four o'clock, the team gathered in a circle to perform a breathing protocol for the mountain. This involved relatively quick but deep breaths followed by an inhale hold, while using the skeletal muscles to create pressurized contractions that would assist in rapidly adapting to altitude. To get the breaths in, I used a combination of the nose and mouth, with heavy emphasis on the mouth to ensure a greater volume of air at a faster speed. As I performed my breathing exercises, I intentionally focused on mentally mediating the neurally induced tension that can occur even at altitude. Using the mind to assist the body in moderating the action state of the nervous system is one key factor that helps prevent becoming light headed when increasing breath speed and volume. Feeling good, we continued.

Thirty minutes later, at 11,500 ft, we stopped to do altitude adaptive breathing. Weeks later, reviewing video from that day, I remembered the clarity I had at that point. With minimal effort, we had all been able to get our saturated blood oxygen levels into the high 90s. The muscle tissues also got a boost anytime we engaged in our breathing protocols. Deep breathing, managing speed, and carefully timed contractions while moderating the emotional/neural action state allowed for rapid reoxygenation of the blood *and* tissues. What's more, thanks to my consistent practice, performing this combination in real time was proving to be effortless.

By a quarter after five, my body glowed pink from cold thermogenesis: heat production induced by the cold. Shirtless against the elements, which at this point included declining temperatures, a howling wind, and light rain, we finally neared the day's break point: Horombo Hut, elevation 12,276 ft.

In that final push to Horombo, I started to sing softly, playing with the breathing rhythm. I added humming and vibrational noise to ease tension in my nose, mouth, and throat. A study published in the *American Journal of Respiratory and Critical Care Medicine* in 2002 showed that simply humming could increase nitric oxide production by as much as fifteen fold, compared to quiet exhalation.[2] As this gentle aid facilitated increased nitric oxide production and, with it, oxygen delivery to my system, I felt my sinuses open wider and my heart beat more easily. A restful ease settled on my consciousness like a comforting blanket while I walked unflinchingly forward, delighting in my steps. A final check of SpO2 and SmO2 at the hut came in 90 and 63 percent, respectively.

It would be at Horombo Hut—which is actually a series of small structures—that we would spend the night, rest, and take some hours to adapt. Our responsibilities were not over for the evening, however. It was important that we remain cautious, aware of our blood oxygen levels lest they begin to slip. Anything below 90 percent blood saturation would be deemed unacceptable and require active breath protocols to facilitate a return to proper balance.

I greeted the team members who had preceded me to the hut: both Rauls, Marcin, Pi, Mark, Rafa, Steven, Sergio, and two of our guides. We talked jovially for a few minutes, waiting in the wind to see who might be coming along the path. Some trailed in over the course of the next hour; others took more than three hours to arrive.

Cold set in. It was time to get clothed and shepherd ourselves into shelter. The weight of the day came down hard and fast.

Horombo's wood-slatted huts have green tin roofs, making them look like playhouses forged from giant LEGO blocks and Tonkatruck metal. Each is equipped with six bunk beds, so half a dozen of us piled into one playhouse and the remaining members split into two more units. Our plan was to depart between five and six o'clock the next morning. We needed to eat to refuel, plus we would be waking up at midnight to do another breathing protocol to help us adapt to the altitude.

In challenging situations, it is easy to lose track of plans made earlier, before emotional ties had been taxed by an exhausted body and mind. As we sat at dinner, discussing the need to interrupt our sleep to check oxygen levels and do group breathing, dissent began to emerge. Jozef no longer wanted to take part. Brief flashes of hostility breached the air as everyone else became quite vocal about the need for all to partake in the prophylactic breathing, as originally agreed. It was not the time to make alternate plans simply because someone no longer felt like doing the required mid-climb maintenance that was a hallmark of Wim's past success. It is a scientific fact that oxygen saturation levels drop during sleep. Combatting this phenomenon requires extra precautions; hence, our agreement to wake at midnight to breathe. Withdrawing would be tantamount to putting the group at added—and unnecessary—risk. We could not afford to lose team members or have someone hold the group back because they had failed to take all the necessary steps.

We had no formal leadership. That choice was intentional at the outset, but now it appeared to be questionable. It was up to each individual to bring to bear his or her best self, to follow through on the agreements. As one member, Steven, put it, what we were doing was very risky, and the least we could do was to take measures to control the risk. The debate was still ongoing when I opted to try to go to sleep.

Sleeping that night turned out to be less of an option than we had anticipated. Sleep is one of the most important performance and recovery tools known. Neuroscientist and sleep specialist Matthew Walker, PhD describes at length the necessity of it in his book, *Why We Sleep*, with regard to high-level motor function. Despite sleep's importance, as you ascend to higher altitudes, it becomes more and more difficult whether you like it or not. In order to sleep, it is important for the nervous system to transition from a sympathetic action state to the required parasympathetic rest state. At higher altitudes, this transition can be interfered with as the body tries to figure out how to prioritize survival. The heart rate remains elevated and the brain triggers faster breathing, all to maintain sufficient oxygen delivery. This alert, action-oriented state discourages the needed slumber.

As we attempted sleep, many of us faced low-level bouts of nausea and headaches, early signs of a drift toward AMS. In order to combat this, breathing deeply became more necessary. After just a couple hours of rest and possibly some disturbed sleep—the kind that leaves you unsure if or how much you have actually slept—we all awoke in our respective cabins to raise our oxygen levels. Jozef, despite his initial resistance, joined in. Everyone was relieved.

When I checked my blood oxygen levels, I saw a reading of 79 percent. I was in deficit and needed to give my body a boost of oxygen and the means to adapt to the altitude. The slow breathing I had been using to try to encourage sleep had left my body starved for the oxygen it needed. We did several rounds of WHM altitude protocols over a fifteen-minute period. At the end of it, I was up to 97 percent, and the others had similar results. Lying down once more, I finally drifted to sleep. Although my rest that night fell was far short of what most would consider sufficient, my body still got the small respite it needed.

To Sing is to Delight the Gods

Our original plan to depart at six in the morning was severely delayed. I woke at five, but by seven, it was clear that our team wasn't ready to depart; the guides and porters with us had not yet roused and packed, and the cook was still making breakfast. Clearly, the timeline we had set was quite foreign to everyone's typical habits. So we adapted and found patience as everyone organized themselves. I checked my morning oxygen levels: As of seven o'clock, I had 91 percent blood oxygen and 54 percent muscle oxygen. Not bad, I thought. The midnight protocols had really proved helpful—and I would need that help. The day would be a steep, intense push to ascend more than 7,000 feet of elevation gain into extreme altitude territory.

I headed to the mess hall to fill my body with the nutrients it was sure to need. The conversation mostly centered around the poor sleep everyone had gotten, the slight headaches and nausea starting to set in, and the breathing required to get rid of it.

Finally, near nine o'clock, everyone was ready to go. As the team watched, our guides and porters all gathered in a half-circle and began to sing and dance in the mid-morning light. Joy emanated from each of them as they harmonized, the choral layering filling the mountain air. Bart walked into the empty space and began break dancing, to everyone's delight. The singers' volume increased as we and they interjected cheers for the live art synergy that was happening.

Even with our rapidly compressing schedule, taking ten minutes for art and beauty was immeasurably worthwhile. It injected us with appreciation, gratitude, and a vast well of energy that would carry us forward that day.

It was time to breath load. We circled to do our prep protocol: breathing deeply with contracted retentions, allowing our breath to empower our bare skin. The previous night, my hips had been sore, aching from the day's ten-hour climb. Each time had I rolled over in bed, my legs had cramped, locking up, each adjustment sending painful sensations. I had not taken any pain killers: just drank water and tried to breathe through it. I managed the night, but not without worry that I would struggle to recover in time for the next day's demands. But as we progressed in our morning protocol, increasing the speed of adaptation, getting the circulatory system moving, I improved. Instead of starting the morning sluggish, fatigued, and sore, I began fresh with literally no soreness to speak of. I was surprised at this reality, but grateful. Once our morning protocol was complete, we set out, Raul R. and Marcin nearly stepping on the guides' heels in an effort to go faster. The rest of us formed a long line and focused on trying to remain steady in our steps.

In a video from around ten o'clock that morning, March 4, I can hear my laborious breath as the camera shows a rocky, grey trail with sparse vegetation. I speak into the microphone, noting that my SpO2 is 82 percent and my SmO2 is 63 percent at an elevation of 13,100 ft. Raul R. and the guide are the only characters in frame. The sky shows incoming and receding clouds, like a slowed heartbeat obeying the commands of time on its own massive scale. As the camera flips around to show me, it captures my rhythmic and lilting breathing. Although I had started the practice of humming and singing earlier on the route, it was on this second day that the rhythm expressed by song became a primary source of focus. Deep inhalations were followed by long exhales as I varied intonation.

The group split up, separating from sight despite the open moorlands. With only Pi and Bart visible behind me and Raul R. steadily in front, we pushed the pace of the guide who led us for the next couple of hours. Then, just before we entered the saddle, the five of us who were leading slowed for a few minutes to let the other team members catch up.

The saddle of Mt. Kilimanjaro is a valley where notorious winds rip sideways through the desert-like landscape. There is almost no vegetation, just tiny scrub brush surrounded by brown, red, and grey rock. The wind causes temperature fluctuations, adding to the chill already in the dry air. Together, the whole team walked strong through the valley, breaking 14,000 feet in elevation.

By a quarter past eleven (as the video I shot can attest), my lips were chapped, and my bare skin was reddened from a combination of the sun, the cursed wind, and the cold thermogenesis of my body's response to the lowered temperatures. Impressive wrinkles had formed around my eyes and on my cheeks, indicating the start of dehydration. As I recorded that video, I recounted how important it was to remain totally focused on the present. To concentrate on letting my mind become one with the wind, as if this wind were some kind of god to appease. To focus.

By the time we hit a little stopover with restrooms, not far from Kibo Hut, the windchill factor meant the temperature was below freezing. My bare hands were frozen, my brow sun-beaten. As I gave testimony of my condition to the camera to document the moment, the wind was so loud you could hardly hear the words I was saying. Nevertheless, I felt positive at that moment. As the stress on my body increased, a high-performance flow state was emerging to counteract it. My internal rhythm had formed a shell of unity composed of breath, tension, heat production, and what felt like optimal hormonal support to keep driving me forward. I checked my oxygen levels: steady at an SpO2 of 90 percent and an SmO2 of 63 percent. I smiled at the camera, Kili in the background, contriving to look like nothing more than a little mound. How deceiving 4,641 feet of elevation—all that then remained—can look from the wrong vantage point.

After waiting a few minutes at the stopover, I felt a strong urge to resume climbing. As if my nervous system could see something going awry if I were to remain there, it prodded me to get going. Listening to that inner feeling, I began walking to the trail. I noticed Raul R. talking kindly to a lady who looked out of place. She had set up a stand to, what? Sell something? Give out brochures? Try to induct passing trail climbers into a cult? Fuck if I knew. But something about it registered as not right, and I had no intention of getting caught up in a conversation. I caught Raul's R. eye briefly and told him I was heading on, thinking he would quickly follow. He didn't, a decision that would later cost him dearly. One by one, the others fell in behind me and we made our way to the next resting spot, Kibo Hut.

At 15,520 feet above sea level, Kibo Hut serves as base camp for summit attempts on the Marangu Route. We arrived and checked in. Our rest quarters were an unheated wood cabin with thin windows and no insulation. We couldn't complain though, as others had set up tents in this frozen desert area. The air was thin. Around one o'clock in the afternoon, I, along with the ten other members of the group who had arrived, got dressed in warm clothes and laid down to do some breathing. It would take a great deal of time for the remainder of our team to catch up. Our plan to meet the forty-eight-hour deadline required that we rest and acclimate until a departure time of around midnight. So for those of us already at Kibo Hut, that would mean a rest time of eleven hours.

After breath loading and restabilizing blood oxygen levels in the 90s, it was time for some lunch. At that altitude, however, hunger all but disappears, so getting needed calories is difficult. I ate what little I could and left the rest there.

As we sat at the mess hall table, Rafa, Marcin, and I started talking about the possibility of going for an earlier ascent. Although cold and windy, the weather looked otherwise stable. We felt that we had momentum. There was also an undercurrent of impatience by that point and a desire to summit as fast as possible.

After talking it over with the other team members, we realized that we were the only three who wanted to go early. Loose talk of a double summit—one with the three of us and another with the team as a whole—was thrown about as we tried to reconcile two desires: one for group unity, the other for an expedited summit attempt.

Rafa went and talked to one of the guides, Salim, who had been with Wim's group back in 2015. Salim agreed that he was ready, able, and willing to guide an early summit if we wanted. We decided to talk it over with our whole team one last time. This was an unintended and unanticipated split. We didn't want to cause a breakdown in the group dynamic.

The team members were very clear that they had no intention of going up early, but they were all highly supportive of our expedited attempt. We gathered our equipment and notified Salim. With more than 3,800 feet of elevation remaining to reach Uhuru Peak, the summit of Mt. Kilimanjaro, there was no time to waste. At two thirty in the afternoon, with little more than an hour and half of rest and recuperation at Kibo Hut, we set out on a trail that looked like a lunar surface, barren and rocky.

Signs posted in Kilimanjaro National Park along the route show estimated hours and distances to each point. The posted time between Kibo Hut and Uhuru Peak is six and a half hours to travel roughly four miles. The reason that it is estimated to take so long is a combination of the steep incline and the extreme altitude that makes everything a challenge.

I began the route softly singing and humming with each breath. The delight of song propelled me forward. I was smiling. It is wonderous how something as simple as smiling in the face of adversity can swell the human spirit. It lifts you, regardless of pain and suffering. The feeling may only last for moments, but those moments serve as stepstones along an uncertain path. They are the rocks that can save you from falling.

Just after four o'clock, at an elevation of 17,300 ft, the temperature sank and it began to snow sporadically. Sun filtered weakly through the grey clouds that were trying to dominate the afternoon sky. As we ascended, gray rock mixed more with reds and blacks, giving an impression of Mars. Fitting, I thought: Mars was also the Roman god of war. And we were certainly in the midst of battle. I performed the requisite check of my oxygen levels: SpO2 80 percent, SmO2 59 percent. My heart rate was 78 beats per minute. Like the proverbial turtle, slow and steady would win the race.

Jamaica Rocks is a section of the route just below Gilman's Point that requires deep lunge steps and the assistance of your hands to stabilize and pull yourself up. Lose focus there and injury can surely follow. To make things worse, the layout of Jamaica Rocks is misleading: The climbing feels close to ending at all times, yet the challenges keep coming. It is mental fuckery and physically draining. For us, the weather also complicated things. Clouds and snow constantly threatening to swallow us before receding at the last moment, only to do it again minutes later.

The rapidly shifting weather felt like the changing personality of the mountain. To find safe passage, I had to think of myself as one with the place. This may sound odd—and granted, it feels woo woo to recount—but never have I felt so close to inanimate objects, nor to the subtle nature of energy flow and exchange as I did that day. With every step, I expressed gratitude to the mountain as if it were listening and responding. I felt the heartbeat of the mountain in tandem with my own.

I concentrated on humming breath and vibration to relax muscle tension. I breathed evenly and vigorously as needed. Any headache, side ache, or nausea that tried to creep in was countered by my intentional increase of the depth, volume, and speed of my breath, the power of which expelled the ailment on command. My emotional/neural control of my breath was the general leading the army of my body to surpass its known limit.

At 18,300 ft, just below Gilman's Point, a decision had to be made. Sideways snow had set in, the sun was low on the horizon, offering little support, and our energy stores were vastly depleted. Without words, Marcin, Rafa, and I stopped to take ten power breaths. In sync, each of us reached into our packs and pulled out our coats. Instinctively, each knew the others' choice. We wanted to summit, which meant layers were in order. There was no hesitation, nor comment. We just did it: threw on our jackets and kept climbing.

Finally cresting the top of the seemingly never-ending Jamaica Rocks felt like victory in itself. We looked at the sign post that read

Gilman's Point, 18,600 ft, then looked beyond it at the expansive crater. To the left of the crater was the glacier shelf, a surprisingly large, white block that looked out of place as it glowed, the thick ice nurturing the edge of a wound in the mountain.

Gilman's Point only stands below Uhuru Peak by some 800 ft. The trail gradually slopes up as you walk around the crater rim, ice shelf on one side, massive hollow of brown-red dirt on the other. I felt suspended between two worlds, walking a tightrope. All I could think about was the summit. It was 5:26 p.m. We had made it there from Kibo Hut in less than three hours, an incredibly fast climb.

Mountains of Kilimanjaro's size are notorious for having their own weather patterns. Within moments, the weather can shift from one extreme to another. There is little warning, only hints that offer the opportunity to predict or adapt. The sideways snow that had dogged us through the Jamaica Rocks suddenly gave way to receding clouds and the last of the day's sun rays. We stood above the world, looking down at the thick cumulonimbus clouds that billowed like smoke, gathering energy.

As we traversed the crater rim, every few minutes I would stop to do rapid breaths, pulling deep into the bottom of my lungs. This would briefly stave off the headache and nausea that were trying to worm their way into my body. The breath was the repelling force that kept them at bay. Mouth breathing, with a slight restriction by the tongue, was my primary mode of controlling the inhale flow and ensuring sufficient volume. It had served me well up to this point, and any attempt to take breaths solely through the nose was futile anyway. These were not the circumstances to rely on nose breathing alone.

It is not uncommon for it to take more than two hours to traverse the crater rim from Gilman's Point to Uhuru Peak, which stands at a lofty 19,341 feet. Our determination and focused mindset, supported by rhythmic breathing, careful footing, and controlled speed, allowed us to move through that obstacle of extreme altitude at a swift pace. In a little more than one hour, we arrived at the final destination.

Total time from the Marangu Gate to the summit was a mere thirty-three hours and fifty-two minutes—almost 30 percent faster than the ascent we had planned. Our exhaustion at the summit is evident in the pictures. Our smiles are genuine, but they appear to be held up by invisible strings or scaffolding. We didn't have the wherewithal to take a group photo or do anything special once we arrived at the summit. We stayed up there for just over twenty minutes, emotionally elated and spent. I looked around and placed a small black rock from the summit surface in my pocket as a memento. Then, as the sun faded in the background behind the edge of the earth, we gathered our equipment and our fractured wits. It was time to descend as night closed in.

The Ghost of Night and Snow

Descending a mountain, you can often count on improving your speed. It typically takes a lot less time than the ascent. We had climbed from Kibo base camp to Uhuru Peak in roughly four hours, a substantial reduction from the approximate climbing time listed by the park. On the descent, however, Kibo was a ghost drifting in a nighttime blizzard.

The emotional shift that occurred as we started down was hard to manage. No longer were we driven by anticipation of a successful summit; rather, we were managing a previously sidelined undercurrent of fear that we may have forgotten to leave enough in our respective energy tanks to get back to Kibo. We walked heavy around the crater, passing once again the sign of congratulations at Gilman's Point. Back at Jamaica Rocks, there was no light in the sky to speak of. Clouds bringing snow had swarmed the mountain like a wraith. Our headlamps illuminated our path as best they could, just enough to keep us in sight of one another. Dizziness and fatigue were close friends, practically tangible. Each step was supported by everything we had at our disposal to maintain balance and footing: trekking poles, hands, and seated positions. A thought came across my mind: *This is how climbers die on the descent. They have forgotten a critical piece. The ascent is only halfway.*

Moments later, in the midst of the dangerous Jamaica Rocks, my headlamp went out. I yelled to Rafa and Salim to hold up. They stopped and turned, the sideways blizzard scattering the light of their headlamps as they looked back at me. I felt at once disheartened and proud. I was prepared for this issue: I had a whole package of AAA batteries in my pack. I just had to replace the batteries, an easy task. No need for me to feel put out by this inconvenience.

I set my pack down, pulled out the reserve batteries and took my headlamp off. Every move of this seemingly simple task was hard. Rafa and Salim stood close by, directing their lights to give me the maximum visibility they could. I fumbled for several minutes without success. I felt like I was in a slow-motion dream, the kind where you are impotent to overcome an oncoming force. No matter how hard you swing, punch, run, scream, you just can't win. I focused intently to keep my emotions tethered, my heart rate low, my breathing in check.

I felt in control but still couldn't muster what was needed to change the damn batteries. I couldn't even open the headlamp. Salim stepped in to give it a try. He, too, struggled for a couple minutes. Then he looked at me, took off *his* headlamp, and handed it to me. "You wear this," he said. "No," I replied. "You have to lead us. I'll walk in the dark." "You won't make it," he persisted. "*I* know the way. You shine the light for me." His insistence was clear. I reluctantly took the headlamp. Rafa and I coordinated to shine our lights in front of Salim to light his path as best we could. We ploddingly proceeded that way for an hour or more before finally emerging to encounter a snow-covered sand-and-rock slide.

I recalled this part from the trip up. It had been difficult to get sufficient traction to climb, but going down was even more challenging. Salim called out, "If you see an overhang of rock that looks like shelter, let me know. It will be on our right." We slipped down, losing our footing regularly. In thirty minutes or an hour—it was hard to judge—I looked to my right and there it was, the rock overhang. It would shield us from the snow and looked like an ideal place to rest. My legs and body were sore, tattered. My mind, which had been consciously focusing for so many hours, focusing on every breath and every step taken, would finally be able to rest. It was so close to us, fifty yards maybe. I yelled out to Salim, "There! There it is! It's right over there!" My voice sounded hoarse and hollow, fading in the blizzard wind. Salim didn't turn around. He didn't even acknowledge that he heard me. He just kept descending. I yelled a second time, "Salim!!" I gave it everything I had. He turned briefly and nodded his head. Then he just kept going. I didn't understand. Why wouldn't he stop? We could take shelter here. Yet if I was going to get down, there was no choice but to abandon that line of thought. The whys didn't matter. Salim was leading; I was following. I only had the capacity to focus on a few things at that point, and it needed to be my steps, my breath, and my intent to get off the mountain.

Sometime later, after what felt like an infinite number of steps, a light broke the darkness, illuminating the white snow from afar. A true beacon if there ever was one. *That must be Kibo*, I realized. A surge of energy pumped into me. My shaky steps became a little firmer.

Then, over the black hill at the edge of our sight, came one light, then another, then another, and still more. Little spot lights penetrating the madness, coming toward us in a broken fashion. The lights got bigger, brighter, and steadier as we each closed the distance. It was four or five guys—porters, guides—who had come to help us. They grabbed our packs, lifting those hefty burdens from our shoulders. Less than twenty-five minutes later, we stepped out of the blizzard and into the main barracks at Kibo Hut.

Elevation is Elevating

Later, when I reviewed my HH data from the day of the summit, I found record of muscle oxygen as low as 41 percent and as high as 76 percent. However, the marked altitude curiously stopped after 17,657 ft. The oximeter still recorded data for another six hours after that, but it didn't log the associated altitude, so it was unclear exactly what matched what. I don't know if this glitch was because of the temperature or because of the altitude, but whatever the cause, the device stopped working perfectly approximately 1,700 feet below the summit.

However, I had last video recorded my oxygen readings at about 17,300 ft, where my blood oxygen was 80 percent and my muscle oxygen was 59 percent. After that, taking oxygen measurements was no longer on my conscious agenda—I was having to exert too much effort just to climb and breathe.

When Marcin, Rafa, and I arrived at Kibo Hut, our team members all gathered around us, the concern on their faces only partially relieved by our presence. They still needed confirmation that we were ok. We learned that when the porters and guides had left base camp, it had been on a rescue mission to locate lost climbers: us. Fortunately, we were not so much lost as severely delayed.

Reassured that everyone was safe, our team members asked questions and cared for us, offering hot soup and water. My utter exhaustion, as well as the high sympathetic stress level my body had maintained for the past eight-plus hours, made it difficult to want to eat. I forced a little soup into my body, but that was all I could manage. I could not recall a time when I had felt so depleted. The physical, emotional, and mental toll had reached its crescendo.

It was nearing eleven o'clock at night. Some team members were trying to rest; others were trying to determine when they would start their own summit attempt. The original schedule had called for a midnight departure, but with the blizzard still venting its wrath upon the mountain, it looked dicey.

Steven, assessing the conditions, gave his opinion that they should all wait until weather conditions improved. He elaborated that since the risks they were taking were already substantial, it would be careless to start out in a near whiteout. The rest of the group agreed, some a little reluctantly, others more enthusiastically. And so they waited. Most rested; few slept. Steven kept checking the weather through the window, again and again. Every twenty to thirty minutes he would confer with the guides. They were looking for any window that presented itself.

Finally at three o'clock in the morning, their chance came. Steven called everyone to action. From our bunks, Rafa, Marcin, and I gave them support and encouragement. Weak as our voices were, our hearts were with them. They walked out strong. Any residual fatigue faded immediately as they began their ascent toward Uhuru Peak in that freezing devil's hour. We would not see them again until we met at the lower elevation of Horombo.

After the stressful ordeal we had pushed our bodies to do, recovery was in high order. However, as I lay in my bed trying to sleep, it was apparent that my body wanted to remain on guard and alert. At 15,520 ft, there was still too little oxygen to allow for a deep and restful sleep. Two separate times, my levels fell so low that I had to oxygen load using breathing protocols. Excitement still vibrated in my bones, even if I was too exhausted to show it. I had just completed an extraordinary endeavor in my life. My heart rate remained elevated, my blood pressure was high, and my stress hormones continued to pulse throughout the early morning hours, despite my need for sleep.

Clearly, appropriate measures needed to be taken so that I could make the necessary transition to sleep and recovery. So at six thirty, I spoke with Salim and told him I wanted to descend to a lower altitude to facilitate my body's shift to rest. The ten team members still on the mountain would be making a full descent to Horombo anyway, only passing through Kibo. Salim agreed. I rallied Marcin and Rafa, who both appeared to be struggling with their own downshifts.

The descent from Kibo to Horombo took little time and proved easier than I had anticipated. My daughter, a delightfully obsessed rockhound, asked only for me to bring her a rock or stone from Kilimanjaro. I checked my pocket, feeling for the small, black stone from the summit. It was there, still secure. As I walked, I found two more: a sharp-edged stone of Venetian red and a rock of burnt umber shaded with bluish specks. I smiled as I put them in my pocket, knowing they would make her happy.

I checked my HH to get a muscle oxygen reading; it was 47 percent, still low. Every step downward, however, supported my body in its efforts to recovery. The soreness and fatigue felt more and more manageable. My muscle oxygen steadily ramped up during the first thirty-five minutes of the trek down to reach 63 percent saturation, where it more or less held steady during the two-hour and twenty-two-minute descent to Horombo. A video that I shot just prior to reaching Horombo recorded an update of my progress. It shows me smiling and joking with Rafa. My heart rate—which had been 100 beats per minute since we had arrived at Kibo, even while at rest—was dropping as we descended at pace.

Once we arrived at the lower-elevation huts, which sit at around 12,250 ft, I took an inventory of my body's condition. My hips, shoulders, and knees ached, not only because of the climbing, but also because of the pack I had been carrying. Trying to balance lightweight materials with good capacity, I had elected to bring my Black Hole 25-liter pack. I love this pack but it had been the wrong choice for this situation, as it lacked the stability I needed. It did not include a hip belt, so the relatively heavy weight of it ended up resting solely on my shoulders. As I shifted from side to side on the uneven footing of the climb, my knees, hips, and lower back bore the unnecessary burden of the less secured load.

I dropped my pack in our room and felt relieved. Marcin, Rafa, and I smiled at each other. We talked about our experience: the difficulties and the highlights. We rested, walking around the hut site slowly. I took pictures of everything that caught my eye: the verdant vegetation, the hillside, a stout magpie that caught my attention, even a heart-shaped hole carved out in the dirt. I was in full hippie mode and unashamed.

The Return

Night was settling in, and finally, just before eight o'clock, our other team members began to arrive. A few of us gathered in my room, two of who had been carried down on stretchers. They recounted what they had gone through.

Raul R. was one of them. As he sat in a chair, exhausted, he explained how the extra time in the saddle talking with the random lady had cost him his focus. He had never fully caught up, which had led to his decision not to attempt the summit with me, Rafa, and Marcin, even though he had been the leader though virtually the entire climb up to that point.

Raul R. is a fierce spirit and when he got to Jamaica Rocks, he found the opportunity to show it. He told us how his heart rate had hit 237 beats per minute and his oximeter had read in the 30s. In all probability, he'd been near some sort of heart failure amidst deep hypoxia. But he did not give up. He had resolved to making it to the top. The risk of that decision was extreme, but for him, the limit was predetermined. It was who he was as a person. There was no way he was going to back down.

As Raul R. told his story, I couldn't help but think of the principle that once you get behind, it is nearly impossible to catch up. There, in the safety of Horombo, he humbly recognized his error in the saddle. It had taken everything he'd had to summit and get back to Kibo Hut. From there, the porters had put him on a stretcher and carried him down to Horombo. Fortunately, Mt. Kilimanjaro did not cost him his life.

Raul R. soon fell asleep, but I continued talking with Marcin and Rafa. We had been mulling over the timing of what we had accomplished and what we would change if we did it again. It was right around this discussion that Jozef knocked on the door. He looked to be in bad shape.

Porters had carried him down on a stretcher as well, and he described how their every step had caused brain-rattling shakes that had reverberated through his head and body. A sinus infection he'd gotten the day before summit had intensified to the point that it was contributing to serious health deterioration. Up to the summit, Jozef had managed to keep the infection at bay, focusing almost solely on grit and power breathing to assist him to the top of Uhuru Peak. Before the climb, he had told me that he wanted to do the Kilimanjaro challenge with very little preparation, using only WHM—specifically power breathing—and mental toughness. He hadn't done any exercises or prepared in any way before he came to Africa, but he is a fit guy with substantial muscle mass. Until I saw him after the summit in Horombo, he had fared remarkably well with his approach.

But the choice to not prepare had come very close to costing him his health and his life. When a storm had set in on the descent, Jozef had had to exert an unexpected amount of energy under worsening conditions with a sinus infection taking greater hold. Within an incredibly short window, he'd begun experiencing a variety of AMS symptoms, some verging on severe. A deep headache had set in and with it, significant nausea. He told me he'd begun stumbling like a drunk and his skin color had become pale. These symptoms all indicated that staying at altitude would be *extremely* dangerous. Apparently the guides had tried to intervene, but Jozef initially had refused their help. He had to walk down himself, he'd told them. He'd been escorted down the mountain by the guides, who'd kept close tabs on him all the way to Kibo Hut. There, Jozef had tried to lie down, but the guides had absolutely refused to let him remain at that elevation and rebuffed his every plea. Jozef, physically exhausted and mentally compromised, had been strapped into a medevac stretcher, and four porters had carried him down to Horombo Hut. He was very lucky that he was able to make a full recovery over the following few days.

The next morning when we awoke, we saw that everyone had returned safely. We gathered for a farewell ceremony on the mountain, starting with a cold plunge to soak our worn bodies in frigid water. Once we had eaten breakfast and gathered all of our gear, the guides and porters formed a large circle and cheered for us. They sang their lyrical poems, filling the sweet-smelling, sage-filled air with melodic voices. We thanked them sincerely for all their assistance.

Then Steven offered them a gift of learning: WHM breathing. Everyone sat in a circle and we demonstrated how and what to do. Some were focused and eager; others looked suspicious but joined in halfheartedly for the first round. By the third round of standard

WHM breathing protocol, everyone was participating vigorously. We were united, breathing on the mountain together.

As we set out on the trail that day, Rafa, Marcin, and I, led by Salim, cruised at an increasingly faster pace as we descended. Within a quarter hour we were jogging, hopping over rocks, stones, and uneven footing. Within a half hour, it turned into a run. Salim smiled, showing his bright white teeth, and Marcin and I smiled back as we all dashed along. Rafa slowed, later telling me he had wanted to enjoy the scenery down rather than rush things.

As we ran, each step felt like it fueled my human spirit. I experienced waves of gratitude for my life back home. I felt thankful for the experience I'd just had—and was still having. I was grateful to have learned just how far I could push my body physically, mentally, emotionally, and spiritually.

With each leap over a stone, each tree root avoided, I felt my spirit lift while my breath pulsed in the rhythm of running down the mountain. The shifting landscape mirrored the shift inside, because I was one with everything I touched with the soles of my shoes. I could feel the connections all around me, a network of infinite strands that spanned the space between me and the mountain. Such a description does not fully encapsulate the experience. The bonds felt both known and unknowable; they were a glimpse of the true beauty of something indescribable. I was truly inspired.

Flashes of summiting Kilimanjaro shot through my mind like a strobe light as I ran down thousands of feet. My brow sweated. My heavy pack swayed back and forth. None of it mattered. I felt the soul of the mountain and mine connecting with it. In less than two hours and twenty minutes, Marcin, Salim, and I descended, arriving at the park entrance with smiles as large as those of great white sharks.

Back at Moshi Town

Once the entire team was back in Moshi Town, drinking beers, we learned that Bart had gotten sick at one point, briefly lost consciousness, and then managed to regain his faculties to finish strong.

We learned that Raul H. had had the strength to help his friend Raul R. through his most trying moments in Jamaica Rocks and wildly celebrate on the summit, but then he had faced the worst breathing challenges of the entire climb on the way down. We learned that Steven had surprised himself by remaining fully alert, focused, and capable of coordinating the group, despite not having slept at all the night before.

Eight of the ten climbers had supported one another and battled their way to the peak as a group. It had taken them nearly eight grueling hours to summit from Kibo Hut. They had managed to reach Uhuru Peak just a little more than fifty total hours after leaving the gate, despite the three-hour delay due to the snow storm.

We learned that as that group had started to descend around the crater rim, Dustin had come into view. He was climbing unguided and would eventually reach the summit alone. Dustin told me that early in the day, he and his partner, Natalie, had gotten behind. Dustin had been climbing with her the entire route. When Natalie had started to fall behind, he'd slowed his pace to stay with her, as did a guide. Apparently, Natalie had slowed to the point where it became increasingly clear that she would not reach the summit. She was battling but falling asleep on her poles. They had been at extreme altitude for too long. It was getting dangerous. When they had finally reached Gilman's Point, Natalie could go no farther. Dustin had realized he couldn't take the guide with him, so he'd told him to stay with Natalie and left before he could protest. "I walked from the Gilman's to the summit like I was walking through the mall. I was at 80 percent SpO2 and 72 percent SmO2. That is fucking crazy." We all laughed while sitting around the patio table in Moshi Town.

The results were in: twelve of the thirteen of us had fully ascended, reaching Uhuru Peak in remarkable timeframes: Marcin, Rafa, and I in thirty-three hours and fifty-two minutes, the eight team members in fewer than fifty hours, and Dustin, who power walked across the summit at the fifty-two-hour mark. Natalie, the thirteenth team member, made it all the way to Gilman's Point in just over fifty hours. All were notable achievements, deserving of the accolades we showered on one another.

A Breath of Inspiration

It took me quite some time to unpack all we had experienced. Once I was back stateside, I called several team members to get their insights. Although everyone's were powerful and lent great perspective to the elements of suffering, mindset, and emotional regulation we had experienced, as well as the impact of conscious breathing on performance, my talk with Marcin stood out.

Marcin and I felt akin to one another during this experience. We had summited together and run back down to the park gates next to each other. Even after we had returned to our respective countries, there was a fluidity and ease to our phone conversations.

Marcin, a very cerebral, regimented young man in his 30s, approached his preparation for Kili very seriously and it paid off. When I asked him for details, he described his physical preparation, training that included different types of breathwork, and endurance training. But the mental work, specifically around goal setting, was more of an internal obstacle for him.

For Marcin, goals on the mountain were initially undesirable and confusing. He told me that if he didn't know the goal of life (which he didn't), then he saw no point in trying to set lesser goals. He felt like it somehow, "violated the spontaneity of life," as he put it. Of course, even without a refined goal-setting regimen, Marcin has managed to accomplish a great deal in his life through sheer will and discipline. But the discipline he invoked was essentially self-tyranny: There was no one with whom he was more strict than himself. However, once he discovered that arbitrary goals could be useful to pull him forward, he was willing to take a second look.

He began to challenge his own ideas about goal setting as the cold reality of summiting Kili crept closer. He realized his training was being sufficiently guided by the goal of a rapid summit that would surely push him to his limits. This carried him for a while, until more thoughts got in his way, this time relating to human competitiveness and his own tendency to compare himself to others. The very concept seemed negative to him.

"I wanted to do well for myself. But how did I know I did well for myself? I knew through the fact that there are other people around me who are also pacing me. It was comparative to a certain extent. At any point, I had trouble accepting the part of me that wanted to do well comparatively. I found myself having thoughts I did not understand, and then I was being a tyrant to myself for having these thoughts."

This kind of negative thought loop is at once common and stressful. What many experience, but do not fully understand, is that a goal's arbitrary nature gives it a game-like quality but does not diminish its power. Big goals, even comparative goals, tap deeply into the neurobiological systems in humans. Having the ability to accept yourself and your desires, as well as to put them in their proper context in relation to others, leads to a great deal of psychological freedom.

Marcin, after wrestling with this, was eventually able to find self-compassion and along with it, the acceptance he needed to find peace and empowerment.

Those of us with the strongest desires to push ourselves to the limits have within us an equal desire to do comparatively well. Jordan Peterson, PhD, professor of psychology, recommends that we compare ourselves to who we were yesterday and compete, if you will, with that person rather than those around us. This is often a great tactic to apply in daily life. It is also helpful, however—even necessary sometimes—to allow your competitive nature to drive you forward in contrast to your peers. Just don't lose sight of yourself in the process.

This is perhaps the greatest difficulty because it requires nuance. How and when we express competition matters. Don't let it blind you. Don't let your goal setting, along with the inevitable successes and failures, be defined by your peers. Don't let competition keep you from learning. To master the stress response, you must not only engage in goal setting, but partner training and competition as well.

Finding the balance and nuance is key.

Like good therapy sessions, talking with other team members trying to digest what we had done was beyond helpful. Most of us felt estranged when we got back to our respective homes. A dip into brief depression hounded us all. This was a natural reaction to returning to life without the comradeship and shared adversity we had experienced. Although on all accounts it will take us yet more time to unpack all we went through, many insights have been forthcoming already.

Steven, for his part concluded that, "the mountain is a metaphor [that can serve as a life principle] about having a big ambitious goal and then having the discipline—the daily discipline over an extended period of time—to reach that goal ... Be clear on what you want, focus on doing it, and surround yourself with people who support you. We should all have our own Kilimanjaro." Good words of wisdom, summed up.

I chose to climb Mount Kilimanjaro to find out the truth around breathing techniques and performance under high stress. What I took away was a deep confirmation of the power of human adaptability, especially when guided by an intentional, conscious direction. The human design, as it has evolved over thousands and thousands of years, can yield incredible results. The right training simply needs to be in place for optimal expression and development.

It is easy to overstate a single mechanism within the human body as allowing us to succeed in the face of adversity and to maximize our potential. The body and mind compensate and interlock in so many complex ways. However, training each component accordingly and then stacking the parts together to maximize advantages leads to unknown heights of potential.

But a few words of caution: Be honest with yourself at all times. Do not expect overnight results. Keep in mind that a trained body and an untrained body often behave very differently. Expect the need to frequently reevaluate. Don't expect progress to be a gradual incline curve. It is a series of steps, and it is nearly impossible to predict how long and big each step will be. Don't forget that progress sometimes goes backward. This is simply an indication that you should revisit your training routine and rest and sleep periods. It is also impossible to remain at one type of peak performance constantly. But it is *not* impossible to grow continuously over a lifetime.

Taking intentional breaks and changing things up is very important in any routine. Distinguish between the needs for different types of performance at different stages of your training and your life. Experience a full range of intentional performance for maximum growth, expression, health, and longevity, and discern each accurately to rise to your potential.

There are times to see what you are made of, what you are capable of, what you can endure, or what you can overcome. Riding the knife's edge, however, should be temporary, not standard. Intentionally engaging in peak potential will allow for more peaks over the course a lifetime, thereby expanding your life's breadth and depth. This will also amplify your comfort zone and capability. If you push for peaks daily, you will likely find yourself injured, sick, or dead. But when coupled with the necessary periods of rest, recovery, and reflection, the steep curve of pushing limits is wonderful.

Finding balance using mechanisms designed to deal with extremes—what I call survival stress tools—is the most developmental human process of which I know. Why? Extremes require all facets of human capacity to rise to the necessary occasion. To paraphrase Marcin, an extreme challenge increases the baseline of the human experience, because it pushes the parameters of what you define as base.

The Kilimanjaro challenge, and the experiments it prompted in the months after, was the final component I needed to share the understanding of stress presented herein. On that mountain, a lifetime of stressful events, endeavors, and circumstances culminated into razor-sharp focus. And with that focus, I offer you a clear methodology to master the stress response.

Book I Endnotes

1. I find it highly interesting that Bannister's arguably most lasting contribution was not in running, impressive as his eight-year running career was. It was in the field of medicine that Banister made the greatest impact. Following his 1954 retirement from running, Roger Banister dedicated himself fully to the field of neurology. This would remain his focus for nearly sixty years. His primary interest was the autonomic nervous system (ANS) and specifically failures within this system. He would be a leader in this field, helping to redefine and clarify syndromes that led to breakthroughs in understanding autonomic nervous system dysfunctions. The principles of WHM involve access and certain control of the ANS, which is part of the nervous system that typically governs many of the automatic processes of the body and brain. Breathing, heart rate, and hormone production are three examples that are primarily directed by the ANS (https://www.ncbi. nlm.nih.gov/pmc/articles/PMC4879455/).

2. Weitzberg E, Lundberg JON. 2002. Humming Greatly Increases Nasal Nitric Oxide. American Journal of Respiratory and Critical Care Medicine 166(2):144-145.

BOOK II

WHAT IS THE STRESS RESPONSE AND WHY DO WE WANT TO MASTER IT?

THE WINTER OF 1986 stands out as a prominent time of my youth. I was eight years old and living with my mother, brother, sister, and step-father in a cul de sac of a northeast neighborhood in Albuquerque, New Mexico. Our house backed up to sage brush and creosote amid a natural desert landscape that gave way to a large arroyo, which would carry water from the mountain elevations down to the valley during heavy rain. When it would storm, the lightning would be fierce, the thunder would clap so loudly it felt like you were under a splitting sky, and the torrential rains race through the arroyo at a frightening speed.

One night, when my sister and I were asleep in the room we shared, we awoke to a thunderous clap that sounded like a familiar monsoon. It was not one of nature's storms but rather another type that had recently frequented our home. Jolted from sleep, I could feel my eyes narrowing in the dark. My heart began to pound inside my chest and my muscles tensed all over my body. I could hear my laborious breathing, even though I was just sitting up in my bed. An eerie feeling crept into my belly that made me feel slightly sick but fully energized, ready to spring to action.

Sitting silently in the dark, I waited to clarify what woke me. I looked over at my sister, who was also now awake. We stared at each other. Suddenly we heard screams and the sound of doors being slammed with intense anger coming from down the hall. It was my mother. This was the signal my body had been waiting for. I leapt out of bed and began to pack a suitcase. My sister did the same. In a matter of a minute or two, we had all the things we needed. We had become expert packers by then.

The screaming and yelling continued, accompanied by more slams. We came out of our bedroom to discover our mom running toward us with my baby brother in her arms. An intoxicated tyrant lurched clumsy but violently some distance behind her. My mother passed next to us with a sharp command, "Now kids. Go!" As she went through the kitchen, I ran right behind and held the door open for her and my little brother with my free hand. The door led to the garage, where our small white Ford Escort lay waiting. The drunk close on our tails. As I was urging my sister to come quickly, I saw her eye the woodblock of knives on the kitchen counter. I held my breath; my body and brain felt overloaded. The feeling was so strong that I was momentarily incapacitated. My eyes narrowed to the point that it was difficult to see. My sister, two-and-a-half years older than I, lunged for a butcher knife and turned to face the lurching man, who was now less than four feet behind her. "Get away!" she yelled, as she drew the knife up and back into a striking position. The drunk stumbled to a quick halt, then backed up considerably. "Let's go!" I shouted, my voice mobilizing my body back into action. She ran toward me and through the door. I ducked out of the house as the door shut and ran to the car, throwing our bags inside as I jumped in the backseat. Car locked, my mom started the engine quickly. The drunk stumbled through the door just as we started pulling out. A screwdriver flew through the air, rotating as though in slow motion. When it hit the windshield, there was the loud crash of glass breaking. Our windshield became a spider's web of cracks. We drove away.

Even after we had arrived at a safe place, my body was full of energy and anxiety. My vigilant action state remained elevated for hours. Finally, as the morning light arrived, so did exhaustion, and I fell into a sleep that was shallow and unsettled.

There can be silver linings to the challenges we face in life. Over the course of my life, I have met many who have dealt with situations similar to mine or worse—sometimes much worse—who have faced their pasts bravely and used them as fuel.

This was not the last incident of its kind in my young life. When I was older, these and other experiences would motivate me to help others confront high-stress situations, and not just violent ones. There exists a wide variety of high-stress situations, all of which share so many of the same components to which the body and brain respond in predictable ways.

What I know now, but did not understand then, was that my reaction that night was what is known as an extreme stress response.
The human stress response can emerge in varying degrees and be
stimulated by a great number of factors, as we shall explore. But as
a base definition, the stress response is an adaptive response to perceived internal and/or external demands that triggers a rapid series
of arousal state functions. In other words, the stress response is a
mobilizing force that the body goes through, physically, emotionally, and psychologically, to prepare for action.

When the nervous system perceives a demand—which can include mild discomfort, pain, or even life-threatening circumstances—it begins an internal process to make the necessary adaptive
adjustments to deal with the issue at hand. Our brains and bodies
do their best to rise to the perceived level of demand. The accuracy
of the stress response is based largely on an individual's experience
and habits.

Your nervous system's sympathetic and parasympathetic nerves
fire to innervate various organs and brain structures. Your brain's
hypothalamus quickly activates the pituitary gland, which signals
for hormones like adrenaline, noradrenaline, and cortisol. This system is also referred to as the hypothalamus pituitary adrenal (HPA)
axis pathway. While this is happening, your nervous system also
relaxes the bronchioles in your lungs so that you can take large
breaths. Your heart beats faster. Your pupils adjust so that you can
focus on the thing directly in front of your eyes. Your nervous system adjusts body tension and redirects blood flow in your vascular
system, stabilizing your blood pressure and sending blood to all the
competing areas of your muscles and organs that need it.

The HPA is an example of a neural circuit, a pathway that operates as a messaging system in the complex interactions of the mind/
body. Understanding that it is a circuit—rather than just one part
of the nervous system, or just one part of the brain—is extremely
useful, because it highlights how the body communicates in small,
rapid messages to accomplish its intended goals. These messages
travel from mind to body and body to mind through electricity and
chemistry.

The stress response occurs when you are stressed due to an external danger: hearing that you must give an impromptu presentation at work, running into a mountain lion on the hiking trail, or being unexpectedly confronted by an abusive step-father in the middle of the night. The stress response will even activate when you get a brief scare, such as a group of friends jumping out to surprise you for your birthday. The stress response will continue throughout the danger or perceived danger period. So long as a threat, demand, or perceived demand remains, the mind/body will continue to operate accordingly. Then, when the threat or perceived threat is gone, your body will begin to adjust, regulating that response and moving toward the next perceived internal or external demand. Recovering from this high-action state can take minutes, hours, or days. Many people suffer from chronically high-action states that persist for years, which can lead to a reduced quality of life filled with anxiety and depression, as well as significantly contribute to heart disease, cancer, autoimmune disorders, and suicide.

To fully understand the potential range of the stress response, it is important to view it as a continuum, one that begins at elevated alertness and progresses to an all-out response, which can include fight, flight, or freeze.

For purposes of this book, a situation causing the stress response is defined as anything that mobilizes us for action, whether the action needed is small or big.

Figure 1 is a visual way to understand the basic idea of the body's stress response. Throughout the day, we travel this spectrum of stress, back and forth, depending on what or who we encounter and how well our minds and bodies deal with the different points along the continuum.

When the stress response is quick, both in terms of onset and recovery, we call that acute stress. When the response has a lengthy or continuous cycle, we call that chronic stress. Chronic stress leads to deregulation of the mind/body because of the lopsided prioritization of perceived demand. The mind/body cannot give the needed attention to the many other vital processes in the body, such as proper digestion to extract energy and nutrients, or proper sleep to restore, repair, and recover. Acute stress, on the other hand, is often welcomed by your mind/body. Evolution has prepared us well for this type of adaptation.

The mind/body is forever seeking balance; it is in constant flux in an effort to operate as successfully as it can amid the complex interactions and competing demands and priorities that life places on us to survive *and* thrive. This balance, when achieved, expresses itself as tightly controlled parameters referred to as homeostasis. To really hone an understanding of the complexity of the nervous system and its interaction with the mind/body, we need to view the nervous system as a process, rather than something that is fully on or fully off. This is why a continuum makes sense.

The physical, mental, and emotional processes all affect the thousands of complex interactions of the mind/body. In addition, these interactions are affected by the things that happen to us, the things we choose to do, and how we perceive the events. Such variables include the food we choose or choose not to eat; the type, duration, and intensity of exercises we engage in; and the environments in which we choose to work, play, or challenge ourselves. It greatly matters whether we enter a situation gladly or unwillingly, excited or fearful.

Why Master the Stress Response?

There are three overarching reasons why mastering the stress response is so important. Outlined below are introductions to each in no particular order: All are of equivalent importance.

One reason is to reduce the myriad of accidents and situations that can arise due to inexperience and the unknown. Since such novel occurrences (hopefully) do not happen very often, practice is a quality training tool. Drills and exercises are necessary to prepare your mind and body for the advent of infrequent situations.

The second reason is to enhance performance and recovery, specifically for a job or physical endeavor. Mastering the stress response will elevate your performance and integrate your mind and body. Unlike infrequent situations, performance tends to be a

STRESS CONTINUUM

FIGURE 1.

known, everyday occurrence. Learning to harness the nervous system to create a controlled high-action state consistently is an advantage for anyone, be they layperson, CEO, or professional athlete. The flip side of this coin is that in order to develop and maximize consistent high performance, the ability to increase the speed of recovery post-activity is a critical skill. A master of the stress response understands how to turn off the heightened state, maximize sleep, rest, and recover. One cannot be separated from the other.

The third reason is for health: to maximize your active functioning hours as well as your sleep, rest, and recovery hours. This includes gaining mobility and plasticity throughout your body, optimizing oxygen and the exchange of oxygen and carbon dioxide, balancing hormones, efficiently clearing metabolic waste, and resetting the nervous system's functionality. It also includes clearing brain plaque, organizing necessary information, and forming important memories through rest, recovery, and sleep.

As living beings, we are under constant attack. The very nature of life is to occupy a narrow space between existence and death. Everything inside and around you that is alive is fighting for its place: trillions of trees, flowers, and bushes; little varmints; the quintillion of insects and bugs; and trillions upon trillions of ubiquitous bacteria and viruses. Fortifying your health by mastering the stress response will allow you to function optimally within this great life arena. Stress that is beneficial will create strong roots and a resilient trunk, as well as branches, flowers, and fruit. Stress that impairs you will rot the roots, leave the trunk exposed to illness, shrink the branches, and leave little or no hope of flowers or fruit.

The next section will dig into each reason at greater depth. It will include stories that will further illustrate the importance of mastering the stress response. It will also highlight what happens if we don't.

To Grow or Perish in the Face of Stress

In the last section, we identified three primary reasons that it is important to master the stress response. Here, we will cover each in greater depth, providing examples to further illustrate the benefits of managed stress as well as the drawbacks of an unmanaged stress response.

The first reason—to avoid tragic accidents and situations—also means to perform effectively in life-and-death circumstances. In 2014, a rookie police officer, Peter Liang, was patrolling a high rise in New York City with his gun drawn. He was startled and accidentally discharged his weapon. The bullet ricocheted off the wall and hit an innocent twenty-eight-year-old man, fatally wounding him.

Unfortunately, similar incidents are not uncommon. Although there is not a single agency that tracks and releases statistical data on accidental discharges that result in injury or death, The Associated Press has attempted to collect reasonable estimations by pulling from a variety of sources, including public records requests and media reports. An article published in December 2019 cited more than 1,400 accidental discharges by United States law enforcement agencies nationwide over a seven-year period. Of those 1,400 accidental discharges, 21 resulted in fatalities, 134 resulted in officer self-harm, 34 hit innocent bystanders, and 19 hit suspects.[1] Experts aver that such a large number of accidental discharges is largely associated with a lack of training that simulates the harsh conditions that police face on the streets.

I wish to note that my comments are not intended to indict police. I have grave empathy for the difficulties and continuous stress they meet trying to protect the public. Dealing with continuous stress at extremely high levels, knowing that a routine traffic violation might turn to a life-and-death situation, will wear steadily on any individual. I can only imagine the emotional and mental challenges that a police officer must bear in order to avoid turning resentful and corrupt when the very public they wish to serve has so many unknown factors and individuals who may threaten their safety.

However, this acknowledgement is not meant to excuse the higher standard to which we should hold our public safety officers. There are a number of factors that can affect how an officer carries out his or her job, including inherent biases, precinct culture, and police academy training programs, as well as ongoing training and requirements. At the root, however, there is the individual and his or her ability to handle stress—extreme survival stress—and still remain highly operational and safe.

Police confront high-stress situations regularly, but they are only likely to encounter extreme-stress situations where a gun needs to be drawn once or twice a year. Creating officer training programs accurately that simulate these infrequent circumstances of extreme survival stress is challenging at best. Such programs are also expensive, both in terms of time and taxpayer dollars.

Officers suffer greatly from the limited degree of training available; simultaneously, they are expected to display near-perfect decision-making abilities under the extreme stress. The results can be tragic. Offering inexpensive training tools that help the body adapt to survival stress on a regular basis should be of great interest to both the police and the public.

As stated, the human nervous system experiences a continuum of arousal states; survival stress situations can take the action state to its greatest limits. When uncontrolled, the survival action state can quickly reach panic or freeze condition, at which point the individual becomes blind to what they are doing.[2] When humans panic, involuntary actions take over, and a state of extremely narrowed focus occurs. Missteps and tragedy often ensue as a result.

In a presentation to my martial arts students in 2014, attorney Brian McKenzie, who represents the Seattle Police Department in court proceedings when guns have been fired, explained that it can take up to three seconds for an individual to register what he or she has done in a survival stress situation. Three seconds may not sound like a lot, but consider that an experienced shooter can discharge sixteen rounds from a semi-automatic handgun in three to four seconds. In other words, from the moment of pulling the trigger to fully registering that one has done so, it is possible to empty the entire magazine.

A great many potentially tragic accidents and situations can occur for a wide variety of professionals who face life-threatening situations to carry out their jobs: soldiers, firefighters, and body-guards, to name a few. EMTs and other medical professionals can also regularly experience extreme stress in their attempts to save others' lives. They are not generally called upon to put their own lives in danger except under extreme circumstances, such as a disease pandemic. Nevertheless, their burdens are great, and they must be able to control their stress responses in order to be at their best and avoid the potentially catastrophic situations that can result from panic or freeze states.

Being Threatened or Attacked

The safety of our own person and those we care about stems from a deep desire to live. Life relentlessly pursues itself with a drive that exists in all things living. Any threat—actual or perceived—to life can quickly lead to being overwhelmed and unable to take action, with catastrophic outcomes if one is unprepared.

As a professional teacher of survival self-defense, I've seen thousands of students over the years. They come to my school for various reasons. Most often, they have a desire to preemptively learn how to protect themselves, should they ever encounter a violent threat. Others have already experienced attacks, or extremely close calls, in which they found themselves ill equipped and suffered the consequences of street violence.

The need for survival self-defense comes in many forms. Sometimes a situation emerges slowly before it erupts into violence: an argument that takes place prior to a sudden blow; a violent predator coaxing or charming a victim in a way that allows him to exploit the created vulnerability. Other situations don't offer much time to react. The violence explodes with little warning: seemingly random stabbings, shootings, and violent empty-hand (non-weaponed) attacks on random targets fit this description.

One of my students, David, originally came to my school for training in 2011.[3] Not long before, he had been assaulted when he'd asked someone to leave his home during a gathering. The person had been intoxicated and acting belligerent toward other guests.

When David had asked him to leave, the man had quickly thrown a punch, connecting hard with David's head and knocking him to the floor. As we discussed the incident upon his initial school visit, David described how he hadn't responded at all: He'd simply froze in the moment. The result had been a trip to the hospital and costly medical bills. Approximately one year later, David was out in his neighborhood on a Friday night. He had been visiting with friends and enjoying the evening at a local bar. At the end of the night, as he stepped out into the summer night air of the Capitol Hill area of Seattle, he heard a man yell close behind him. David quickly turned around to see a man he didn't know coming toward, making violent gestures. David first responded with his voice—"Stop!"—but also didn't hesitate to crouch and shield himself from the violent perpetrator as he connected. The clash created distance between David and his assailant. David, in addition to yelling "Stop!" again, immediately assumed a readied position. The man cocked his fist back while moving forward aggressively. David responded by closing the distance between them while throwing overwhelming counter punches, a technique he had been practicing for the previous twelve months. The conflict had carried them into an alley adjacent to the bar entrance. David put some distance between himself and the perpetrator, who then yelled out to a nearby friend, "Over here!" David turned around and saw another guy in the street behind him. He appeared to have been chasing another individual, who was running away. The new assailant turned toward David and took a couple of steps. Just as this happened, two police officers who had been driving down the street turned their car's lights on. The perpetrators ran as soon as they saw the lights. David exhaled, relieved he was ok.

When we talked about the incident the following day, he described how the two guys had apparently been randomly attacking people throughout the area that night. The police had been looking for the two culprits when they came upon David's incident. David had been able to react in a way that allowed him to stay calm enough to counter the threat until help arrived, a marked change from one year prior. His significant progress in managing the stress response contributed to his ability to keep himself safe that night.

Shootings

In 2007, I was on a date with the woman who would become the mother of my daughter. It was an early winter evening in Salt Lake City. While standing in line at a movie theater waiting to buy tickets, the loud screech of a car's tires disturbed the otherwise peaceful air. The car hit the inclined entrance to the parking lot driveway, the metal scraping the ground. It turned abruptly into a stall twenty yards from where we were standing. A man leapt out of the car and proceeded to unload the entire clip of a semi-automatic pistol, aiming at the intended target less than fifteen feet away from us.

When the first shots were fired, everyone standing in line froze; some turned away but beyond that, they didn't move. My hand immediately took the shoulder of my date and pulled her behind a pillar that offered cover, small as it was.

The gunman jumped back in his vehicle and sped out of the parking lot as fast as he had come in. The man he'd been aiming at had not been shot and no innocent bystanders had been hit. As these things go, it was a very fortunate outcome. Whether or not my date and I would have been hit if I hadn't pulled us behind the column is an unknown, but there can be no doubt that my ability to control my stress response greatly improved our chances of safety.

The threat of extreme violence can be overwhelming. The ability to act under such circumstances can literally mean the difference between life and death.

Mass Shootings

There are multiple records of an individual being able to react in a situation while others remain frozen. Whether intervening against a gunman or escaping the chaos of a mass shooting, action is very often critical for survival. In 2019, there were more than 400 mass shootings—shootings that include four or more people being shot—throughout the United States. That is more than one per day in that year.[4]

In mass shootings, it is often the case that those who are able to take decisive action live and those who freeze perish. This is the darkest side of an unintentional nervous system freeze. Stephen Porges, PhD, author of *The Polyvegal Theory*, describes the freeze as a reaction to prepare one for death. The person's nervous system becomes overwhelmed to the point that they shut down and begin to black out. I do not write this to blame the victims in any way. I write this to explain how having the ability to manage the stress response can help an individual avoid an unintentional freeze and survive such a tragic incident. This sort of preparation offers the best chance of survival in an extreme situation, as full mental, emotional, and physical control is retained by the individual.

The Everyday Grey

Of course, most situations in modern society are not so extreme. However, very few create no stress at all. Most are intermediate situations that do not have life-or-death consequences but must be dealt with to navigate the world safely. In virtually all such circumstances, the individual is benefitted by a calm mind, an observational nature unhindered by over-vigilance, and the ability to act with decisiveness. The knowledge of what to do and when to do it can be greatly enhanced by specific training over a period of days, months, or years. However, being able to apply that knowledge when you need it will have an even greater effect on the outcome of a stress-inducing situation. In order for this to happen, you must remain calm enough to access what you know.

Consider times when you, personally, have faced threats or fear-inducing situations and found yourself with an impaired ability to respond effectively, or at all. There may have been times when your mind felt foggy and your body felt shaky, and you simply couldn't remember what would otherwise have been easily recalled. How you manage stress influences posture, awareness, judgment, and decisions - all of which impact your ability to handle and respond effectively to the infinite grey situations of life.

Now consider the fact that dangerous situations can often be avoided or forestalled by small things: assertive posture, a brisk walk, or the willingness to look someone in the eye. In their perennially cited seminal study, *Attracting Assault: Victims' Nonverbal Cues*, psychologists Betty Grayson and Morris I. Stein interviewed convicted perpetrators of violent crime and asked them to watch videos of pedestrians walking down a crowded street. Grayson and Stein asked the perpetrators to choose would-be victims from the people they saw in the videos.

To the psychologists' surprise, the same victims were chosen again and again, and the choices were not those expected. Size and gender did not appear to play a major role: In fact, sometimes a large male was chosen over a small female. The commonalities among the chosen victims were the following: poor posture, a downward gaze, and a fidgety, anxious, or distracted demeanor. Also targeted were those who had strange gaits, kept their hands in their pockets, or looked fearful.

In addition, while it may seem counterintuitive, those who go about with overt vigilance are often targeted for violence. Such individuals often appear vulnerable and incapable of responding, largely due to their overextended focus: They cannot distinguish between a threat and a non-threat because *everything* feels threatening. This level of awareness greatly diminishes perceptual ability, resulting in clouded judgement and nervous system overload.

The part of your nervous system called the autonomic nervous system is responsible for mediating the tension in your vascular system. It does this in a number of ways, using various hormones and neurotransmitters to direct blood flow, nutrients, and oxygen to the parts of the body that most need it.

The chemical in your body that is primarily responsible for action-oriented behavior is called norepinephrine. As discussed in the introduction, it is a type of adrenaline produced in both the brain and a gland atop the kidneys. Norepinephrine concentrations are lowest during rest, specifically sleep, higher during wakefulness and alertness, and highest during a perceived or actual survival situation.

Norepinephrine is the main neurotransmitter used by the sympathetic nervous system, a part of the autonomic nervous system.

The sympathetic nervous system is the action system of the body, and it uses norepinephrine to signal target organs like the heart and liver to improve action-oriented functions. For example, increasing doses of norepinephrine signal the heart to beat faster and trigger the release of glucose from the liver for increased energy.

Norepinephrine is involved in many processes that occur as part of an action-oriented or sympathetic response. During a stress response, norepinephrine constricts your vessels to reroute blood to the muscles and organs that have a prioritized need for action. As vessels constrict, the heart beats faster and blood pressure increases. Influenced by norepinephrine, the irises of your eyes dilate so that they can take in more information. It signals fat cells to be used as energy. It inhibits digestion and relaxes the bladder. It signals skeletal muscles to increase glucose uptake, so that they have more available energy. Norepinephrine causes your airways to relax so that the lungs can pull in more oxygen. It increases your pain threshold and shifts your immune functions to prioritize the possibility of imminent action.

Norepinephrine, along with epinephrine and other stress hormones, can increase very rapidly in the body during a stress response. The results can include hyperventilation and increased skeletal muscle tension, even before such responses are warranted. If you remain in a vigilant state over an extended period of time, restlessness and anxiety take root. If vigilance escalates to hyper-vigilance, things can start to become foggy. When the neurochemical composition in your body is mismanaged, you end up feeling debilitated instead of empowered. This is when fight or flight becomes freeze.

Furthermore, the body requires sufficient amounts of vasodilators—such as nitric oxide, which aids in oxygen delivery to the smooth and cardiac muscles—to balance vascular tension and proper blood flow. Vasodilators can be acquired by increasing breathing depth and volume and managing skeletal muscle tension. Hypertension, or high blood pressure, as a short-term response can be very helpful, but if it is sustained or increased without accompanying vasodilators, it can quickly lead to poor performance and an overwhelmed system.

These responses are primarily governed by the sympathetic branch of your autonomic nervous system. However, they are also affected by your conscious attention, your attitude and perception, voluntary muscular contractions, and your breathing. All affect the body on different feedback loops that can and should be trained. Otherwise, we are at the whim of our conditioned fears and habits, and our perceptions are likely to be overwhelmed. A regimen that includes purposeful and intentional vasodilation and vasoconstriction while simultaneously practicing a mindset that supports optimal balance can help train the system to respond accordingly when the unknown confronts you.

Whenever we are dealing with the unknown, extraneous tension, poor breathing habits, and poorly tempered perception will lead to stress-induced mistakes. When life-and-death consequences are at stake, we could all benefit greatly from having simplified training tools that help us learn how to deal with survival stress. Learning how to effectively manage survival stress improves reaction time, heart rate balance, blood flow, muscle tension, breathing rate and depth, vision scope, memory, and auditory clarity. All of these functions are needed to effectively address unknown circumstances, give yourself the highest probability of excellent performance, and reduce the chances of tragic accidents and situations. Mastering the stress response will maximize your chances of dealing with the unknown successfully.

Performance Required

What do the financial trader, the fashion designer, and the public speaker have in common? They, like countless other professions, need to perform under intense pressure and respond in real time. Today's world is one of constant demands and ever-shrinking timelines. Although the 'life-and-death aspects' of these professions are of a more abstract nature, the necessity of performing under high stress is of no small consequence; it taps into our primal feelings of survival.

When I was in my early twenties, I was invited on a trip to see the trading pit at the Chicago Board of Trade. I had been to the floor of the New York Stock Exchange on a previous trip and found the buzz exciting: everyone on their telephones taking orders worth staggering sums of money. But to see the Chicago traders huddled together in their octagonal amphitheater, using small hand gestures, yelps, and calls to make trades worth millions of dollars, was electric.

Being down in the pit, I could feel the relentless high energy emanating from everyone. Emotions flared; eyes darted around the room only to lock with another pair, creating an invisible connection amid the chaos. Quick hand signals would follow and then, in a flash, the chaos would return, filling in the space where the connection had been: The transaction was done. Costly mistakes due to inattention were not tolerated in this environment. With so much on the line, a sustained state of high alertness and emotional intensity was the cultural norm. These guys worked long days in an extremely stressful environment and seemed to balance it by consuming large amounts of alcohol at the end of the day.

After the day was over, I went out to grab dinner and drinks with some of these men. As we all drank our whisky, most of the pit traders talked of the job as if it were just a routine endeavor. *You get used to it* was the attitude. These guys no longer seemed to register the hectic pace I had witnessed. For them, the speed of the day was a constant velocity and as such, almost unrecognizable. As alcohol entered our bloodstreams, the emotional intensity of the day shifted to jovial conversation. I got the impression that they liked having me there. As if my youthful naivety and excitement afforded them a glimpse of how they'd felt when they first began their jobs. I liked them too, and thanked them for having me along.

Years later, as I reflect on the memory with the advantage of more life experience, I recognize that operating at the high-level buzz of their collective occupation over days, weeks, and years has its price. I wonder how many of the traders I saw that day used alcohol as the primary means to counteract their stressful jobs. Given my impressions of the trading pit, I suspect the answer is many.

Only a couple of years earlier, the *New York Times* had reported that deaths from heart attacks among New York Stock Exchange floor traders was sixty percent higher than average for eighteen- to fifty-five-year-old men, numbers cited from the national health statistics. The Chicago pit traders I saw that day would likely have fit the same pattern.

Heart attacks are not the only symptom of high-stress jobs. Those in the fashion industry, for example, are laden with the demand for creativity and innovation while operating under tight deadlines and extreme hours. Virtually everyone in the industry, whether designer, model, or secretary, is subject to intense and constant scrutiny, and the necessity of always being 'on' takes a toll. The result is a significant impact on not only physical but mental health: It is an industry riddled with burnout, eating disorders, drug and alcohol addiction, and suicide.

When my sister, Lady, got her first job in New York City with a boutique designer, I got an inside view of what beauty could cost. My sister and her colleagues would work fourteen-hour days with few breaks as a matter of course. Then, in the weeks leading up to fashion week, eighteen-hour days became the norm to prepare for the season rollout, which typically culminated in a fashion show in Manhattan.

The fashion show I attended was as exciting as it was eclectic and beautiful. The artful and elegant displays of dresses, shoes, and accessories flooded the runway while photographers and videographers scrambled to capture the moments. Months of laborious love shone in the tents of fashion week, but the displays of creativity were there and gone after a mere thirty minutes. The inevitable emotional, mental, and physical crash would follow the show. My sister and her co-workers would be utterly exhausted. However, after little more than a day or two of downtime, they would be back at it. Even the 'downtime' often required ten-hour days.

My sister fortunately never succumbed to eating disorders, deep depression, or alcohol or drug abuse. It is to her credit that she managed to avoid these and other pitfalls of the fashion world. I have seen her close to burnout many times over the course of her career, but she is a remarkable woman and has always been able to push through. Many in her industry have not been so lucky. According to the Centers for Disease Control & Prevention (CDC), suicide is the number one cause of death for females in fashion. Furthermore, between 2012 and 2015, suicide rose thirty-four percent in that demographic.

A touch of madness may be required for those who wish to immerse themselves in creative work, for which they will be expected to endure unending hours of toil and be constantly critiqued. Therefore, any strategy that maximizes the body's ability to rest and recover, while simultaneously delivering flow state creativity and innovation, should be not only welcomed but highly coveted.[5]

Whether to sustain high-energy days of Chicago pit trading, or to encourage innovation and emotional stability, the capacity to seamlessly and rapidly shift between high-energy outputs and rest-recovery states is a must. Furthermore, any reliance on drugs or alcohol to do so will erode the body's power to adapt in the long term. Learning to master the stress response aids such shifts and helps those who participate in high-stress cultures to flourish.

Creative Demands, Scrutiny, and High Performance

I have been giving presentations of varying size and type for more than twenty-five years. Whether acting in front of audiences in my teens and early twenties, or later, advising groups of clients and corporate stakeholders on various programs to meet their financial needs, the need to be 'on' in front of peers and critics with real time feedback has been ever present. Each role has had its own challenges: acting required entertaining an audience, while financial seminars required that I carefully weave content with question and feedback engagement.

When I purchased a martial arts school in 2010, becoming an entrepreneur, I found that those early speaking roles had helped prepare me to stand in front of groups to teach on a daily basis. Over the years of practice, it has gotten progressively easier to stay present in the moment, working on timing, projection, and clarity while remaining creative. I have found it to be highly stimulating to speak and work with groups and individuals, to watch how learning and performance shifts due to any number of influential factors. Using a combination of various pedagogical methods— priming, mediation, visualization, rote learning, shuffling variables, purely adaptive techniques—I have been witness to the positive effects certain combinations consistently yield.

So when Wim Hof asked me to host one of his Wim Hof Experiences in Vancouver, British Columbia, as well as to lead some basic physical exercises in front of 250 people, I was keen to say yes. After all, how different could it be?

Two hundred and fifty people may not sound like a lot, but the number certainly applied pressure to perform on a scale that I had not yet known. Partly because of the number of attendees and partly because of the need to connect to the audience in various ways throughout the event, I had been asked to tailor a few physical exercises, lead warm-ups before and after the cold immersion ice baths, and introduce Wim and the other speakers. It was quite a motley array of responsibility.

Public speaking is often cited as one of the scariest things a person can do. According to the public speaking group Toastmasters, as well as psychologists the world over, public speaking consistently ranks as a top fear, sometimes beating out death as the number one fear. My public speaking experiences prior to the Wim Hof Experience had not been nearly that frightening. But as the event approached, every time I thought about it I got an incredible surge of adrenaline. Fortunately, I also had an established toolkit to support me. On the day of the event, I went through a preparation routine to control my adrenaline and access the calm within the heightened state. The occasion turned out to be a success by all measures.

I was asked back a short time later to do similar work. Over the following two years, I was offered increasing responsibilities that required planning, memorization, real time creativity, and strenuous physical exercises. To date, I have conducted consciousness guidance events for groups numbering up to 1,200 people at one time. At these events, I guide the group to help individuals achieve their personal flow state and therefore, access to their peak performance.

To be able to create individual and group flow state experiences is no small task; it takes a great deal of energy on my part, both before and during. On top of that, I've led groups in different parts of the world—North America, Iceland, Australia—often on little sleep and almost always in a different time zone, all of which has created a multitude of challenges. However, sticking to developed, proven routines has allowed me to engender these individual and group flow states consistently. My routines have become a methodology, one that has provided invaluable insight into the benefits of combining physical, intellectual, emotional, and spiritual training into a single body of work. By applying the methodology, I cannot only fulfill my role at these group events, I can, upon my return, resume my work and responsibilities as a full-time single father with few to no rest days in between.

The need to remain in a high-performance state while reducing the chance of negative health consequences is of great concern to those with demanding jobs that require long hours. The entrepreneur with his start-up working fifteen-plus-hour work days; the pro-athlete traveling time zones and playing a remarkable number of games while still putting in practice hours; the airline pilot's long hours compounded by her responsibility for hundreds of passengers; the executive in a cutthroat marketplace, constantly positioning and repositioning; the news reporter pushing harder and traveling farther in dangerous territory to find a compelling story to fill the twenty-four-hour news cycle: The list goes on and on. The bottom line is that the world is moving toward greater demands, reduced downtime, and ever increasing competition. The stress is rising and we need tools to address it.

Our Health: Optimized or Jeopardized?

All of the above and more have profound implications for our health. There are the obvious issues I previously mentioned—heart disease, mental health, and suicide— but there are others as well. In certain situations, an unwanted freeze state can be injurious or even fatal: Being involved in a major car accident—of which there are thousands every day in the United States alone—comes to mind. Even if you are not directly involved in the incident, witnessing one of the 38,000 fatal crashes per year[6] could cause post-traumatic stress for days, months, or years to come.

There are countless stress-related threats to our mental health. Perhaps you are one of the more than 16 million people here in the United States who has suffered a major depressive episode in the last year, or one of the 264 million who suffer from depression worldwide. Maybe you fall into one of the other categories, such as general anxiety disorder, social phobias, panic disorder, or OCD (obsessive compulsive disorder). When added up, an estimated 26 percent of the adult US population suffers from a diagnosable mental health disorder, including depression, general anxiety disorder, bi-polar disorder, substance abuse, social phobias, and others[7]. While the causes of these problems are complex, there can be no doubt that all are exacerbated by excess stress and sometimes induced by it.

The stress response is something shared by all humans. Modern life confronts us with so many disruptions to our natural balance and ability to focus: the stress of long work days and family, excessive artificial light, twenty-four-hour news cycles, and body systems weakened by constant climate control, all with minimal rest and sleep.

Under constant stress loads and relentless responsibilities, we are increasingly obese and prone to hormonal imbalances. We are seeking out drugs and alcohol at epidemic levels in an attempt to ameliorate the symptoms of chronic adrenaline, cortisol, and other stress hormones—not to mention boredom or a desire to state shift from the discomfort and suffering that life sometimes imposes. Unfortunately, the path of drugs and alcohol only reinforces the stress, fracturing any rest and recovery we do get and offering few benefits other than a temporary respite.

Autoimmune disorders, such as Crohn's and multiple sclerosis, certainly have a genetic component, but they are also steadily on the rise due to lifestyle-related factors: Chronic stress is near the top of that list. This is a problem that is up close and personal, affecting people of all types of genetics, occupations, and backgrounds.

Another common symptom of stress is inflammation and the pain it brings. While it is often treated as the root problem, there is another possibility: that inflammation is the result of stark imbalance within the body, a chronic cry of broken internal messages ignored for far too long. In later chapters, we will come to understand the role of inflammation in the body and ways to reset it and restore the body's proper balance.

With such a litany of ailments to lay at stress's door, the potential benefits of ameliorating stress becomes apparent. Using tools to increase resiliency and provide stress adaptations to strengthen our minds and bodies in a natural way is paramount if we are to battle today's challenges and harness the future. And just imagine if we achieved such a balance not only individually but collectively? A balance of time, health, and the wherewithal to intentionally contribute to the design of our future evolution while devoting proper energy to consciousness development. What if we could maximize our directionality to fuel growth, innovation, and creativity? To harness millions of years' of evolution and boldly orient the future with a lifestyle? Mastery of the stress response just might be the key.

What is Mastery?

There is no single philosophy that I can point to and say, "I embody this fully, completely, and to the exclusion of all else." Indeed, I have intentionally eschewed dogma, as I believe it to be the root of stagnation. I am a seeker of truth grounded in direct experience, both my own and that of those who intelligently point the way. This need to explore has been with me as long as I can remember and has been greatly responsible for the breadth of my experience. As I have explored, I have found connections within myself, with broader humanity, and with nature.

How long we stick with a pursuit dictates whether we get just a taste, explore certain intricacies, or study until we understand and incorporate that pursuit's essence. Once that has been captured, we can even take further steps. Through diligent practice, we may become experts; through deep desire, time, and dedication, we may become masters. All endeavors sit on a continuum and must be coupled with an inescapable time factor; it is always a balancing act between how much time you're willing to commit and how deeply you wish to pursue an undertaking.

As a young student of life, I desired to possess the essence of things: to know and intimately understand the deepest parts of whatever I was exploring. In this search, my passion was inexhaustible. However, the same could not be said of my time. It was always a challenge to reconcile the reality of how much time to invest in a pursuit when I also had competing interests and responsibilities.

Many philosophies have strongly influenced my life. Perhaps the simplest—and the one I have abided by most—has been the maxim that, "There are only two mistakes in life: not trying, and once trying, not going all the way." The only variable in this approach is how far is "all the way"? Must I be a professional, expert, or *master* at anything I tried? Or, can it mean something different?

In my life, I have chosen to interpret and incorporate this philosophy by digging in and learning until I have captured something's essence. I know that I will never stop learning. One could take the smallest, narrowest of subjects and spend a lifetime on that one thing. Slicing the world that thinly however, can lead to more harm than good. In fact, it has been my experience that with such narrow focus, context is missed. And there's the irony: focusing so closely that the expertise is actually lacking, because it fails to incorporate a practicality and relational connection. It fails in context. To paint in a single color, a single shape, on one canvas just doesn't make any sense.

The first organized athletic thing I did was karate. My father, a martial artist who competed as an amateur in both karate and American kickboxing, enrolled me in his dojo when I turned six years old. My parents were newly divorced, and I was going between two households. Regular attendance became more and more challenging, and when my father stopped competing about a year later and took a break from the dojo, I, too, took a break. My father decided to enroll me in soccer in the fall just before my seventh birthday. I didn't go back to martial arts for some time.

From playing soccer every day for hours on end, I progressed to skiing, which gave way to basketball, then wrestling, and still more soccer. Soccer eventually segued into dancing, which finally came full circle to martial arts over the course of fifteen years or so. Though I got good at many things, even to the level of expert in several, it would be a long time before I could claim mastery of any one of them.

Mastery comes with a combination of diligent practice, refinement, and integration. It is the expression of an art over a learning curve until one is capable of consistently displaying a truly high level of *expert* competence under high-pressure circumstances. Mastery is also an aim. It is the understanding that as one reaches a bar of competence and fulfills his current potential, that potential swells to offer a new, ever-reaching goal. It is to strive for perfection even though perfection will never be realized.

The natural question might come up, *who judges mastery?* When the goal being judged, such as the mastery of self, is not easily rated by outside observers, then it is for us to judge. Our internal worlds are vast, and their external expressions are quite limited. Sure, certain aspects of ourselves can be put to external tests, but ultimately, we, and only we, will know if we have mastered ourselves.

There is a warning we should all heed before we claim we have mastered something. The great physicist Richard Feynman is famous for his statement: *"The First principle is that you must not fool yourself—and you are the easiest person to fool."*

Mastery can be elusive, and to self-judge such a thing is often quite difficult, although with practice it is possible to arrive at a closer approximation of the truth. At a minimum, mastery takes a great deal of time and effort spent on developing the skill itself; moreover, it requires proper practice, quality feedback, and a true desire to know one's own failings. Only by following such a path is it possible to attain higher and higher competence. Knowing one's own failings is of especially great importance. We must be willing to fail long enough and often enough to ascertain an accurate view of ourselves without discounting the progress we have actually made. This is not an easy thing.

There are myriad inexperienced individuals, clueless and ignorant to the point that proper self-assessment is all but impossible. For example, in 1995, a man by the name of McArthur Wheeler set out to rob two different banks in the Pittsburgh area. He did not wear a mask to hide his face, but instead relied upon chemistry: He smeared lemon juice all over his face in the belief that it would render him invisible to the video cameras, or so he thought. He walked brazenly into each bank and starred confidently at security cameras as he carried out his robberies. Upon his arrest, he was stunned and at a loss as to how he could have been recognized.

There is a fun kid's science experiment that allows children to reveal secret messages using lemon juice. If the juice is mixed with water, it can be used as ink to write a message on white paper. Once the liquid dries, it will be more or less invisible. Shine a light on the paper, however, and the diluted but oxidized substance will reveal the message.

The best explanation for Wheeler's behavior is that he had come across this or a similar experiment and come to the conclusion that lemon juice could render his face invisible as well: There is no way to describe this conclusion except as incredibly dumb. However, it did prompt two psychologists to investigate the reasoning behind such an idea. And in 1999, they published their cognitive bias study showing results that would come to be known as the Dunning-Kruger effect.

The Dunning-Kruger effect highlights the inaccuracies of people's self-assessments, particularly their qualities or skills. The distribution works out such that those at or near the bottom of the competence scale greatly overestimate their abilities, while those at or near the top end tend to underestimate their own abilities. In other words, bias and lack of clear self-assessment can exist for novices and experts alike. Although later research by other psychologists has pointed out that relatively accurate self-assessment can be learned, it is important to note that this phenomenon is quite common in the untrained self-observer.

I have seen this pattern often in my involvement with martial arts, meditation, or any number of other skills I have personally tried to learn over the years. Whether evaluating my own progress or watching my students evaluate theirs, I have witnessed inherent biases and ignorance at the beginning, when the person is at the bottom of the spectrum. Then, as one becomes more and more competent, there comes the ever-growing realization of how much there is to learn within a given field. This is exacerbated by the fact that skilled practitioners of any pursuit gravitate increasingly toward each other, producing new biases because the vast majority of who they see are other skilled practitioners. I would argue that truly skilled people tend to want a challenge, and they therefore search for groups in which they know less than the others present.

Quadrant Learning Theory

If we apply the facts of the Dunning-Kruger effect to a skill-based learning model, it becomes evident that at the beginning of learning something new, not only do you not know the skill, you also don't know what you don't know or how to apply what little information you do have. In other words, you are unconsciously incompetent.

Let's take learning the piano. The first lessons will involve an introduction to the piano itself and how it works: the keys and how they are arranged; the pedals and how they shift the sound. You will likely learn a little bit about music and how to begin reading it. Very likely, you will learn some highly simplified music and learn to play just one hand of it. You won't just sit down and start playing the most difficult pieces of Chopin, Stravinsky, or Liszt. In fact, you won't even know about the many different skills involved in playing the pieces from these composers. You will probably have some idea that to play such a piece is very difficult, but you won't *really know* anything about it. And you won't know how to perform any of the skills required to make such sounds come out of the piano. So you begin, unconsciously incompetent. You don't know what you don't know.

As you learn more, you begin to recognize your deficits and become more acutely aware of your incompetence. This is where the transition to stage two occurs: the transition to conscious incompetence.

The right hand still moves sluggishly and perhaps awkwardly. Numerous mistakes happen as you try to play, even slowly. Each time you take your eyes off of the piano to try to read the music, you lose track of your hand. You stop frequently to read the notes, trying to memorize a few that will be coming up. Back and forth, reading the notes, you practice with the right hand. And so it goes. If you stick with training the skill, you start to get better at it. You begin to perform, albeit inconsistently. It takes a great deal of effort, focus, and conscious attention to be able to do the things that you want to do. But keep at it and you will enter the third stage: conscious competence.

You must still consciously track the skill to remain competent, but with conscious attention, you can do what you want to do. You can read the music and play the right hand part of it. The music becomes fluid, the timing and pace and the dexterity of the finger movements all working together. Even though it requires intense focus to perform, it feels good.

The longer you stick with practicing this skill, the faster, more fluidly, and consistently you are able to perform, and with far less effort than before. You don't think about it, you simply do it. Your hand moves with ease, traveling through the required notes to play to the simple tune. You are unaware, but performing nonetheless. This is the fourth stage: unconscious competence.

Teachers have varied methods and schedules for introducing added complexity. Perhaps you will begin to learn the left hand after you reach the fourth stage; perhaps it was introduced at an earlier stage. Regardless of when it happens, adding the new variable sends you back to stage one, unconscious incompetence, and you begin the journey again. With each new skill introduced, this return journey takes place as that skill is integrated into the whole. The same process occurs as song complexity increases. These four stages become a fluid track that you travel, back and forth and back and forth, as the microskills of playing the piano are learned and integrated.

These four stages are what is known as the quadrant learning theory, and I have found it to be a very useful framework to understand how to build and assess progress within a given skill set. The greatest utility of this type of framework is in understanding that as skills are layered upon and integrated with each other, the process more or less starts over. As pointed out, even though two skills may be grasped independently, combining them often results in having to go through the stages again. When examining the pursuit of a skill set through the lens of the quadrant learning theory, it becomes clear why it can take something like 10,000 repetitions or 10,000 hours to become an expert at a subject.

However, even to become an expert is not to be a master; that requires a still-greater degree of expertise. This is why I say that mastery is an aim, a continuous striving toward perfection. Only after sufficient training at an expert level—and what constitutes sufficient varies from person to person—can you truly claim to have mastered something. And even once you have arrived there (wherever there is), it is just another interval on the path to the perfect ideal for which mastery aims. Much of the step-by-step guide in the second part of this book delves into specific tactics for development and marking progress clearly. In any case, before claiming mastery, do your due diligence, temper your ego, and enjoy the process—because *every-thing is* about the process. Fully engaging in the process over a period of years gives you the opportunity to become a master in your chosen field. Engaging in the process on the way to mastery is what makes actual progress possible. Mastery must be accomplished through a lifestyle, not a checklist.

What is Self-Confidence?

Self-confidence is needed to master the stress response, but what is it that truly makes someone confident? I propose that there are three aspects to confidence: the mental, the emotional, and the somatic. Mental confidence as defined herein is the belief in yourself. The emotional component is how you feel as you confront the infinite variety of situations you must navigate in life. Somatic confidence is the command of your physical body, whether it is still, poised for action, or in motion. Applied to all of these must be a clear understanding of both your present limits and your abilities.

Regardless of the situation, possessing confidence in these three ways greatly reduces the mental and emotional anguish that contributes to stress and the anxiety that naturally follows. Much of our mental and emotional pain comes from failure or fear of failure. The paradoxical aspect of self-confidence is that it is often developed through the lessons of failure. Therefore, there are two acts that you must engage in to develop true and lasting self-confidence: 1) expanding the zone in which you are comfortable, and 2) creating the habit of taking action, whether that action fails or succeeds.

Your ability to tolerate the discomfort and fear associated with these two acts will directly impact your ability to create lasting self-confidence. The two are highly interrelated, and both require courage: action despite fear. There can be no courage without the presence of fear.

For younger children, fear is often mediated by caretakers: parents, siblings, aunts, uncles, grandparents, family friends, and so on. We are more or less fearful of situations depending on the reactions of our caretakers. Slowly, the environment shapes our perceptions. As we become more autonomous, early environmental conditioning plays a key role.

The good news is that no matter our natural inclination for taking risks, or how early environmental conditioning has shaped us, there is no fixed state that guarantees a level of belief in ourselves. In other words, self-confidence is plastic, moldable to the extent that we are willing to mold it.

To begin to remold ourselves, two goals are helpful. The first is to become aware of our existing conditioning and learn to get out of our own way: Stop the negative self-talk. The second is to devise a technique that improves our willingness to take action and learn to optimize risk: a way to show up, face fear, *and* see ourselves through it.

The Negativity Bias

The negativity bias is our brain's default behavior. It is estimated that one negative experience requires five positive experiences to balance it and regain neutral. This has some clear evolutionary advantages. In the world of survival, a negative experience could mean death, so it's better to learn the lesson the first time. But our brains also thrive on new experiences, and many first times are bound to be less than ideal. Therein lies the dilemma.

The negativity bias has a strong tendency to reinforce inhibition. Simply knowing this can help us understand the brain's natural tendency and help us make intentional choices to overcome that bias. Entering a new situation with an attitude that is prepared for challenge or hardship can turn this bias on its head.

We can also apply techniques to help improve our outcomes, especially early on in training. If you are venturing into unknown territory, don't start with the hardest thing you can find because you "need the challenge." Challenge is wonderful, but start with small wins whenever possible. This technique will help balance the equation in the short term and help you build resiliency over the long term.

As you become comfortable in the training model, it becomes easier to approach failures and problems as challenges to overcome, rather than pure setbacks that leave you with a distaste for the skill. I often have my students develop the training habit of seeing incremental failure as a positive result, one that demonstrates that you are indeed on your way to ultimate success.

Combining small wins while facing discomfort, failing, learning from failure, and ultimately succeeding can be a basis for retraining the negativity bias. The process can help make this natural physiology a useful tool rather than an innate hindrance. The approach will help you develop confidence, despite the challenges encountered.

Managing risk stems from experience. Start small. You can always build from there.

When approaching a skill with this understanding in mind, your conscious brain becomes a helpful driver. But be aware that what lies outside your conscious attention will still affect you. Therefore, to be maximally successful, it is important to address training in such a way that you directly engage in its emotional, mental, and physical aspects.

For example, if you only train physically, then you may develop great somatic and physical confidence. Some of this may even transfer to the emotional and mental side, as it usually takes some degree of both to support physical practice. However, this is not guaranteed, and when you find yourself under pressure to perform, your skill may suddenly not be readily available.

A better approach is to make sure that you practice the emotional and mental components of a skill independently: like the right and left hands of playing piano. Then, when you are ready, you can integrate varied facets. The resulting skill will be resilient, and your confidence in reproducing the skill will be exceptional.

Another important piece when developing true confidence in a particular skill is to make sure it has a relational component. This means training with or against another person or group of people. There are psychological, emotional, and physical reasons for this approach.

Let's assume there's a skill you are attempting to acquire. When practicing cooperative or competitive physical exercises, you must learn to communicate and set boundaries through verbal communication. This will build your trust and confidence in your emotional ability to assert yourself. The physical training will be greatly improved because you choose to practice this emotional component intentionally.

The human brain has a natural negative bias that, when combined with the fear of rejection, can lead us to avoid the discomfort of a witness to our failures. This bias taps deeply into our survival awareness, since rejection or being ostracized from the group has meant increased vulnerability or death in many eras.

This fear has the same root as fearing to speak in front of people. There is no inherent danger in having someone witness your failure, just as there is typically no inherent danger in saying something amiss while in a group in modern culture. However, these fears did not evolve within the framework of the modern era: they developed over millennia and register on a primal level.

Within each of us we have potential. That potential can be realized and expanded just like a muscle can be strengthened. All of our body systems are like this: improved by use. This is especially true when you combine the variables of emotional, psychological, and physical pressures to perform. This approach to training forces adaptability, and adaptability fosters growth.

The Power of Belief

The power of belief is a critical junction on the path to self-confidence. Without believing that what you can do is possible, your mind and body will be unable to muster the effort to try, fail, and try again. To have faith that what you are moving toward is possible creates a growth mindset. It tells you that you are not at a fixed station: that, with hard work and effort, you can improve and grow.

Our thoughts and beliefs govern our willingness to even try. As anyone who has plowed the furrow toward mastery knows, failure is an inevitable part of the process. So, how do we remain confident that we will eventually get there? How do we overcome the discouragement of failure and still believe our efforts to be worthwhile?

Belief relies on our ability to subject ourselves to the discomfort of our peers witnessing our failures and triumphs. To strengthen belief, we must be willing to expose ourselves to the scrutiny of others. If we can accept this often discomforting experience, we empower ourselves by turning the negative into a positive. We prove to ourselves that we can endure such an incident, thereby increasing our belief in ourselves. In addition, our belief is bolstered by the encouragement of our peers, whether it takes the form of praise or constructive criticism.

Belief in your abilities is fundamental. Performing with and in front of your peers to endure the emotional and mental anguish when you fail is irreplaceable in its benefits.

What You Focus on Makes a Difference

Where we focus our attention ultimately directs where our energy goes. If we focus on a mindset of excitement and anticipation, then we are much more likely to take action, overcome self-doubt, and succeed, leading us to feel more confident over time. The more successes achieved, the more failures overcome, the better the chance that we will do this again and again.

Chaining together successes reinforces the resilience needed when we meet inevitable failure. In a training approach, therefore, it is important to balance a major challenge, where failure is bound to happen from time to time, with mild to moderate challenges, where success is likely to be found.

The practical approach to this is to start your day doing something moderately difficult. Choose an activity that requires risk and effort when you are fresh in the day, ideally after a good night of sleep. Overcoming the challenge will set up your day for success, even if you encounter other challenges that end in failure. Over time, this approach will translate to the ability to not only recognize failure as a natural part of the success model, but to learn where on the curve you need to encounter failure in order to keep moving forward.

The question becomes, how do I use various training methods to foster my confidence? What is the principle, what is the timeline, and what result am I looking for? The process of learning a martial art has a number of good examples of how it helps students to develop and maintain confidence.

- Many skills within martial arts are difficult to learn, and overcoming these difficulties or challenges builds one's confidence in ultimate success.

- Martial arts tap into our survival mechanisms, offering experience with a range of emotions and hormones, physical demands, and mental focus. The result is an increasing ability to encounter and control chaos. As the control improves, our perception of what is happening changes tremendously. An experienced martial artist can see and feel things that a beginner cannot discern.

• A good martial art school builds a foundation of trust among training partners, which in turn increases the confidence of the individual students. Both can extend the danger potential without compromising the students' relative safety.

• Good training methods require that the student be fully engaged, or present, in the *now*. Much of self-doubt comes from staying in a personal circle of seemingly endless thoughts and half decisions. Being in the moment and having a requirement to act now, whatever that action may be, naturally eliminates the head talk over time.

Martial arts training is not the only option, but it is a rather useful example, as it easily touches on so many useful areas of learning mastery and training the mind and body.

It is important to understand that mastery requires a mindset that training is a way of life. It is not something you do but something you become. You must become the training; otherwise, every day is a quest to find the motivation to do something, and over time that motivation will wane. If you wish to become confident and pursue mastery, you must become your goals.

If your training becomes who you are, then the decision is already made. It is simply a matter of time. The amount of energy this releases is tremendous. No longer do you spend your precious mental, emotional, and physical energy trying to decide if you will train. Instead, all that drive is applied to your training directly. This also frees up precious time to balance the rest of your life with your training.

You must build on a strong foundation. You must be willing to test your assumptions and disrupt them, to put yourself on the edge of discomfort. If small failures are relished as feedback, they will strengthen your confidence in the long run. If you are not failing, there is a good chance you have accidentally taken a wrong turn and are no longer on the path to mastery. Stay on this wrong path too long, and your confidence will be undermined and suffer as soon as you hit a formidable obstacle.

Be willing to start again. Don't be afraid to fail. Accept it fully.

As I train my students using these principles, a natural question often surfaces. Must we always be pushing the envelope in every setting to stay on that edge and maintain confidence?

The answer is surely no. Actually, pushing too hard often leads to injury or situations in which the danger outweighs the benefit. There are many reasons to attempt things that have never been done, to try to break records, to explore new territory simply for the challenge of doing so. But such acts do not, by themselves, build confidence, and this approach will not necessarily lead to mastery.

You must learn to pair patience with diligence. Confidence is a practiced emotion reinforced by results. It is found on a tempered landscape of trial and success, trial and failure, more trial and success, and so on. Once you have built a strong foundation based on your acceptance of an action's potential for both success and failure, you will be willing to continue to take action toward a meaningful goal. Your confidence will grow, and mastery will be only a matter of time.

We need many assets to tap into self-confidence sufficiently to sustain failure long enough to achieve mastery. We need the right neurochemistry: enough testosterone in the blood to be willing to take a risk, and enough dopamine and norepinephrine to have good focus, attention, and movement toward our goals. We need enough serotonin and oxytocin to keep us emotionally satisfied, secure, and willing to try again when we fail. We need endorphins and anandamide to feel pleasure and stem pain along the path. We need mental fortitude developed through emotional control, which means we need to have learned to confront failure and proceed despite it. We need courage to take the next step, despite our fears. We need practice that is regular and recurrent enough to give us an accurate view of our abilities. We need control of our breath, which allows us access to the nervous system and steers our conscious experience.

We must explore the deepest parts of ourselves and integrate them as one.

The Timeline Problem and Stress: Viewing the Past, the Present, and the Future

Is it best to simply live in the present? Or is there a more complete truth that doesn't require abandoning some of our mental facilities' best uses, such as planning and reflecting? How can we improve strategies for solving problems, increase the speed and capability of adapting, and rise to the myriad challenges we face in modern life? How does our basic view of the past, present, and future direct so much in life?

To answer these questions, let's examine some typical timeline challenges. Living solely in the future, for example, often creates a sense of anxiety, fear, and worry. Knowing that we have to provide food, shelter, college tuition, car payments, or whatever else the future holds can be daunting and mentally exhausting. Knowing that someday—an unknown day that could be tomorrow or decades away—you will die, you wonder: Will I leave my loved ones enough? What will my legacy be? Did I accomplish what I set out to do in this life? All of these worries can cause a deep sense of insecurity and fear, not to mention keep us up at night. To live in the grip of the future is to suffer.

On the other hand, living in the past has its own drawbacks. Many people revisit acts that should have been done differently and things that should or should not have been said. Others escape to the past, to a time when things were better than in the present. But living in the past can make us feel lost or uncertain, naively romantic, and distracted. It can make us want to sleep the day through, neglectful of current responsibilities and wishing for times long gone. To live like this, as a remnant of the past, is also to suffer.

If to live in either the future or the past is only to suffer, surely the solution is to live in the *now*. Stay out of your head, live in your body, and take action, and you will get the most out of life, the argument goes. Is this truly the solution?

It is true: The now is absolutely necessary and often neglected. Our brains get looped into a default mode that alternates between replaying the past and focusing on the future; the present remains ever elusive. Naturally, to rectify this problem, it makes sense to seek to reside *here*, in the present moment. As you begin to make this shift, you will notice that your suffering does, in fact, recede. The stress you experience is temporarily alleviated. You feel a lightness of being. To exist in the present is to somehow escape the constraints and pressures of time.

However, living solely in the present should not be our final goal, and to do so is a regressive human developmental action. What do I mean by regressive? All three mental states—past, present, and future—are significantly limited by themselves. But combined, they allow us to effectively adapt in an uncertain world.

As humans, we possess the ability to reflect on the past, learn from it, and apply our new knowledge to present and future actions. There is incalculable value in knowing, learning, studying, and remembering the past. Reflecting on history, both personal and societal, can yield clear insights to help us avoid repeating the mistakes of our ancestors and our younger selves.

Contrastingly, in imagining the future, we can evaluate possible actions and solutions before we plunge forward to experience the consequences. By looking into the future, we can plan for tomorrow so that it is less uncertain. There is power in evaluating the future.

The ability to review the past and plan for the future is what lends human beings some of our greatest insights and adaptations. To rid ourselves of this talent is tantamount to giving away a key that unlocks vast reservoirs of power. The past and future should not and cannot replace the present, but they are excellent resources. What is important to realize is that the past and future operate in our conscious experience much more slowly than does the present. It is important to evaluate when and how existing in this space is useful and when it is not.

The circuitry of the brain that involves visualizing the past and imagining the future is part of the Default Mode Network (DMN): those parts of the brain that light up when you daydream or think about a past event. When you think about yourself or others, this circuitry is activated. When you reflect on your emotional state to investigate how you are feeling, this network is activated. And none of this is bad ... unless you spend all or most of your time in the DMN. And therein lies the rub: most people do exactly that. It has become a part of us that we abuse, and through that abuse, we suffer greatly.

At this very moment, important things are happening all around you. To be able to focus on the task in front of you, you must act in the present, not the DMN. To be available in your life, to listen and respond, to foster true connections with friends, family members, partners, and business associates, you must direct conscious attention to the now. To act maximally and be successful in this world, you must learn to have presence of mind, be accessible, and eliminate distractions. It is a matter of building the proper pathways and reinforcing them to the extent that they function at a master level.

What is required is a better way to handle these temporal foci. We need to be able to more readily and intentionally shift states: in other words, to adapt. We need to reduce the depression and anxiety that existing solely in one state can bring, as well as the poor habits that are often a result. We must understand our neurochemical and biological needs that can foster balance, and with it, growth, innovation, creativity, and problem solving. Understanding and being able to intentionally implement state shifts can help provide the emotional resilience, intimacy, and joy we crave.

As countless life philosophies and religions have aptly pointed out, life involves a great deal of suffering. While many "isms" try to mitigate or even eliminate suffering, such a goal is always elusive. But what if we embrace it?

If you get "better" at suffering and *accept it fully*, you just might be amazed at how much less it negatively impacts your past, present, and future. Such acceptance can help you act appropriately in the moment, your emotional, physical, and mental faculties intact as they carefully address the present. It can let you face the future with a renewed faith in your own abilities, and it can help you examine the past with improved perspective. You will be able to glean wisdom from your reflections, and you will have the presence of mind to use the information when you actually need it. Full acceptance of suffering knits together past, present, and future.

Denying or pushing a part of yourself away is the surest path to stress. No matter how you try to rid yourself of it, it will creep back in. However, by fully accepting and integrating suffering, you will be able to both confront and welcome life and the stress it brings.

Truly integrating the three mental states of past, present, and future and using each to its fullest potential can increase your learning speed and improve your decision-making abilities. It is important to know how and when to use each state. By developing a clear path to harness the potential of each, you will maximize the brain's capability for learning, integrating, and applying information.

Information is not useful until you know what to do with it. This is achieved when we are able to apply information in the moment we actually need it. By engaging in the three-step process of learning, integrating, and applying, information becomes knowledge and knowledge becomes a powerful tool.

For example, when I first began training in martial arts, I did not understand the extent to which past, present, and future affect our lives. The insights of my own experiences often seemed contradictory, and most books I had read stressed living in the now as the ultimate goal. But through training, I discovered a very different answer, one that relied on context.

I found that by taking the time to reflect on what I was being taught, to see how or if it made sense—how moves were applied in certain situations and so on—I could more clearly extrapolate principles that applied to many situations instead of isolated incidents. If I visualized future applications, my consciousness would help build the necessary pathways to make that movement more readily available in the moment. And when I stepped in front of an opponent, I could simply let everything else go and be fully immersed in the present. Of course, this did not happen overnight: It took many years of practice to discover how each mental state can serve a higher purpose.

Once past, present, and future have been integrated, all are understood as purposeful and suffering becomes tolerable. Using learning methods to disrupt existing patterning in the nervous system and foster deeper integration is a worthwhile endeavor for its own sake. But maximizing our conscious attention in the present, as well as using visualization to both reflect and prepare, fosters exceptional learning and releases us from the constraints of the timeline problem. To master the stress response, we must engage in full acceptance of who we have been, are, and may be.

What Does it Mean to Live in Modern Society?

In modern times, there are advantages more glorious than at any other time in human history. But those advantages have come at the cost of some very important unmet needs. The result is a great deal of stress.

Modern society operates at an ever-increasing rate, wherein the demands upon time and attention increase likewise. The information you need to be successful in life is very different than it was even thirty years ago. Recall, the Internet was not widely used until the World Wide Web was invented and made publicly available in 1991. Since then, information and tools in virtually every industry have seen huge technological advancements. Entertainment, sales and marketing, computer technology, medicine, news, global markets, publishing, and construction—everything has leapt forward, but the tradeoff has been significant demands on time and attention and rapid learning curves.

When attempting to adapt, it is easy to get lost in the ocean of data, information, and distractions constantly surrounding us. Increasingly, we are gravitating toward one of two extremes: becoming more specialized in an ever-narrowing field of expertise—thinking, learning, and obsessing over a single path of pursuit—or simply checking out, hardly participating in society at all. Modern life affords both of these options and seemingly encourages them. Humanity's current interdependence has made it far less important to possess a wide and varied skill set. Why would I need to know what plants are edible, how to hunt and process meat correctly, how to build and make tools, how to navigate, how to grow food or sew clothes when all of these skills can be substituted at the click of a button?

On the surface, many aspects of modern society appear to be fairly benign. As societies grow and technology improves, the need for specialization becomes a logical efficiency. But it also means that we require less of ourselves and those around us. We are physically, biologically, and chemically wired for survival, and a varied skill set is an essential part of survival, but our need for variety often goes unsatisfied by the actual requirements of today's world. In addition, we can afford to be anonymous regardless of the path we choose, but this anonymity comes at the cost of yet more stress to our emotional and mental well-being.

Depression and anxiety are rampant. According to the CDC, in 2017 suicide was the tenth leading cause of death in the United States. More specifically, for those aged thirty-five to fifty-four, it was the fourth leading cause of death; for those aged ten to thirty-four, it was the second leading cause of death. The World Health Organization (WHO) states that worldwide, suicide occurs once every forty seconds. And these figures do not account for all drug overdoses, an epidemic that is taking lives at an increasingly alarming rate.

We are impatient. Hell, we have to be. Things need to be done and done now. But this stressful attitude actually undermines our ability to learn and adapt quickly. It makes us anxious and often depressed. In modern society, it is hard to know what we actually need in order to deal with life's difficulties and cherish the good moments. We often neglect necessary parts of ourselves: We don't sleep well, eat well, or exercise sufficiently. How do we get beyond the distress induced by our neglect of human needs?

It is no wonder that many of us decide that it is not worth it, that we would rather drift through life or work at a pace that eclipses most of life. Countless individuals default to satisfying the human brain's need for variety and challenge with food, drugs, and passive entertainment. Unfortunately this path also leads to emotional, mental, and physical distress. The immune system becomes impaired as a result. We sicken in every sense of the word.

How do we fuel our human system's needs for challenge, risk, creativity, and intimacy? How do we face the fear necessary to experience these life aspects while valuing fear's evolutionary role? To survive and thrive as human beings, we have many needs: true intimacy; meaningful human interaction beyond the workplace and social media; expressions of creativity; time for quiet and deep thinking; a sense of purpose; physical outlets to test and understand our own strength and capacity. In all, we need a wide range of skill sets and experiences. And intermixed with all, we need a healthy outlook on fear and an understanding of its utility. *We need them all but instead, we are busy working furiously or checking out like zombies, and our biological, neurochemical, and physical states can barely support us.*

As modern humans, we are presented with two very important tasks. One is finding balance in our biological, neurochemical, and physical states in a world operating twenty-four hours a day, seven days a week. The other is defining what that balance is. The fact is, many of us don't know who we are in modern society, so we either spend too much time trying to figure it out, or we just check out.

We need an understanding of ourselves in light of our current circumstances. We need effective tools that balance our evolutionary makeup with the demands and stresses of modern life. What we need, in fact, is to master the stress response.

The following chapters lay the crucial groundwork for the existence of certain principles of mastering the stress response. With this knowledge, you will be able to understand the inner workings and design of each tool presented in the final chapters of this book.

Who We Are

A Very Brief History

We are human beings: great apes who have learned of our own inevitable demise through the consciousness we simultaneously value and despise. We are extremely limited and vulnerable while simultaneously possessing untold potential. We are the product of those who came before us, the individuals who learned to adapt in an incredibly unforgiving world.

We are part of a legacy that has had to innovate, create, plan, communicate, and negotiate with thousands of circumstances just to survive each day. It is only within the last 10,000 to 12,000 years that we have started to have time enough to look beyond the day's survival. It is only within the last few thousand years that we have developed a method of storing large quantities of data: writing. It is highly plausible that it has only been roughly 3,000 years since human consciousness itself emerged and was codified to its current extent.[8]

Then there are the last 100 years. In the last century, we have seen exponential progress in terms of tools, technology, poverty, disease, and general innovation. With such changes have come new stressors like air pollution, constant light stimulation, incessant information input, reduced sleep quality, excessive eating, reduced movement, and a deep shift in what mental facilities we use and emphasize. *Our advances and technologies have permitted us to outpace our own biological and psycho-sociological adaptations.* Only with a concerted, carefully designed effort can we find the balance we need to thrive.

To understand who and what we are as humans, it is helpful to have a certain understanding of the individual parts of the human body and brain and how they interrelate. From an evolutionary perspective, our closest relatives in the animal kingdom are the other great apes; however, it is easy to see some of the ways in which we differ. For example, on average, the chimpanzee (one of our closest relatives) has a brain weighing less than one pound, while the human brain weighs close to three pounds. Additionally, the white matter in the temporal cortex is far more dense in humans, giving us a notably better ability to process information than our close relatives.

Human brain size has increased over the course of our evolution. The Smithsonian has wonderful displays showing how early humans spread over the globe, encountering new environments and new challenges. As ancient humans came up with the necessary innovations to survive, brain size increased substantially over a period of millions of years. But it is important to note that when it comes to the brain, it is not *just* about size. The Neanderthals, a close evolutionary relative to us, had brains that were larger than ours. Yet the only remaining legacy of the Neanderthal is the small percent of their DNA found in some humans.

As we have evolved, we have made certain tradeoffs between the growth of our brain and the capabilities of our bodies. The size and strength of our muscles is comparatively limited. We lack hardened skin, sharp teeth, and claws, all of which are common adaptations in other apex predators. But the human brain, as most of us have been told throughout our lives, is truly the distinguishing characteristic that has propelled us to the top of the food chain. And not only the brain's size, *but how we have used it*, both knowingly and unknowingly.

How much conscious influence we have had over thousands upon thousands of years of our own evolution is unknowable. However, the study of our nervous systems and bodies in modern times yields data that illuminates the potential of investing in ourselves.

We are deeply social beings capable of cooperating with large numbers of strangers, primarily through language and established social parameters. We are agile and dexterous beings, capable of performing incredibly varied extreme physical feats. We are deeply cognitive beings, constantly inventing new ways of examining the world, such as mathematics, art, and engineering.

The human brain, and more broadly the human nervous system, exhibits a unique aspect of plasticity. Our brains can adapt to a changing environment at a pace and extent that is, to the best of our knowledge, unmatched on this planet. Valuing this plastic-adaptability is essential to understanding human function and evolution.

The human brain is part of the central nervous system. The central nervous system is composed of the brain and the spinal cord. Nerves elsewhere in the body comprise what is called the peripheral nervous system. The human nervous system in its entirety is the most complex thing we are aware of in the universe.

Other animals share our basic structure of central and peripheral nervous systems, but the finer points are quite different. Let's begin with the physical differences, specifically the trait of plasticity. In principle, plasticity means that small changes in the brain's wiring can lead to large changes in its functionality. Here is a very brief summary of what is and what is not specific to the human brain.

Two things that are NOT specific:

- *Size*. Certain whales have larger brains than we do. Their brains can also contain a much greater number of neurons, even accounting for relative size.

- *Structures*. Other highly intelligent mammals possess brain structures remarkably similar to ours, including the neocortex. In fact, the term 'neocortex' has traditionally been used to refer to the human brain, but this is a misnomer. It is simply a highly intelligent mammalian brain.

Four things that ARE notable as specific:

- *Interconnectivity and density*. Links and communication among certain types of brain cells is a uniquely human feature, as is the thickness of certain neural connections.

- *Regionalization and abundance*. Another unique feature is the organization and profusion of certain features in the brain that have to do with neurotransmitters such as serotonin, dopamine, and acetylcholine.

• *Structural and functional reorganization based on experiences.* The human brain's ability to reorganize parts of the brain, particularly certain motor control and dexterity functions, is very rare, although it is shared by some other animals. Basically, what you experience and what you do about it rewires the brain in unique ways.

• *Growth and expansion.* Distinctive to humans are certain features that enhance the ability of the brain to actually expand physically, especially within the neocortex.

These and other facts established by scientific research are indicators of the level of human plasticity that makes us a unique species.

I do not highlight the exclusiveness of our species to place us somehow outside or above nature. We are nature, inseparable from it, reliant on our interrelation with it and all its other components: bacteria, fungi, trees, grasses, animals, rivers, oceans, rocks, and other elements. We could not exist without this integration. But our uniqueness in terms of certain factors and their sum value can hardly be overstated. There exist incredible similarities and adaptive capabilities throughout nature, but our combination of abilities puts us in a truly separate category, one that is not different in degree but in kind. This is a double-edged sword; with it comes tremendous responsibility to ourselves and our species, as well as to the world with which we coexist.

Eating and Diet: Adaptability and Non-Specialization

We are omnivores, adapted to eat a wide variety of foods. Our species evolved this way to feed the brain's growth while supporting the body's development. As Michael Pollen keenly points out in his *Omnivore's Dilemma*, our bodies developed shorter intestines and bigger brains. The advantages of a larger brain have already been discussed. Shorter intestines allowed for a reduced digestive time, permitting ingested energy to be allocated as needed as quickly as possible, such as to the development of our unique brain-and-body connection.

But human health is not just about eating a wide variety of items. *Not* eating and limiting the time(s) when we eat is also an important feature when considering health development and longevity. Peter Attia, MD, a doctor specializing in longevity, recently gave an interview wherein he stated that the only thing that has been demonstrated to enhance longevity significantly is fasting.

Evolution for humans is usually expressed on the order of millennia, and over this time, many of our eating habits have required fasting. It wasn't optional—it was survival. This has been true until very, very recently.[9] It is essential to remember this fact when considering the modern era, when food abundance is the norm in industrialized nations.

As food has become more than plentiful, we have become unsure of how to deal with it. Our society has even produced jobs to tell us how to use food correctly: various sports coaches, nutritionists, and dietitians. Putting aside life-threatening allergies, which are on case-by-case basis, the bottom line of the current data is twofold: One, we are simply eating too much based on the average person's activity level. And two, food with added hormones, antibiotics, and other chemicals wreaks havoc on our systems, exacerbating an already overly dense caloric input.

There is no one diet likely to be optimal for everyone—and thank goodness for that, since variation as diversity plays a key role in our species' ability to adapt to a wide swath of changing environments and stressors. But there is growing evidence demonstrating the roles of stress and recovery and how they impact whatever diet we choose. So rather than focusing on the carnivore, omnivore, vegetarian, or vegan diet, let's begin by concentrating on when and how much.

Mounting evidence around fasting and various diets suggests that it may be less about what we feed ourselves, and far more about *when, how much, and in combination (or not) with what metabolism-increasing exercises.* In other words, are we using the fuel or storing it? If we are storing it, are we storing too much? At what times of the day are we taking in fuel? Before or after what type of activity(s)? At what frequency?[10]

Intestines are part of the nervous system called the enteric nervous system. There are nerves in and around the gastrointestinal system that communicate to the central nervous system. The central nervous system then interprets the messages and makes the necessary adjustments throughout the body.

We need to understand how to truly listen to our bodies to determine if a diet we are following is actually serving us, and moreover, if it is doing so optimally. Learning to listen to our bodies involves paying attention to the nervous system's response to what and when we are eating.

As humans, our brains make up approximately 2 to 3 percent of our body size but demand 18 to 25 percent of our energy, *even at rest.* Comparatively, other apes use only about 8 percent of their energy to fuel their brains while at rest.

The process of digesting food requires energy allocation in order to extract energy. If this is happening all day, especially with foods of different complexities (fats take longer to break down, as does protein), the ongoing energy allocation affects the development of other parts of the body and brain. Recall that one of the reasons we developed as we did was to reduce the amount of time needed to digest. Add to that the understanding that our body clock, called a circadian rhythm, plays a key role with how we partition food for use or storage. Our circadian rhythm can be affected by the heat increase that accompanies food intake, especially in the evening when the body is producing melatonin, trying to signal the body to decrease temperature in preparation for sleep. Additionally, the state of the nervous system affects the body's ability to digest food. Various arousal states, such as action or rest states, prioritize certain functions over others. This means sometimes you digest and use food very well, and sometimes you don't.

When we are in higher-stress states, our bodies do not digest as well, or—depending on the height of the state of arousal—not at all. It is in a resting state that the body digests best. Then, it can allocate blood flow and nutrients to the intestines, as well as have time to produce saliva and the digestive enzymes that assist with that process. When the body is in a sleep state, any digestion interferes with optimal rest. Sleep should be considered a time of clean up, restoration, regeneration, and integration, but digestion distracts the body from these essential tasks. In summation, constantly trying to digest food competes with the other needs of the brain and body and deregulates us.

We often try to get around all of this in modern society, and it ends up causing mayhem in our systems. It disrupts hormone balances, fuel partitioning, sleep quality, wakefulness, and so on. We are increasingly eating too much, at the wrong times, with reduced activity, and alone.

Those promoting different diets may point to various groups in an effort to support their causes. They may claim, for example, that the most centenarians are found in Okinawa, Japan, where they eat a very alkalizing, vegetarian diet. But that is not the full picture. There is conflicting evidence, including much larger group studies showing that vegetarian and vegan diets don't fare any better than other diets in prolonging life.

So why do people on Okinawa live so long? A more complete explanation might take into account other vital contributors to health and well-being, namely social bonds, exercise, how much is eaten, and when. The Okinawans have almost no obesity in their society. They are active, social, and spend time outside. They have a lifestyle and sociability factors that contribute to lower stress. In other words, it is not just diet; rather, it is management of the stress and rest states and allowing the body to find true balance.

Dan Buettner, a researcher for National Geographic, outlined the now-famed Blue Zones: areas of the world with the longest-living people. These zones do not form around a diet, but around a combination of factors that allows for effective stress management and energy allocation. Whether those factors take the form of regular diet and exercise, cooperation and healthy relationships, psychological well-being, or a value for all members of society, the commonality is a more balanced stress response and an extended life span.

France is an excellent example. This is a country that adores its indulgences: food, smoking, alcohol, etc. Yet the French generally have better health than those in the United States. Is it simply that they eat less processed food and walk everywhere? Far likelier is that it is due to managing the stress response differently; for example, the French take their time when eating so as not to overeat. Less value is placed on the food than on time spent relaxing with friends and family.

So, does that mean you can eat whatever you want so long as you take your time? No. What's more important is learning to listen to your body, learning to adapt and shift states rapidly and consistently. And the only way to accomplish this is to become aware of and rebalance your action and resting state continuum, so that you have the ability to listen in the first place.

Here are a few easy recommendations. If what you eat gives you a headache or hives, that is a negative type of stress, so don't eat that anymore. If you feel tired right after you eat, you are likely eating too much or at the wrong time. If you crash after eating or need to eat all the time not to be "hangry," you need to rethink what you're eating. If what you eat gives you brain fog and lack of clarity, you're either eating at the wrong time, eating too much, or eating something that your body perceives as stressful.

What you need to eat to feel clear and energized will vary depending on your training, exercise habits, personal goals, stress levels, and more. But paying attention to the messages that your body is sending while and after eating will set you down the path to far better outcomes and quality of life. Those in touch with the stress response are equipped to do this, even amid the myriad stressors in modern society.

We Are Emotional Beings

We are emotional beings strongly driven by social bonds. We need love, intimacy, romance, and connection with other living beings. We must have acceptance, direction, purpose, and stability within our emotional framework to function at the highest levels. There are thousands of things we do and experience that affect our emotional health. We experience an incredible range of feelings through our emotionally directed experiences.

What we choose to do, both knowingly and passively, in daily life affects this emotional landscape: the food we eat; the drugs, alcohol, or medications we ingest; the organizations we join; the friends we choose; the exercise(s) we do, the challenges we face; and so on. These inputs make up our environmental conditioning and play a major role in our development as humans. Being mindful of the various inputs and how they affect the brain and body allows us to make better choices, as well as to learn to command our emotions. A deep understanding of what we can and cannot control is of critical importance. In the area of what we can control, we need to know what to do to maximize our chances of the best possible outcomes.

So what are emotions? Our definitions and categorizations of them have developed and redeveloped over time. Depending on how you approach them, there are between six and eight base emotions.[11]

Dr. Robert Plutchik, professor emeritus at the Albert Einstein College of Medicine, took a psycho-evolutionary approach that included eight basic emotions: fear, anger, sadness, disgust, surprise, anticipation, trust, and joy. He further broke down these emotions into more and less intense variations using a color wheel chart.[12]

Plutchik's model provides good insight into the range of overlap and possibilities of emotions. As our language and culture continues to develop, such charts and tools will no doubt continue to evolve. But what will remain consistent will be the underlying core of emotions and how they influence our actions and our stress levels.

There is a great deal of survival strategy within our emotional machinery. Emotions have a great deal of bearing on our ability to bond and collaborate. They offer adaptive qualities in changing situations and social constructs and increase our reproductive fitness. Strong emotions help us learn to be wary of dangerous situations, things, or people. Emotions like love, joy, and serenity help us to bond with each other or to repeat an activity to further elicit those pleasant emotions. The richness of human life is due, in large part, to our emotional capacity.

However, emotions left unchecked can result in numerous issues, including a diminished capacity to respond in dangerous situations, a lack of willingness to be responsible for poor decision making, and sometimes even suicide. Genetic makeup and childhood environmental conditioning have a large impact on the negative vulnerability of particular individuals. However, understanding where to begin and how to develop greater command, awareness, serenity, and quality of life is extremely empowering. We may not be able to choose our genetic makeup and early life circumstances, but we can choose to maximize our capacities as humans and reach toward optimal living by harnessing our emotions and painting our desired landscape.

Understanding our emotional machinery and how it operates and recognizing our ability to train and influence it will mean a great deal in terms of the quality of life that we experience. At the core is the need to master the stress response. It is via this ability that we can operate at our clearest and express our best selves. This is as true in relationships as it is in the face of survival.

Neurochemistry

Neurotransmitters

Let's define some language that will help in reading this book. Most all of us have probably at least heard of neurotransmitters, but we may not understand their role. Neurotransmitters are the chemical signals released by the nervous system. They are basically messengers between neurons throughout the brain and body. Depending on their classification, there are as few as 40 to more than 100 neurotransmitters in the human body.[13] The two main classes of neurotransmitters are excitatory and inhibitory. Various neurotransmitters function independently and/or in tandem to assist and control wakefulness, sleep, thought, pain, memory, attention, focus, mood, learning, aggression, impulsivity, pleasure, energy, or movement. Neurotransmitters are vital in our bodies, and *how* they work is one of the things that makes us different from many, if not all, other species on the planet.

The first neurotransmitter identified was acetylcholine. Over the years, scientists have learned that acetylcholine plays a vital role in learning, memory, movement, and REM sleep. Like many neurotransmitters, acetylcholine has different roles in the brain than it does in the body. With regard to the stress response, acetylcholine is important for a diverse set of neural functions, most notably with regard to activity in the brain that boosts attentiveness when faced with uncertainty. Acetylcholine is also the main neurotransmitter of the somatic nervous system.

There are a few other neurotransmitters that are of high concern for those of us looking to master the stress response. Among them are serotonin, dopamine, and anandamide. Many of today's news articles talk about one or another of these and how current medications, drugs, or alcohol affect our brains specifically through these messengers. Most, if not all, of these neurotransmitters participate in highly complex functions throughout the brain and body. However, for our purposes, I will simplify some of the roles that they play.

Serotonin plays a role in how we feel about our lives and whether we feel satisfied and secure. Serotonin is also linked with our circadian rhythm, contributing to daytime function. Our goal with this neurotransmitter is to facilitate its production during waking hours in a balanced and healthy manner. Often, it should be produced in combination with oxytocin, the bonding hormone, as we are a deeply social species.

Dopamine is central to the reward system in the brain, responsible for driving us toward behavior that makes us feel good. Activities that combine high levels of dopamine, norepinephrine, and testosterone promote high engagement and high reward. Harnessing this combination helps us complete tasks and reach intended goals.

Anandamide, the so-called bliss chemical, is an endocannabinoid, meaning it assists in pain modulation and pleasure. It uses the same receptors that *cannabis sativa* does. Anandamide is also associated with energy output rewards, such as the "runner's high." This chemical contributes to flow state activity and optimal performance. Engaging in healthy activities that promote anandamide release contributes to quality of life and the emotion of joy.

Hormones - Another Type of Messenger

Hormones, too, are often in the news today. We hear about everything from added hormones in food, to hormone therapy, to popular talk show hosts discussing how it's "all about your hormones."

Hormones are part of the endocrine system. They are produced by endocrine glands and released into the bloodstream, where they travel to their target cells in specific organs or tissues. Once they connect to their target cells, the intended reaction occurs. Common hormones primarily affect growth, development, and reproduction, but they are also involved in pain regulation. As different levels of hormones circulate, they can affect mood too.

Though many hormones ultimately play a role in stress and recovery, we will focus on just a few. Primary to our topics of interest are seven hormones: cortisol, insulin, melatonin, oxytocin, testosterone, estrogen, and vasopressin.

Cortisol is a hormone that contributes much to our circadian rhythm. Its levels are typically highest in the mornings, since it assists with waking up, and lowest during the night. It is also known as the primary stress hormone, because its level increases substantially during periods of stress. Cortisol plays a key role in assisting the body to prioritize high-activity responses, including increased blood sugar, reduced insulin sensitivity, reduced inflammatory responses, and other immune modulations; it also assists with strong short-term memory formation. In proper doses and timely rhythms, it is a high-functioning hormone that greatly contributes to the body's optimal performance.

If cortisol levels are chronically high or low, there are profound implications for overall health and well-being. High cortisol levels reduce grey matter in the brain and eventually lead to Cushing's disease, while low cortisol levels eventually lead to Addison's disease. Both describe deeply impaired states of health, performance, and well-being.

Insulin is released by the pancreas. Its primary function is to control glucose levels in the blood. The easiest way to think about insulin is that it tells the sugar in your body where to go. It works with other hormones to partition fuel for use or for storage, as well as to promote glucose homeostasis. Our goal is maintain highly functional insulin by regulating eating times and maintaining insulin sensitivity. Mismanagement of this hormone leads to significant health consequences, including diabetes, cardiovascular disease, and potentially cancer.

Melatonin is responsible for initiating responses with circadian rhythm activity. It is essential in the sleep-wake cycle, signaling the body to reduce its temperature and prepare for sleep. If serotonin is the daytime chemical, then melatonin is its nighttime counterpart. Engaging in timely activity that promotes balance between serotonin and melatonin is one of our goals.

Oxytocin can be viewed as the bonding chemical produced by childbirth, breastfeeding, and shared stress experiences, including orgasms. This hormone is present during shared struggle as well. Engaging in activities that healthfully promote this essential hormone is a major concern in mastering the stress response.

Testosterone and estrogen are the primary sex hormones. Engaging in activities that are known to promote the healthy balance of these sex hormones is important for energy levels, desire, intimacy, and reproduction. It is also critical to maximizing our relationship to the stress response.

Finally, vasopressin, also known as the antidiuretic hormone, is responsible for regulating fluids in the body, such as blood and urine. However, in the central nervous system, vasopressin also acts as a neurotransmitter by contributing to the regulation of our circadian rhythms, thermoregulation, and adrenocorticotropic hormone release (ACTH). ACTH's main function is to regulate cortisol, which helps the body respond to stress. For our purposes, vasopressin can be understood as the fear and attachment chemical. When we are afraid and experiencing significant stress, vasopressin is present in high quantities in the central nervous system. Alcohol reduces vasopressin, which may help explain the concept of liquid courage. But interestingly, vasopressin also plays a significant role in emotional attachment between humans. Higher levels of vasopressin correspond to lower levels of testosterone production, facilitating an attachment to a partner or child. Our goal with vasopressin is to understand its complex roles so that we have the awareness to upshift or downshift its production as we engage in a variety of activities and behaviors and form stable relationships.

So, What's the Difference Between a Hormone and a Neurotransmitter?

For our purposes, there are a few key differences between hormones and neurotransmitters. Neurotransmitters are part of the nervous system and communicate directly with neurons (nerve cells), some glands, and certain muscle cells such as the heart.[14] Communication between neurons happens fast, most often within milliseconds. Hormones, on the other hand, travel via the bloodstream and are therefore slower to act, sometimes taking minutes or even days to take effect.

Some chemical messengers can act as both a hormone and a neurotransmitter, depending on the capacity in which they serve. Of this type of messenger, central to our discussion are vasopressin, as previously mentioned, as well as endorphins and the two types of adrenaline, epinephrine and norepinephrine.

Endorphins are the body's natural pain killers, released during periods of stress, but they are also associated with pleasure, sex, love, laughter, and other good feelings. There are several types of endorphins released by the body and brain.

Epinephrine and norepinephrine are central to the stress response. The level of their release changes based on perceived or actual demand to increase function in learning, focus, memory, and high-output activities. They affect the speed of your heart rate as well as how hard it squeezes. Both chemicals increase blood sugar levels to prepare you for an increased demand of energy. There are also some differences between the two types of adrenaline. For example, norepinephrine can cause blood vessels to narrow, which increases blood pressure. Epinephrine can relax some of the smooth muscle in your airways, which improves breathing.

Epinephrine and norepinephrine are best known for their roles in the stress response, but they also play roles in mood, immune function, and inflammation. Too much epinephrine in the body can lead to heart palpitations, high blood pressure, and anxiety. Too little can contribute to sleep problems and pain disorders such as fibromyalgia, as well as depression and anxiety.

Balancing the activity of all of these chemical messengers in the body is critical for a high-quality life—and it all starts with understanding the fundamentals of the stress response. As we seek to find balance and promote an optimal level of each chemical at its respective time, a coordinated rhythm should take place. Like a grand symphony of instruments with each playing its part, these chemicals can create the music to which we compose our lives.

Messengers and Coordination Under Threat

The nervous system is essentially an ultra-fast electrical-chemical system of communication. The endocrine system, of which hormones are a part, is a chemical messenger system that relies on the relatively slower channels of the cardiovascular network. *When working properly,* the nervous system and the endocrine system function together to maximize conditions within the body to prioritize survival.

When your body feels it is under threat, these and other systems in your brain and body coordinate to collect information and send it back to the brain, which then responds appropriately. Your nervous system is intensely reactive. For example, if you put your hand on a hot stove and burn yourself, what happens? Assuming your systems are all working correctly—that you don't have paralysis or some other condition preventing normal function—your hand immediately recoils from the hot stove, *even before you consciously process what has happened.* This is because non-conscious processing happens in circuitry of the brain that controls more basic functions. If you burn yourself, these functions are immediately prioritized to maximize your survival. Your brain doesn't have the time to process and interpret all possible meanings of the situation before it reacts to protect you. Interpretation and processing can safely happen at a later stage.

Your nervous system's next priority is to mobilize any necessary resources to respond to the threat. Responding to the nervous system's direction, the hormonal system responds and there you are: fully alert, heart pumping, and perhaps slightly queasy from the adrenaline release. Then your higher-level, conscious brain gets involved. Your optic nerve seeks out the important information, such as the red color of the burner, and your brain interprets what happened: that your stove is on, the burner is hot, and you accidentally put your hand on it. All of this sounds like a lot, and it is, but it all happens in a matter of seconds. At this point, your conscious brain is in control, and you take whatever steps you deem necessary based on the seriousness of the situation.

All of Our Senses Play a Role in the Stress Response

How many senses are you aware of? Most of us are cognizant of only five: taste, touch, smell, hearing, and sight. But our lives and experiences are made up of input from other senses as well, senses that influence how we react, perform, and coordinate our ongoing efforts to respond to the world. These other senses are essential to our survival and connection to each other and our environment. Proprioception, interoception, and our vestibular senses all provide critical awareness of our own bodies. Utilizing and honing all eight senses is essential to maximizing our own emotional, cognitive, and physical development as human beings.

Let's begin, however, with the five commonly discussed senses. If we take a simple example, such as food, we can quickly see how each sense plays its role. Taste offers us a way to experience pleasure, as well as help in determining whether something is energy rich or potentially dangerous to eat. Taste can also help to determine salt content, which is essential to the body's homeostasis. Smell is also heavily involved in helping us to identify whether a food is good or bad to eat. Touch informs us of the food's texture and whether it is hot or cold. Sight helps us identify things to eat and plays a role in how we hunt or gather potential food items, as does hearing. Listing these senses, I am reminded of hunting trips where my senses of smell, sight, and hearing worked sharply to alert me to the proximity of an animal.

How food looks, smells, and feels also impacts our emotions. For example, how food is plated has an impact on the dining event. Anyone who has been to a four-star restaurant will be familiar with the care taken with the arrangement of the cuisine. The chef does so because well-plated food taps into our emotional perceptions and feelings, heightening the experience.

With regard to mates or partners, all of our external senses play vital roles in the selection process. The most obvious is sight, of course; that's usually the first thing to attract us to a potential mate. But also important is the sound of their voice, the taste of their tongue, and the way we touch each other. Smell can also be a key indicator to help determine immune function compatibility between two people.

Most of us are familiar with applying our sensory input to things like food and mate selection. However, attuning and sharpening the external senses to the fullest extent possible is essential to mastering the stress response. Well-developed senses provide us with better input, thereby giving us, and therefore our nervous systems, a clearer picture of reality and expanding our frames of perception.

There are a variety of ways that external senses can be heightened and applied. For example, the sense of touch, with its receptors to detect temperature, pain, pleasure, and pressure, can be honed through practices like thermogenic training,[15] breathing exercises, and pressure training. In martial arts, pressure or touch can be used to track an opponent and reduce reaction time. In sex, love, and intimacy, understanding how different pressures heighten excitement increases pleasure, as well as allows nerves to reload sensitivity. Taste buds can be re-sensitized and sharpened through fasting. Hearing can be sharpened through both fight training and intimacy practice, and sight is profoundly augmented by martial art training. The survival stress tools outlined in later chapters will offer further analysis to assist in such efforts.

In addition to the five common external senses, there are three internal senses: proprioception, vestibular senses, and interoception. Proprioception is your orientation or awareness of movement and position in space, most commonly with regard to your muscles, limbs, and joints. The vestibular sense is also your orientation and awareness of movement in space, but specifically with regard to balance or while inverted. Interoception governs your awareness of your internal urges and workings, such hunger, thirst, heartbeat, or other processes of the body.

As humans in modern society, we spend much of our time focusing on external demands, which we process using our external senses. We rarely pay much attention to the internal senses, much less talk about them. Yet when neglected, they impede our ability to manage—much less master—stress.

Almost none of my students have been familiar with the term interoception prior to my introduction of it. Outside of certain academic circles, it tends to be unknown. Even google agrees, defining it as a *lesser-known* *sense that helps you understand and feel what's going on inside your body*. But the need to understand interoception is of utmost importance. To do so intellectually, meditatively, physically, and even culturally can help in honing internal awareness and fostering improved decision making. Becoming acutely aware of this sense supports us in understanding the stress response, feeling it, and responding appropriately.

It is a matter of learning to listen to the internal body in the most intimate and real way. So many messages from our bodies go unnoticed due to distraction, complacence, or denial. If we are unaware of the body's internal processes, our ability to handle and deal with stress is greatly diminished, if not negated altogether. Ignorant of how external inputs are affecting our internal states, we find ourselves anxious and bored, eager to rely on short-acting pleasure loops that often don't offer real pleasure instead of fostering lasting experiences of joy.

Hunger is often the easiest example to use. Internal awareness of hunger is primarily driven by the interoceptive sense. Hence, a lack of connection to this sense can have dire consequences. Although there are hormonal mechanisms that assist in managing the states of hunger and fullness, these mechanisms can be overridden and often are. Many in modern society simply eat for the sake of eating, often out of boredom. They are not eating because they are hungry, but because they want something to do. Meanwhile, they are unaware of the neurotransmitters and hormones that play a role in shaping and reinforcing this unhealthful habit.

Incessant snacking can lead to all sorts of issues, including insulin resistance, unnecessary weight gain, and a host of other problems. These problems often lead to others: issues with self-confidence, a reduced ability to perform physical challenges, and mental fogginess, as well as hormonal deregulation and a narrowing of the pleasure-reward centers of the brain. As weight changes and self-confidence diminishes, the body continues to seek balance, which has profoundly negative consequences in terms of managing stress. Too often, the result is just more eating.

This is a vicious circle. Learning to listen to the internal messages of the body and building skills that support such an awareness can help us retrain the brain and body for more optimal expression.

Nervous System

The Nervous System Parts as They Relate to Function

When I defined the nervous system earlier, I differentiated between the central nervous system, which is the brain and spinal cord, and the peripheral nervous system, which is composed of all the jelly fish-looking tendrils throughout the body that connect to the brain and spinal cord.

Figure 2 can help us examine how we can divide the nervous system for improved clarity.

Generally, we should think of the nervous system as a messaging structure that uses electrical and chemical messages to scan, regulate, and coordinate all systems throughout the body. It is highly complex, extremely adaptive, and very responsive to both internal and external stimuli. It prioritizes responses based on perceived demand at any given time, while also obeying certain rhythmic patterns. The nervous system needs a healthy balance of both consistency and spontaneity for optimal functioning.

One component of the larger nervous system is the autonomic nervous system. Part of the peripheral nervous system, it is responsible for governing the automatic processes of the body: heartbeat, digestion, liver function, pupil dilation or constriction, non-conscious breathing, and a great many more processes that occur automatically in order to keep you operational. You don't have to be awake, aware, or engaged in any way for these things to happen. You simply have to be alive.

Within the autonomic nervous system exists the sympathetic nervous system, which is responsible for the high(er) arousal states, such as being alert, exercising, and activating the fight or flight response. Then there is the parasympathetic nervous system, which deals with the low(er) arousal state: resting and digesting. Finally, there is the enteric nervous system, which governs the gut's behavior.

For the sake of simplicity, let's focus on the sympathetic and parasympathetic systems for now. You will notice that I described both in terms of the *arousal states* that they govern. In this book, arousal states are points along a continuum that covers every human condition, from being in a deep sleep to full fight, flight, or freeze.

Although the sympathetic and parasympathetic systems each have their separate responsibilities and often work to oppose one another, they work in tandem as well, constantly recalibrating as

CENTRAL AND PERIPHERAL NERVOUS SYSTEM

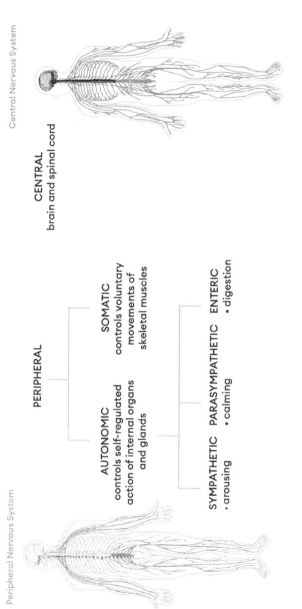

Peripheral Nervous System

Central Nervous System

CENTRAL
brain and spinal cord

PERIPHERAL

SOMATIC
controls voluntary
movements of
skeletal muscles

AUTONOMIC
controls self-regulated
action of internal organs
and glands

SYMPATHETIC
• arousing

PARASYMPATHETIC
• calming

ENTERIC
• digestion

FIGURE 2.

needed. Many articles, books, and other resources discuss these two systems as if when one is on, the other is off. This is not really the case, and it is not a helpful way to explore these two facets of the nervous system. Review Figure 3.

As an example, note that there are both sympathetic and parasympathetic nerves that innervate your heart. Each time you inhale, the sympathetic nerves are dominant and speed up your heart rate. With each exhale, the parasympathetic nerves are at work and lower your heart rate. The difference between these two states is known as heart rate variability and is both a health and athletic performance indicator.

So although each set of nerves has a different function, they work together to meet the demands of the body. Sometimes certain nerve pathways become more or less dominant to meet the needs of a given situation, making the sympathetic or parasympathetic system more dominant. It is not that only sympathetic nerves are firing or only parasympathetic nerves are firing. Rather, the expression of the nerves and the associated chemistry are more dominated by one system, which elicits certain responses.

For example, the parasympathetic system is responsible for constricting the pupils in your eyes and the airways in your lungs, whereas the sympathetic system dilates your eyes and relaxes the airways in your lungs. This is easy to understand when examined in the context of perceived demand. If you are safe in your home, cooking a meal and relaxing, then your body's arousal state downshifts to conserve energy, initiates the production of digestive enzymes, and generally prepares you to start digesting your food. There is no demand for energy output or high levels of alertness in this space. You don't need to increase your visual field and hone in on a potential predator. You don't need to run or fight. So constricted airways, a slowed heart rate, and constricted pupils make sense.

On the other hand, if you are outside of your home in the hustle and bustle of life, or if you encounter a situation in your home where your safety is threatened, then your arousal state demands a much higher responsiveness. Therefore, your airways relax so

SYMPATHETIC AND PARASYMPATHETIC NERVOUS SYSTEM

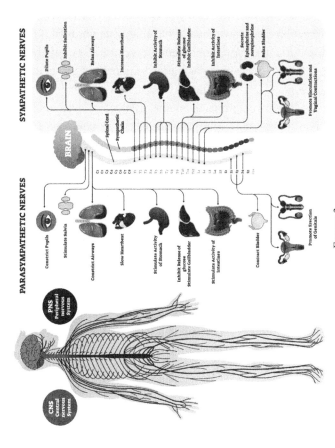

FIGURE 3.

that you can more easily take larger breaths of oxygen. Your heart speeds up to match the increased breaths and assist with faster oxygen delivery. Your pupils dilate to increase and sharpen the visual field. Your nervous system signals the release of glucose (sugar) from your liver to aid in the larger perceived demand of energy needed to take on the task.

Let us take another clear example: sex. In order for a man to get an erection or for a woman to have large amounts of blood flow to her clitoris, the parasympathetic nerves must be highly involved. However, an orgasm or ejaculation requires sympathetic system engagement. To complete the sex act, the two systems perform separate but highly coordinated actions. Hence, we need to harness both systems to maximize performance of the nervous system.[16]

Looking back at the illustration of the nervous system, there is another branch of the peripheral nervous system: the somatic nervous system. Like the other two, the somatic nervous system functions to meet our needs, and it is extremely adaptable and subject to development. This system is a collection of nerves under our voluntary control and is responsible for innervating our skeletal muscles.

Muscles can be divided into three primary categories: skeletal, cardiac, and smooth. Skeletal muscles are what we generally think of when we hear the term. Examples of skeletal muscles are things like biceps, quadriceps, and glutes. But there are also a ton with which you're likely not familiar. There are somewhere between 650 and 850 *named* skeletal muscles.[17]

The degree to which you govern the somatic nervous system largely depends on what you do, how you train, and how refined your movement is. Somatic control is developed through both conscious attention and non-conscious attention using habit and repetition.[18]

The Autonomic and Somatic Overlap

Control of the autonomic nervous system has yet to be well established scientifically. Wim Hof in his now-famous endotoxin study, was shown to actively influence his sympathetic nervous system, but exact mechanisms to control other aspects of the autonomic nervous system—such endocrine function, heartbeat, digestion, and smooth muscle tension—remain elusive.[19]

While specific links still need to be established through formal, controlled studies, I would argue, based on inference and experience, that a highly developed somatic nervous system offers humans greater capacity in and access to sympathetic and parasympathetic regulation of the autonomic nervous system. Isolating the mechanisms to grant this access will likely be difficult and take time. However, what is fairly well established is that perception affects all autonomic responses.

Perception in this case can be understood to mean a series of activities involving sensory input. How we train, our mindset within the training, the degree to which we are physically, emotionally, and mentally developed all prepare us to exert greater control over our automatic functions. If my heart rate increases based off external stimuli, I can counteract this effect using breath regulation and a focused mind, because I have trained myself to do so. However, the untrained individual will be significantly less successful.

Or, to return to the example of food, whether or not I think a meal looks and smells delicious influences my digestion. If I don't perceive the food to be good for me (good, in this instance, meaning aesthetically pleasing, agreeable, nutritious), I will not produce the same amount of digestive enzymes or peristalsis to assist me with digestion. Enzyme production and peristalsis are autonomically governed, yet I can actively influence them for maximal efficacy. The countless smooth muscles in your body are basically responsible for squishing stuff around. They are found all over: in your stomach, intestines, and other organs, in your veins and arteries, and just about everywhere else. Important for our purposes is the fact that these muscles are critical for constricting and dilating your vascular system. The autonomic nervous system signals the smooth muscles to constrict or dilate, based on perceived demand and need. Therefore, the vascular system can be consciously controlled to a certain extent.

Thermogenic training—exposing yourself to extreme temperatures for short periods—bolsters the vascular system. Studies have demonstrated that something as simple as consistent sauna use can *reduce all-cause mortality by up to 40 percent.* Based on recent trends in cold training, I expect studies with similar results to be forthcoming. Right now, there are thousands of individual test cases worldwide that offer testimony on improved health associated with cold training practices. Formal studies have already begun substantiating these positive results.

Homeostasis and Stress

If homeostasis is body and mind regulation to stabilize the internal system within a functional range, then stress is its challenger. And depending on survival priority—which is largely a result of perception—there can be significant competition between achieving homeostasis and pushing it aside to meet external demands.

When we hear the word homeostasis, we often visualize a static system peacefully at rest. However, our systems are always dynamic and active, constantly monitoring and calibrating to accommodate competing priorities. As part of this process, our systems seek conservation and as a result, patterns emerge. Stability in our systems is fostered by consistency. However, disruption in our systems forces them to adapt; therefore, in short bursts, disruption helps our systems recalibrate and improve their abilities to serve us by redefining a base level of operation. This is the concept of short-term stress as a beneficial tool.

However, in the case of chronic stress, homeostasis is disrupted to the point where internal systems constantly deprioritize meeting our internal needs. Under these conditions, pathology, disease, and breakdown manifest due to stress.

The Nervous System as a Protective Mechanism

As established, the nervous system has many jobs. Yet another of its tasks is to initiate specific system defaults in order to protect the body in certain situations.

Imagine you were seriously wounded. For most people, to remain conscious under such circumstances would mean a sustained high-level arousal state, possibly near panic. In this state, your blood pressure would also remain quite high: It wouldn't take long for your heart to pump all of the blood from your body.[20] So as a safeguard, your nervous system has the ability—make you pass out—to protect you. Fainting or syncope is a common response to shock or trauma, physical or otherwise.

The nervous system also protects the body by affecting tension in the muscles. When you try to stretch at the beginning of a workout, for example, your nervous system limits your range of movement to what it perceives as safe. As blood flows to an area of the body and metabolic activity increases, the nervous system adjusts to allow for a greater range of movement, although one still within the confines of its perceived limits. Although the range of motion is dependent on several factors—including how much blood is flowing to a particular area, the overall health and mobility of your connective tissue, any underlying injuries or scar tissue, and muscle pathologies—the nervous system is the primary driver.[21]

Whether or not the protective mechanism of the nervous system serves your best interest depends on context. It is also important to note that some of us have over- or under-protective systems. To draw from the first example above, if you pass out upon being hurt because you begin to panic, that could be good. If, on the other hand, you panic and pass out when you need to run for your life, that would not serve you. Psychologists have documented how those with unresolved trauma are more likely to have an overprotective nervous system: to bypass normal sympathetic function and move directly to a freeze state, their gauge to accurately judge threat being significantly impaired.[22]

In the second example, range of motion, an over-protective nervous system maintains too much tension, while an under-protective one allows for too great a range of motion. Both can greatly contribute to injury. If you brace for impact too tightly, the effects of an impact can be tremendously exacerbated. An over-protective system lacks sufficient bend, so specific muscle fibers and joints end up bearing too much of the load, resulting in a strain or tear.

Contrarily, those who are hyper-mobile, or have under-protective nervous systems, lack control. They often end up exceeding the safe range of motion, which causes injury to their joints and/or muscles as well. Whenever I teach a student who clearly falls into one category or the other, especially a martial arts student, I always attempt to explain the potential for injury.

In both examples, the nervous system tries but fails to act in the individual's best interests. This lack of optimal functionality is due to a combination of physiology and conditioning that simply does not serve us. Training specifically to create balance, adaptability, and strength is a great asset in the quest to maximize stress adaptation for health. It also aids in taking appropriate action when you need it, a worthy endeavor that can help lead you to master the stress response.

Interrupting Versus Aligning the Nervous System

For the last decade, I have focused much of my martial arts training, both learning and teaching, on disrupting the nervous system of an opponent, while maximizing the stability of one's own. This is one of the central tenets of Tsun Jo, the survival self-defense martial art that I teach. The reason this is so important is because it is one of the most effective advantages you can create in martial arts. It allows you to simultaneously maximize your own capability and minimize any superior strength, weight, or speed on the part of your opponent. One simple example of this is to undermine an opponent's balance. An opponent fighting for his balance is not nearly as strong as one with a solid foundation underneath him. In other words, undermining his balance reduces his functional strength. Another basic example is to overload or overwhelm an opponent's senses. Overwhelming an opponent through a barrage of constant counterattacks leaves no time for mental processing and little time for their own attacks. Disrupting the nervous system of the opponent using either method can create tremendous advantage for the self-defense practitioner, when used appropriately.

On the flip side, in order to maximize your own strength, nervous system alignment is critical. This is applicable whether you are attempting to resist or adapt, deliver powerful strikes or grapple effectively. Since I don't expect that all my readers are martial artists, I will offer a different example.

Think about lifting something heavy. If you don't maintain good posture, balance, and mental focus, it is easy to overload and strain parts of the body, often resulting in injury. Alignment of the nervous system means that the body is in a position to handle the stress load of a heavy object. It also means that you are balanced so that as the nervous system innervates the muscles, there is a clear, uninterrupted signal that links your movements together properly. And finally, nervous system alignment provides the mental focus needed to accomplish the job, bringing your present awareness to the task at hand. If you were to be distracted somehow, your attention drawn away from the task of picking up the heavy item, your muscle functionality would lessen. The result could be a dropped load or an injury to yourself.

As briefly mentioned, nervous system alignment involves more than just the physical. Your mental faculties, emotionality, and physicality all contribute to nervous system alignment. The degree and kind of focus needed to properly align the nervous system is discussed further in the third part of this book in conjunction with survival stress tools. There, I outline exercises that cover gross and refined motor skill movement, reaction time, and emotional intensity and control, as well training exercises for meditation, focus, and observation. Much of the training presented combines the psychology and emotionality of base survival mechanisms such as fear, joy, or intimacy coupled with concrete exercises to overcome barriers and maximize performance and well-being. These exercises will aid you in developing substantial control of your nervous system and harnessing it for peak expression.

As a lifelong athlete, meditator, and martial artist, training and teaching by optimizing nervous system alignment has provided deep insights into the human expression of bodily processes. If you wish to command the stress response, to learn to turn it on and off like a switch, you must first know how to align the nervous system or disrupt it to your benefit.

Consciousness and the Nervous System

The Human Brain-Mind Relationship: a Simple Explanation

What is the human brain? The simplest answer is that it is an organ of the central nervous system, a tangible lump of matter. And what is the mind? Again, the simplest answer is that it is a nonphysical, non-tangible conceptual framework of thoughts, intentions, and expressions. Clearly the two are connected, able to communicate with and influence each other. As between a pair of intertwined dancers, the communication is continuous. There is still a great deal unknown about this interaction between the physical brain and non-physical mind. However, what we do know is helpful in gaining a deeper understanding of this relationship.

Let's consider a few aspects of the brain-mind partnership. According to Rick Hanson, PhD, and author of *Just One Thing*, a book on the neuroscience of mediation, what you pay attention to, what you think and feel and want, and how you react to things all sculpt your brain in multiple ways. Dr. Hanson cites the example of genetic activity within the neurons of people who regularly relax.[23] Those who habitually engage in relaxing activities have demonstrated improved expression of the genes that calm down stress reactions.

Another example provided by Dr. Hanson is neural connections, which form more tightly and densely the more they are used. When they go unused, they wither away: Use it or lose it in action. In truth, the reality is more along these lines: Lose it until you invest the energy to rebuild it. In the previous section, I discussed the idea that the nervous system defaults to certain patterning, always attempting to be conservative. This is one expression of that conservatism.

How we direct our intentions, our practice, and our focus leads to physical changes in brain structure. Connections between neurons become more sensitive and new synapses grow, resulting in thicker neural layers. A commonly cited study for this phenomenon is the cab drivers in London. They are required to memorize a great deal of visual-spatial information to pass their exams and receive a license. In a study published in 2000, researchers noted that the brains of these individuals had a thicker hippocampus, an area associated with visual and spatial memory.[24] Other studies have noted that people who practice certain types of meditation regularly develop thicker layers of neurons in the insula, a region of the brain that activates the interoceptive ability to bring about greater awareness of the body and feelings.[25]

Of course, it is not just about thicker layers. The important point is the ability of the mind to activate brain regions and influence autonomic function, and our ability to control this through focus.

Wim Hof, while under observation at Wayne State University, demonstrated the ability to regulate his skin temperature, a known autonomic function.[26] The insular region of the brain was active, as was an area known as the periaqueductal gray matter (PGM), which is associated with autonomic functions such as responding to stress and injury. Depending on how or where the PGM is stimulated, it can contribute to circuitry that expresses fight, flight, or calm behavior. In other words, the mind can help determine how or where the brain is activated, thus influencing the brain's physical expression.

Learning the skills needed to sculpt your brain with mindful intent is a process that becomes easier over time. As thicker cortical layers in the regions of the brain that control attention build up, your inner attention improves. Meditative techniques can literally grow your brain matter. Practicing meditative techniques has been shown to improve immune function, reduce negative thoughts, and ease pain.[27] These techniques contribute to human grit, resilience, and potential.

The stress response often includes negative emotions, thoughts, pain, and discomfort. However, if we can shift the way we perceive the world with our minds, we can shift the inputs to our brains and cause our central nervous systems to respond differently. If we want to maximize our ability to handle and combat stress, learning to direct the brain with the mind is of critical importance. Meditation, mindfulness, and mindset training are three of the most important practices in mastering the stress response. Engaging the mind under various circumstances allows for a steady increase in the ability to control and direct the mind and its effect on the brain.

Within the three groups of mind-based techniques outlined below, there are innumerable variations that one could practice. I recommend using all of these broad types in conjunction with one another to fully develop your mastery of the stress response and maximize your human capacity. Simply choosing a few in each category that resonate with you is all that is needed. The following are my personal definitions of the various categories of these practices.

• *Meditation* is practicing returning to the present moment.

• *Mindfulness* is cultivating awareness of the present moment. Included in that awareness is the existence of what is inside of you and outside of you.

• *Mindset* is orienting the mind to a particular focus with resolved decisiveness while remaining present and open to what is.

Although these three categories certainly overlap, I find the distinctions to be highly useful as I continue to seek a greater understanding of human potential. Learning to focus the mind in a variety of settings—quiet or noisy, peaceful or stress filled—has helped me build incredible resilience and adaptability.

If you are new to these types of practices, meditation and mind-based techniques may be a struggle. Although there are many reasons for this, the following two are the most common: people are unsure of what they are trying to *do* during mediation—"Am I supposed to do anything? Am I just trying to shut off my brain?—and they assume that mind-based techniques must be practiced while sitting down for extended periods of time. When they struggle not to get bored, fall asleep, or be distracted by their thoughts, they get discouraged.

I encourage beginners to shift the perspective. There are three things to consider when practicing mind-based techniques. One, it is important to understand that a mind-based practice is, at its root, simply learning to focus or concentrate in a particular way. Start small and be confident that at a certain point, this will be effortless. Two, the way the brain is wired favors consistency over intensity. You must practice regularly to build the strength needed for focus and attention. Three, you are not trying to shut your brain off; you are just shifting the way you use it.

A simple way to start is with one- to two-minute meditations. Focus on your breath. If you notice you are thinking of something other than your breath, simply try to return your focus to the breath. Do this at least once per day, or aim for multiple times a day. The key is consistency. You can stand, sit, or be moving.

The exercises outlined in the survival stress tools later in this book include mind-based techniques under specific circumstances to maximize your ability to hold attention and control your nervous system. Practicing these techniques will foster the deepest connections to yourself and the world around you. It is through these practices that you will eventually master the stress response.

But don't be afraid to start small with the extremely valuable one- to two-minute meditations. I frequently prefer one minute to ten minutes for many reasons. Most notably, you are more likely to practice consistently and more often. Since consistency is really the key to unlocking the door of potential, this is valuable. Another reason is that shorter meditations eventually enable you to pull your entire being into focus very rapidly. This is tremendously useful in stress situations, as the time you have to focus is often highly constrained. Learning to orient and fully focus as fast as possible, rather than being distracted or questioning what we should do, is what we want to develop as masters of stress. The longer it takes for us to command focus, the greater the chance of diminished response in times of stress.

Once you are practicing regularly and can maintain attention on the breath, expand to other areas of mindfulness. Start choosing anchors within yourself or around you and direct your focus to them. Put your attention on your heartbeat, or be aware of the sounds around you without being distracted by them. When you notice an unintended thought or distraction, notice it, then let it pass by like a car on the street. Don't try to see how many people are in the car, what kind of interior it has, and so on. Simply let the thought go by and return your attention to your anchor.

Try focusing on the movement of your hand as it makes a specific shape. Or focus on what you are feeling inside, without judgement. Notice physical sensations, tension states, or tense places throughout the body. Perceive mental states or focus on a color. These are all simple and effective beginner's tools that will allow you to start building the desired neural connections in your brain. As part of the martial art I teach, every class begins and ends with a very brief mediation, typically lasting from one to three minutes. Regularly performing this activity allows you to get deeply in touch with your brain, body, mind, and the connections among them.

Consciousness as a Flashlight and its Function as a Compass

What is consciousness exactly? Is it exclusive to humans? Is it merely a concept or is it located in a specific part of the brain? While philosophers the world over have attempted to answer some of those questions, scientists have largely ignored getting to the root of consciousness. The pursuit to fully understand consciousness is, in some ways, a dangerous proposition.

When we think of consciousness as simple awareness, then we miss out on all the other things it is capable of producing. Consciousness begins with awareness. Like a starting point around a multidimensional track, awareness is only the gate. Though a full investigation of consciousness is beyond the scope of this book, let us understand it as an operation. It begins with awareness, then directs the nervous system, and finally results in physical expression.

Everyone intuitively understands adages such as "ignorance is bliss" or "what you don't know won't hurt you." While we might be tempted to skip over investigating consciousness, this is not a place where those adages hold true. It is indisputable that clearer information can result in better decisions. Not necessarily more in-formation: just clearer. Humans are notoriously bad at dealing with more than a few variables. The more variables we have to take into account, the harder our decisions become and the more likely they are to have negative outcomes. So how do we get clearer informa-tion? We get it by asking better questions, having a better sense of our own power and limitations, and knowing when to get out of our own way.

The first question we should ask with regard to consciousness is how much do I need to understand its source in order to use it effectively? If consciousness is an operation, then trying to locate its source is largely irrelevant, not to mention futile. We may know what circuitry of the brain lights up when we embody conscious at-tention, but the manifestation of actual consciousness as it impacts and grows capacity remains unwitnessed and thus uncertain. The source of consciousness cannot compare to what it does, achieves, and changes.

The next question should be, what can/does my consciousness direct? Consciousness directs the nervous system to take a partic-ular action. To what extent this direction is effective depends on how broadly and specifically awareness has been cultivated and trained. In other words, if there are multiple possible approaches to an operation, a properly attuned awareness can lead us to the right approach to produce the desired outcome. It is also critical to un-derstand that consciousness exists beyond your sentient attention, especially as it grows in capacity. Realizing that conscious attention is limited, and that holding onto conscious attention detracts from optimal processing of input, is an early step to maximizing your potential in this area.

One of the best metaphors for consciousness I have read was by researcher Julian Jaynes. He noted that consciousness is like a flashlight that shines in a dark room. It only reveals items in the path of its light; it is useful to shine it on things we want to inspect, but it cannot make us aware of items in the room where light does not fall. This metaphor, while accurate, should only be applied to *conscious attention*, not consciousness as a whole.

Take, for example, the complexity of tracking all the sensory information from our environment. Simply trying to be consciously attentive to input from the five common senses is quite the challenge; too many variables are difficult to process. Humans are better off focusing on one or two variables at most, in order to have better awareness. But with a little initial effort and consistent practice, we can train the nervous system to have better awareness *automatically*. The plasticity of the brain permits us to use our conscious attention to create a priority for the nervous system that can then develop and track *on its own*. You haven't lost awareness, just conscious attentive processing. In samurai culture, this is the concept of *mushin*: the empty mind, the fullness of capacity without interfering thoughts.

Of course, if conscious attention is a flashlight, should we not attempt to develop a bigger one, or better yet, install an overhead light that illuminates everything? The simple answer is, no. What is more important, at least at this stage in our human development, is understanding that consciousness is an operation and conscious attention, like a flashlight, has its limitations. Over time, we can grow the flashlight's capacity by developing brighter bulbs and lenses that offer wider angles, but it will remain limited. What is unlimited—or better yet, what has unknown limits—is operative capability of what consciousness can do.

We must strive to work within the limitations of conscious attention by not over-relying on it, but by using it to point the way toward the desired outcome. If we can shine the flashlight on specific aspects of consciousness, we can further develop and refine those aspects through conscious attention. When we are aware of this relationship, we can use our intention to produce staggering results.

Knowingly and unknowingly, humans have been doing this for hundreds and hundreds of years, expanding the baseline potential of our species. The speed at which we can realize our potential rests heavily upon our ability to maximize the relationship between attentive conscious operations and non-attentive conscious operations.

What Holds us Back?

Not all humans exercise the same degree of development. At the outer reaches of human potential exist those pushing the boundaries of human consciousness. As a species, one of our greatest faults is that we invest a great deal in training our minds at the neglect of our bodies or vice versa. This happens because we misunderstand that the fullness of conscious capacity exists in the whole being, not just one part.

Your mind is not optimal without a high-functioning body.[28] A body cannot maximize its potential without a fully functioning mind. When we forget that fact, it leaves us severely lopsided and unrealized in our potential.

We are diverse and as a species, possess different skills. That is a good thing. Those who have a Richard Feynman[29]-type brain for problem solving and those possessed of a Herschel Walker[30]-type body both offer valuable assets. But both—and everyone in be-tween—could greatly benefit from training the other side, if only to support inherent abilities. Only by focusing on the whole being can we develop the awareness needed to maximize the operation of consciousness.

We should strive to strengthen our natural abilities and counter our weaknesses. In this process, consciousness can be a check-in device and directional magnet. As we strive to fulfill our potential, consciousness can assist us in making necessary alterations. It can help us understand the degree to which we should cultivate differ-ent aspects of ourselves in order to maximize what we can achieve. The more we do so, the clearer the direction of our development becomes.

Strive for Intentional Evolution

We are homo sapiens, the only surviving species from the genus *Homo*, of the phylum Chordata, which is of the kingdom Animalia. Sapiens is our species. We are complex, intricate beings that have evolved as apex predators, deeply social apes, and incredibly so-phisticated animals.

131

From a survival point of view, it is important to remember that evolution is not foolproof. It is possible for a species to take on adaptations that end up failing when conditions alter. The ability to survive in a complex, constantly changing world is the great challenge for any species. Our ability to adapt to a wide range of environments, use and invent a large variety of sophisticated tools, and work under combined principles of cooperation and non-cooperation to further our refinement stands out from that of other large, complex species. Our conscious capacity to make good choices can and will have a strong impact on our continued survival. However, while our conscious capability at this stage in our developmental evolution is powerful, it is not almighty. We simply cannot account for all of the variables necessary to operate at an all-powerful level. So let us use our consciousness, and with it our flashlight, to focus our attention, shining and clear, upon the fundamental regimens that are known to engage our natures and encourage the best outcomes.

Book II Endnotes

1.Bellisle M. 2019. AP Exclusive: Accidental shootings show police training gaps. AP News [online], December 9, 2019. Available from: https://apnews.com/article/009ac6cf0a174a58d88d9d01308aedd6.

2. The freeze reaction, done intentionally, has clear advantages. An intentional freeze reaction involves holding yourself absolutely still while breathing calmly and almost inaudibly. Hunting is one situation where this can be useful. On a recent elk hunt, I had crawled into a small area surrounded by leafless branches. The branches offered little in the way of cover, but it was virtually the only cover that offered a 360-degree view. After more than an hour, an elk emerged about seventy-five yards away. She came down a small hill and stopped about fifty yards in front of me. My adrenaline was high; my breath moved slowly. The elk looked intently through the bushes in an effort to detect me. It could not. This is an example of a positive, intentional freeze reaction.

3. David's name has been changed to protect his anonymity.

4. These statistics and definition are from data published by the non-profit group Gun Violence Archive.

5. To clarify, the flow state is similar to what some refer to as 'being in the zone:' operating at your maximum capacity for artistic, creative, or physical expression. There is often an accompanying sense of timelessness and effortlessness.

6. asirt.org

7. National Institute of Mental Health Disorders

8. For a full meditation on this theory, read Julian Jaynes's *The Origin of Consciousness in the Breakdown of the Bicameral Mind.*

9. For the most part, humans have had the ability to eat our fill on a daily basis for less than 100 years. Clearly, this varies by world region.

10. When incorporating some degree of fasting or time-restricted eating, questions may come up: Are we getting enough to eat? How are/should we eat after restriction? Unfortunately, as fasting increasingly becomes the new "thing" in the developed world, those who are already managing

stress poorly may end up not eating or developing unhealthy habits, such as short-term fasting and binging. Eating disorders, such as anorexia and bulimia, which are also a concern, are not addressed here.

11. Some psychologists have tried to pare things down to two to four emotions, but I find that level of simplification less useful. Emotion psychologist Dr. Paul Eckman, whose landmark work in the 1960s and 1970s helped to determine the universality of human emotions, defined six basic emotions: fear, anger, disgust, happiness, sadness, and surprise. As emotion research has been codified into many of the models used today, other psychologists have searched for a more encompassing explanation. Plutchik, is an example of those who offer a more detailed model.

12. I find Plutchik's color wheel useful when it comes to describing the base emotions, as well as how each base emotion flowers into varying intensity levels.

13. Cooper JR. 2001. Neurotransmitters. In: Smelser NJ, Baltes PB, eds, International Encyclopedia of the Social & Behavioral Sciences. pp 10612-10619.

14. Your heart has some 40,000 to 50,000 neurons in it. The complexity of this system is likely why we can feel it when hearts sync up: Marshall L. 2017. When lovers touch, their breathing, heartbeat syncs, pain wanes, study shows. University of Colorado at Boulder.

15. Thermogenic training is the practice of exposing yourself to extreme temperatures for short periods.

16. The primary neurotransmitter used by the sympathetic nervous system is norepinephrine. The primary neurotransmitter used for the parasympathetic is acetylcholine.

17. Naming skeletal muscles is still an active ongoing process.

18. The primary neurotransmitter used by the somatic nervous system is acetylcholine. In the body, it helps muscles to contract. In the brain, it is responsible for higher-order functions of cognitive processing. It also

controls attention.

19. Kox M, van Eijk LT, Zwaag J, van den Wildenberg J, Sweep FCGJ, van der Hoeven JG, Pickkers P. 2014. Voluntary activation of the sympathetic nervous system and attenuation of the innate immune response in humans. PNAS 111(20):7379-7384.

20. On average, the human body contains approximately eight to ten pints for men and five to eight pints for women.

21. A way to test and understand this protective aspect of the nervous system is de-binding. De-binding involves using gravity, time, and breathing to lower your natural nervous system defense and increase your range of motion. On my website, MattSoule.com, you can find videos that demonstrate this concept in its totality.

22. For a full discussion on this topic, read *The Polyvegal Theory* by Stephen Porges.

23. Dusek JA, Otu HH, Wohlhueter AL, Bhasin M, Zerbini LF, Joseph MG, Benson H, Libermann TA. 2008. Genomic Counter-Stress Changes Induced by the Relaxation Response. PLoS ONE 3(7):e2576.

24. Maguire EA, Gadian DG, Johnsrude IS, Good CD, Ashburner J, Frackowiak RSJ, Frith CD. 2000. Navigation-related structural change in the hippocampi of taxi drivers. PNAS 97(8):4398-4403.

25. Lazar SW, Kerr CE, Wasserman RH, Gray JR, Greve DN, Treadway MT, McGarvey M, Quinn BT, Dusek JA, Benson H, Rauch SL, Moore CI, Fischl B. 2005. Meditation experience is associated with increased cortical thickness. Neuroreport 16(17):1893-1897.

26. Muzik O, Reilly KT, Diwadkar VA. 2018. "Brain over body"-A study on the willful regulation of autonomic function during cold exposure. Neuroimage 15(172):632-641.

27. Holzel BK, Carmody J, Vangel M, Congleton C, Yerramsetti SM, Gard T, Lazar SW. 2018. Mindfulness practice leads to increases in regional brain gray matter density. Psychiatry Res 191(1):36-43.

28. I am not suggesting that if you have some impairment, physical injury, missing limb, or other limitation, it somehow precludes you from finding optimal expression. What I am getting at is that your brain and body compose a closed, intertwined system, and that you need to maximize your attention to the whole to reach your peak expression as a human.

29. Richard Feynman was a Nobel Prize-winning theoretical physicist known for his work in quantum mechanics, quantum electrodynamics, the physics of the superfluidity of supercooled liquid helium, and particle physics.

30. Herschel Walker is an American former professional football player, bobsledder, sprinter, and mixed martial artist.

BOOK III

SURVIVAL STRESS TOOLS:
THE TRAINING GUIDE

Training through a lens of survival requires an elevated risk factor that taps more deeply into the nervous system. Unlike other methods, the elevated risk factor creates a greater need to engage and control the nervous system. It forces us to confront a high degree of stress and learn to find peace, calm, and a flow state amidst the chaos. As a result, our ability to handle a wide range of stressors, up to and including the threshold of survival, is vastly improved. Through careful preparation, we can train in a way that optimizes risk without getting burned out, getting injured, or worse, dying. Over time, we are able to master stress. Book III deals with practical tools to use to train through a lens of survival.

As mentioned previously and repeatedly, there are more stressors now than at perhaps any other time in human history. Moreover, the number of physical, environmental, psychological, and emotional stressors are likely to increase as we continue to innovate as a species and shift what the modern world looks like.

How we manage and deal with those stressors is important. Finding effective methods that actually engage, address, and reduce stress in a functional way is challenging. Too often, the methods available are too abstract, dubious, or inaccessible, partially due to our nervous system's operation at a chronically elevated stress state.

Let's return for a moment to the sympathetic, or action, state and the parasympathetic, or rest, state. In the sympathetic state, the bronchioles remain dilated to allow for more frequent breaths. The liver continues to prioritize the release of glucose for the energy expected to be needed. Blood is diverted to specific parts of the brain, most notably the brainstem and midbrain, which govern survival-based functions like the fight, flight, or freeze response. Stress hormones are released into the blood. Blood is squeezed from the viscera and rerouted to the organs and muscles instead of the gut.

In this state, immune function alters. If you have to fight for your life against a tiger, another human, or any other predator, it is fine for the immune function to be put on hold: Any pathogen threatening you can temporarily wait. But recall that the stress response doesn't require life-threatening circumstances to activate. It happens with all perceived dangers, challenges, and difficulties, albeit to various degrees. Remaining in a chronically sympathetic state over hours, days, weeks, or even months breaks the body down, largely because of the diverted blood and prioritized functionality present in this state.

So why on earth would we want to use survival stress tools to amplify this already-heightened state? Because it is the most effective method to relieve the problem. Counterintuitive as it may seem, survival stress tools are, bar none, the best tools available for such a job. One substantial reason is because survival stress tools can engage the system while it is in the sympathetic state. We can actively take the nervous system to a higher state, redefine its baseline of operations, then bring it back to the rest and recovery state. Through this rapid engagement, we can train our systems using a tool from which they are designed to benefit: acute stress.

Entrainment

In my early twenties, while dealing with the grief of my late father's death, I came across a concept called entrainment. Entrainment typically describes various systems that interact and influence each other. For the purposes of this book, entrainment should be understood as two independent systems interacting as they seek equilibrium. Each may have its own vibrational frequency, but eventually, given enough time and interaction, these two systems will harmonize or balance with each other. The following examples are relevant to the point I am trying to convey.

An easy example of entrainment in our lives is music. Music can have a deep impact on the nervous system's state. Your nervous system operates at a particular vibrational "frequency." When it is at a high vibrational frequency, you are in a sympathetic stress state. When it is at a low vibrational frequency, you are in a more restful state. The emotional palette we experience can contribute to the mood we feel in either state, and that mood can be influenced by music and *its* vibrational frequency.

Musical entrainment then can be described as the following: the interaction between the arousal state, including the often-significant emotional landscape, and the speed, volume, and intensity of the music.

Picture that you are in a serene mood. Everything is butterflies and zebras—a Jimmy Hendrix reference—but you hear harsh death metal music on the radio. It grinds like a chainsaw in your ears, obtrusive and unwelcome. The two systems, you (including your nervous system) and the music, are out of sorts, and you are unable to feel connected to the music. Now, assuming the genre is to your liking, you may begin to enjoy the music after a time, as your arousal state finds a new balance. Most of the time, however, this will not occur before you give up and change the station to something that more closely matches your present state.

But what happens when you don't have the direct control to change the music? Picture, for example, that you have just won a championship. You are high on celebration. Then, filtering through the chaos and joy of victory, you hear a soft, melancholic tune that depicts nothing but gloom. The dissonance of such a situation would be truly abysmal!

We often experience dissonance between ourselves and our environment in everyday life: light, music, television, news, phones, traffic, work, and so forth, are all apt to clash with our internal state, whatever it may be. And trying to shift to a resting state among these dissonant systems is deeply challenging. The discontinuity between our system and that of our environs inputs cannot be dealt with easily.

Although sitting quietly for ten minutes, a common recommendation in meditation, may help a little, all too frequently this short break is filled with the residual recoil of uncontrolled thoughts, responsibilities, and distractions. These distractions stifle us and prevent us from shifting to the desired mental, physical, and emotional space. If we are lucky we get some small respite, but too often we are left with little or no benefit. We get discouraged.

There is no doubt that, given enough time and space, a person can achieve the balance. Ten days of silent meditation, for example, can and does do remarkable things to the nervous system. However, as a practical tool in modern times, this can hardly be relied upon.

Those who keep practicing for many years eventually learn to improve timelines and gain benefits with shorter sittings or movement meditations such as yoga and tai chi. The seasoned meditator, who has practiced diligently, is able to access the ability to shift states with some level of command. But how many actually get there using these methods? Very few, I would say.

There is a better way. Let's return to our musical metaphor. When you experience a dissonance between your "vibrational frequency" and that of the music you are listening to, change the music! You can more readily adapt your nervous system by first selecting songs that match your frequency.

Then, as you gradually change musical genres, your state will also shift. For example, if I want to use musical entrainment to calm myself down after a difficult, high-stress day, I can first put on a song that matches and even elevates my high-stress state. Something with some intense tones, speed, and volume that engages me where I am in that moment. I sing along, my mental and emotional state in tune with the music. Everything is more or less in sync. Then the next song, I lower the intensity. As the music softens, I do the same. The next song is even more moderated. Within three or four songs, I can adapt and shift to a calmer state.

Beyond Music

Using entrainment as a framework for the survival stress tools is the fastest, most efficient way to affect intentional change and master the stress response. Entrainment is a way to harness the nervous system and direct it, not just with music, but through practices that engage the nervous system on its own ground. Aligning the mental, emotional, and physical through entrainment is what training survival stress tools is all about.

Practicing entrainment speaks to the idea of using stress tools to modulate stress as desired. As discussed, there are many physiological, neurochemical, and mental reasons and ways to actively engage our systems. However, entrainment can be applied to all, because it is a stress tool that can penetrate the nervous system very quickly.

So, entrainment can be used to rapid effect. However, when it comes to affecting the nervous system rapidly *and* deeply, *survival* stress tools are key. WHM, which uses extreme cold stress and multiple layers of breath stress—two survival components—to increase energy production and promote adaptation, is one of a wide array of practices to comprise such tools. However, WHM does not just present these ancient tools in a highly accessible format refitted for the modern era, but combines, or stacks, components together for increasing effect. The synergy is far greater than the sum of the individual parts. In a 2016 interview, Josh Waitzkin discussed how his experience with WHM allowed him to access a deep meditative state after only fifteen minutes, rather than two hours of tai chi.[1]

Modulating stress effectively to access a deep meditative state—no matter the discipline—is usually extremely challenging. The reason is that a great deal of training in any discipline involves simply working toward an access point that is a combination of physical, mental, and emotional alignment. Once attained, that access point allows you to investigate different layers inside yourself and produce consistent results. Practice with insight long enough and you begin to uncover deeper truths and states of being. Your ability to navigate these layers improves with time, focus, and knowhow. After practicing for weeks and years, you may be able to reduce the time it takes you to locate an access point to days, hours, or even minutes. But even experienced practitioners spend most of their meditative or focused time simply getting to an access point. Their exploration beyond that tends to be limited, because it takes so much time and effort to get there in the first place.

There are many ways to find an access point, and each allows you to explore different facets of your being. Some of the more common tools include meditation, breathwork, martial arts, yoga, and psychedelics. When I began utilizing the skills I had already developed for mind-based practices in conjunction with various survival stress tools, such as the multiple layers of breath stress found in WHM, the results were dramatic: I was able to reach an internal access point within fifteen minutes, every time. With such speed and consistency, my ability to explore layers of meditative depths was unlike anything I had experienced. In a world where we are bound by so many time constraints and competing responsibilities, faster access to our consciousness to aid in its expansion and thus a more integrated mind and body has a value that can hardly be overstated.

Over the subsequent months and years, I have gone on to separate the components of the method, breaking it down into the underlying parts and combining those parts with many other skills. This has allowed me to apply the gleaned principles to a variety of fields: from martial arts to diet, from thermogenic training to sex and intimacy.

It is through this process that I have come to view the principles of survival stress tools as fundamental to mastering the stress response.

Why Fight, Freeze, Fast, Fuck?

As noted in the introduction, the five survival stress tools—Fight, Freeze, Fast, Fuck, and Breathe—are unique in their ability to offer the best results. Correctly training these tools will result in an improved ability to handle any of life's stressors, no matter the source. These five are exclusive to other modalities as we will come to understand in totality.

So why not dancing, soccer, yoga, or any of the hundreds of other activities demonstrated to improve stress management? Although such other pastimes can have many wonderful attributes—such as expression, mobility, movement, challenge, adaptation, alignment, strength, focus, explosivity, balance, inversion, and spatial awareness—there are overlapping features unique to the five survival stress tools presented here. These features offer the greatest and best chance to master the stress response. By training in these five, we tap into the brain and body in the deepest possible ways and learn to deal with the greatest of possible stresses.

The survival stress tools tap into life and death in a way provided by few other exercises. What is more, they are indispensable to our survival and thus should be trained. This is not to discount the great value that other physical, emotional, and mental exercises can play in our lives. Rather, it is to illustrate that survival stress tools offer a unique set of benefits. Those benefits include combining physical, emotional, mental, and relational development under the greatest possible stress load while optimizing risk, thereby directly tapping into life and death. As we raise the threshold of risk and learn to find peace in chaos, our ability to master stress wherever it shows its face is enhanced.

FIGHT

FIGHT, WHICH WE will come to understand as meaning specific martial arts training, is a relational acute stress tool that endows us with an incredible array of both gross and refined motor skills. Physically, it augments our optic capacity to better see what is happening, at different speeds, by improving our understanding of distance and timing. It refines our ability to detect and respond to various types of pressure, helps us to reinterpret pain, and makes us stronger, better balanced, and more aware of proper alignment. It trains us to identify situations more accurately and to greater advantage. It helps us practice when and how to fight, to discern when resistance is useful and when it will undermine our objectives. It teaches us the power of momentum and the need to squash a problem when it is small, lest it become overwhelming. It improves our sensory perceptions on all levels so that the quality of information received and the speed at which we assess it let us hold fast to our center and resist being easily disoriented.

Physically, but also mentally and emotionally, we learn critical facets of adaptability through the Fight tool. It helps us discern the difference between competition and cooperation and the usefulness of each. It teaches us to resolve various kinds of conflict to ensure the best training practices. It informs how we contribute to and participate in relationships. It demands that we listen with our whole body to achieve desired outcomes. It teaches us to be assertive. It shows us how to build and foster trust and trains us to better judge a person's character.

This training tool improves creativity as well as the speed and quality with which we make decisions. It teaches us how to reduce variables to improve our decision-making process for better outcomes. It teaches us focus and the consequences of distraction. It teaches us to judge situations, intent, and body language nuances. It teaches us the value of confidence and being decisive. It shows us what and when to avoid as well as how and when to engage. It

145

FIGHT | FREEZE |FAST | F^CK | BREATHE

teaches us that full commitment produces fruit, while half measures invariably lead to catastrophe. It teaches us how much energy is required and when to cut our losses. While we should learn humility, discipline, and any number of other invaluable skills and traits, the central goal in martial arts is to understand advantage: All skills directly and indirectly seek to serve this end. This is both its power and its limitation.

Specific types of martial arts training accomplish something more. This kind of training allows us to confront our primal fears around personal safety and harm and to others. As we confront these fears and develop exceptional physical, mental, and emotional control, we find that there can be peace even in the chaos of a physical confrontation.

In a recent James Bond film starring Daniel Craig, 007 is asked what he knows about fear. *All there is, he replies.* This line hit me with an extraordinary resonance, not because of some fantasy of being a secret agent, but because it illuminated a deep truth: that at the root of fear lies freedom. Getting to know and confront fear has long been my mission.

The desire to overcome fear can cause extreme attitudes in people. For my part, early childhood experiences of feeling helpless to defend my mother led to high-risk choices later in life in an effort to confront the fear of helplessness. This behavior culminated in my early twenties when I took on a job as a bodyguard for an escort agency.

A typical night would start at the office, where each escort was assigned one driver/bodyguard. In my role, I used surveillance to help protect my charge, who would hide a bug in her purse that I would use to monitor activity. When we got a call, I would drive my assigned escort to the client's requested location, usually a hotel or house. We had a series of code words that would communicate if I needed to intervene. The clients were unaware of me, a surprise that often allowed me to get the woman out of the encounter safely and with minimal confrontation. At other times, the job required more aggressive action.

The work was extremely risky. My boss had a deep scar across the entire front of his neck; the laceration had been from a smashed bottle during a call that had gone bad. Company policy allowed for only one client to be alone with the escort. In this case, the escort had found multiple men present. When she had tried to leave, they had refused to let her, and my boss had gone in to retrieve her. While getting her out, he was struck with a golf club and cut with the broken bottle.

Despite such stories, I was willing to do the job, which paid well. As a twenty-year-old kid, I outwardly justified the risk by the cash in my pocket each night. Inside, however, I knew exactly why I wanted the job. Thinking that it would allow me to exorcise long-held memories from my youth, I eagerly accepted the steep risk curve that frequently put me in danger. Each time I had to intervene on behalf of the woman to whom I was assigned, I would feel a small relief. Asserting myself as a protector, a natural role for me augmented by parental and social conditioning, was part of a larger catharsis I envisioned on the horizon. The job initially felt like a substantial piece of that effort. Yet the full resolution I had anticipated never quite materialized.

Every organization has its own habits and common practices. Sometimes these are defined through a mission statement or some other formality. Sometimes they simply emerge and adapt as each participant contributes to the culture in his or her own way.

The agency was headed by two bosses whose behavior was unstable. As the months went by, they grew increasingly reckless, both personally and professionally. The new staff hired to be drivers/bodyguards reflected that recklessness, and escorts began to quit. The writing was on the wall. I decided to quit too and take a six-week vacation.

When I returned, I learned that my instincts had proven correct. My bosses had gone to a home with one of the newer drivers after a call had gone sideways. Even though the driver had gotten the escort out safely, the driver and the two bosses returned to the client's home and assaulted him. A police investigation into the incident resulted in the arrest of all three men. When the police had gone to the agency's office, they had also found steroids and other drugs. I hadn't known that they were taking such substances, but I wasn't surprised either. I was grateful that I had managed to put distance between us by leaving at the right time.

In the end, this experience dealing with high-stress situations proved minimally useful in addressing my underlying motivations. I was certainly in a more empowered position, but in many ways I was simply reliving parts of my childhood and becoming desensitized to violence by continuing risk-seeking behavior. To find resolution, I needed to find other ways to address my memories of childhood helplessness.

Martial Arts

In my mid-twenties, I began training with a martial arts teacher in California. It was a style of modern Wing Chun kung fu that integrated both external fighting techniques and internal personal cultivation. This unique combination offered a different lens through which to view my emotional states. It was my first experience with a martial art that fostered practical moves that would be useful in a street confrontation, while simultaneously emphasizing the development of significant internal awareness. Most of my experiences to that point had either focused on physical fighting techniques or erred too far into the internal and abstract. Although each had its benefits, both types of training left me wanting for balance and clarity.

My time in California helped usher in a new way of thinking that would guide me to seek practical martial arts that respected specific internal development. Over the subsequent five years, I trained in various martial arts as I moved around the United States, but I never quite found what I was looking for. I did, however, have the opportunity to study certain practices, such as chi gong, that would contribute to my development of internal awareness.

By themselves, chi gong and other meditative practices remain abstract in their applications to high-speed confrontations. However, when combined with highly practical and intensely physical martial arts, such as Tsun Jo and Brazilian jiu-jitsu, chi gong proved extremely useful. I learned not only how to flip the switch of my emotional state at will, but how to direct my emotional state under the intense pressures of confrontation.

When I moved to Seattle, Washington, I happened across the style Tsun Jo, which was developed at the martial arts school that I now own. This martial art distinguished itself in a number of ways from my prior training. The founder, John Beall, had a varied background, intelligence, and a set of interests that offered unique perspectives on effective fighting, emotional control, and a deep understanding of the nervous system.

John Beall

John Beall had faced a lifelong series of violent events that deeply shaped his view on self-protection. As a martial artist, his goal was to develop a fighting method that would be as efficient as possible in the face of real-life danger. The result was Tsun Jo, a survival fighting method.

John is the son of an attorney and a stay-at-home mother with a bad temper. His formal education stopped in the eleventh grade, but he has gone on to pursue his own studies, create inventions and patents, author a book and videos on self-defense, and contribute to the education of thousands of students in the Seattle area for more than thirty-eight years.

Leaving his dysfunctional home in rural Virginia at the age of sixteen to hitchhike across the country, John eventually landed in the waterfront of Sausalito in the San Francisco Bay area in the 1960s. At once a fighter and a progressive, John had found a hive of similarly minded individuals. Between his makeshift home on the waterfront and tromping through the Haight-Ashbury progressive district, the Bay Area was filled with a great deal of strife in the 1960s. It was the epicenter of youth counterculture and contained a wide variety of groups. There were street gangs from the Fillmore and the "Beat Artists" who were drug conmen. There were the Hell's Angels, who caused general terror. No matter your associates, violence was often very close at hand.

The Bay Area was rife with high tensions and, at times, quick fuses. In 1966, while at a San Francisco park, John witnessed Hell's Angels members storm the area and cause havoc as they assaulted people for what appeared to be no reason at all. He observed how they worked as a unit. Unlike what is often shown in the movies, where individuals take turns punching or kicking unwary victims, the gangs John witnessed worked together, pulverizing victims and any would-be defenders.

John was no stranger to violence in Virginia or California. But in his early twenties, he spent time in prison on a marijuana drug charge. There, he witnessed gang beatings and other incidents of brutal violence that would leave a lasting impression as to the need for and development of a clear strategy for personal safety, and the necessary tactics to support that end. John went on to train in boxing, karate, submission grappling, and a number of other styles, but perhaps his most substantial influence was Wing Chun Do, which he was taught by one of Bruce Lee's first students, James DeMile.

James, for his part, grew up in an orphanage that shaped his own reality of survival of the fittest. As a misfit youth, he ran a gang on Seattle's First Hill. In the 1950s, hoping to steer his life in a more positive direction, he joined the Air Force, where he reigned as the Air Force Heavyweight Boxing Champion for two years, going un-defeated for 128 matches. Later, in the mid-'80s, James served as a hand-to-hand combat instructor for the Special Forces Combatives Program at Fort Lewis, Washington.

When John Beall met James DeMile and heard the latter voice many of his own understandings about violence, John knew that this was a man to whom he could relate. They and the others of their day who had witnessed unnecessary and brutal violence were interested, above all, in how to maximize self-protection. Eventu-ally, after earning his Black Sash under DeMile, John broke off to concentrate on his own ideas about how best to structure a fighting method.

John's only allegiance is to things that work. This has meant exploring all the facets of structural unity, emotional control, and nervous system development. The central theme throughout John's life has been to seek consciousness unity expressed through the mind and the deep physicality of being. He has relied on testing theories using practice and experiments to validate or disprove his own and others' ideas. He has resisted dogmas, replacing them with testable exercises whenever and wherever possible and practicable.

John's desire to break with conventional self-defense wisdom in favor of experiential reality has led him to examine conditioned human processes in an attempt to arrive at truths, wherever they may be and wherever they may lead us. In this way, he has led an exceptional life.

One of his central themes has been evaluating how to use and engage the nervous system to maximize a series of stacked advantages in a conflict. This has included a significant exploration of reaction time. Using relaxed sight, which he would refer to as survival vision, he has trained himself and his students to broaden the scope of vision while paying attention to only the few variables that determine likely attacks. He has combined this with a near-obsession of using distance control to maximize reaction time, or of working to bypass reaction time to use high-pressure contact at close range. He has worked incessantly on verifiable methods to train the somatic nervous system and develop pathways of reliable, repeatable success. John has been relentless in his efforts to deliver the best possible results of success in fighting.

His training has also emphasized how to control the focus and attention of the central and peripheral components of the nervous system, while modulating emotional control and intensity. This means using all of the above-described tools *against* an opponent, disrupting and overwhelming the nervous system to gain a clear advantage in a conflict. The approach is far from abstract: We have trained in this technique on a regular basis for countless hours. From that training, I have developed clear insight into the power of overwhelming an opponent's nervous system—and simultaneously, how to fortify my own.

John has had a tremendous influence on my martial arts training, as well as on my lifelong pursuit of deepening consciousness. He is one of those impactful figures who has not experienced worldwide fame but locally has a highly regarded reputation. Those who have had the opportunity to experience this man's teachings have found them to be truly profound.

Primal Fear

What has been most illuminating through all of my teaching, training, and life experiences has been *how* I have learned to effectively address and resolve primal fear. I did not work to eliminate it but to integrate its highest and best utility into my approach to life.

In order to successfully do this, you must tap into the deepest parts of the nervous system, the primal self, and empower yourself through testable, verifiable practices. Without such tests, you are liable to crumble under the weight of reality when faced with it.

I am proud to say that I have trained 1,000s of others to effectively confront some of the deepest fears we have as humans, fears specifically associated with self-protection: fear of pain or injury, fear of helplessness, fear of embarrassment, fear of harm and death to self, and more uniquely, fear of harm and death to others. Virtually all of us have these personal fears. And virtually all of us fear hurting or killing another. Left unresolved, these fears take substantial hold in our lives.

There are a number of activities one can pursue to get past fear for the self. When this fear is properly integrated into an endeavor, one is not bound by it—it simply asserts itself in its proper place. A bit of a warning: Some of us can be extreme in our attempts to overcome these fears, an attitude that often leads to overcompensation. Be mindful of this extreme attitude. It often produces carelessness, which is not the same thing as fear integration. The egotistical rebel showing off his fearlessness is the embodiment of the careless extreme that does not serve the higher end.

By contrast, there are very few activities that allow us to resolve the fear of hurting, injuring, or killing another. Carelessness in these activities is unacceptable. Only by integrating this fear can one resolve it and put it in its rightful place. A deep understanding of how, what, and when actions are likely to inflict physical harm is incredibly liberating, but a distorted perspective can lead to calamity. Good martial arts training can and does appropriately integrate these fears to enable the clearest possible judgement.

By integrating these fears—that of self-harm and that of harm to another—martial arts allows us to relegate them to their proper place, where they can be used to serve the highest ends. The best training allows us to be at once patient and unhesitating, calm and explosively overwhelming. We can exercise great control without effort, allowing us to show courage in the most difficult of moments and circumstances.

Final Thoughts on Resolving Fear Through Martial Arts

The basic premise of confronting fear through quality martial arts training is to develop tactics and strategies of response to predict, prevent, and deal with violent, potentially violent, or conflict-oriented behavior. Over time, with dedication, your abilities greatly improve. But in the beginning, you must actively tie into and deeply trust your intuitive mechanism to recognize real danger.

Those of us who lead lives of distraction and rarely tap into this space may find we are deeply anxious. We may confuse this state with real fear. It is not. Discerning that reality is critical. Learning to understand the difference between anxiety and fear is a skill that good martial arts training can foster.

Those who have never experienced a truly terrifying situation may find it hard to imagine. The underlying questions that this inexperience produces come with their own primal insecurities. However, to paraphrase Gavin De Becker, author of *The Gift of Fear*, we must start with recognizing that each of us has the capability to access the true message of fear and distinguish it from other non-essential messages that we sometimes confuse with fear. Accessing this capability will aid you greatly on your path to mastering the stress response.

Moreover, being able to accurately identify fear is a skill that is transferable to a great many of life's arenas, allowing us to take action wherever and whenever needed. Confronting fear through martial arts has not only allowed me to express courage when faced with violence or to intervene to protect another, it has also empowered me to risk becoming an entrepreneur, to be on stage to address thousands of people, and yes, to accept death. It has empowered my students to stand up for themselves and others, to unflinchingly help people in need, to ask for a raise, and take necessary risks to get ahead in life.

Which Martial Art Should I Choose?

In order to meet the high demands to qualify as a survival stress tool, a Fight tool training regimen needs to meet certain requirements. At the root of all beings is a desire and demand for self-protection. This is universal and exceeds any sport-oriented aspiration. Therefore, it has a unique presence and value in the human psyche.

While we cannot safely engage in life-and-death training without incurring exceedingly high risks, we can approximate it and significantly mitigate unnecessary risks through the right regimen. The right training more readily prepares us to deal with the harshest realities and thrive despite their challenges.

There are a great number of martial arts out there, and my examples below are not meant to represent all styles or make blanket statements that apply to each and every one of them. There are too many variations in today's world. So, the following paragraphs focus on some of the more well-known arts and delineate why you might consider choosing one style over another as a survival stress tool.

Some martial arts primarily focus on slow development, intentional weight shifting, and internal awareness: tai chi, for example. As such, the majority of tai chi practices—while beneficial in their own right—do not qualify as a survival stress tool.

Other martial arts tend to focus primarily or exclusively on kata. Kata are predetermined, choreographed sequences of movement. Examples of such styles include certain types of karate, tai kwon do, kung fu, and many esoteric martial arts disciplines.

Yet other martial arts focus on self-defense, while others are more sport oriented. Wing Chun, krav maga, and systema, for example, are often in the self-defense category, whereas boxing, judo, and Brazilian jiu-jitsu tend to fall into a more sport-focused category.

Depending on the training methods applied, virtually all of these styles may or may not fit the criteria for a survival stress tool. The teachers of many, if not all, of these styles make claims of transferability to real-life altercations. Though I have my own opinions, rather than address the relative advantages or effectiveness of the martial arts discussed, we will focus on three important requirements you can use to select a Fight tool: the physical, the emotional, and the mental. Using these criteria, it will be clear how important the following supporting concepts are to selecting a martial art for your training.

• The degree to which a real threat is perceivable while training

• Adaptability required by training applications

• The timing of attacks and counterattacks

• The possibility to assess the style through qualifiers, such as the ability to go full speed or not

• Clear consequences of failure

• Optimized risks

The more closely it approximates a real fight, or at least the aspects of a real fight, the better the Fight tool will work. You need a testable truth.

So what type of training does qualify?

You should choose your martial art based on three basic requirements all of which overlap: physical demand, emotional demand, and mental demand unique to the pressure of survival. Use this tool wisely, optimize risk, and be sure to include rest and recovery as essential parts.

The Physical Requirement

In order to meet the survival stress threshold, the Fight tool's training must include a high physical demand. It should help develop functional strength and speed, balance hormones, and develop your cardiovascular system. You should sweat, work hard, deal with resistance, and learn to strengthen your base and shore up your posture. It should require that you control muscle tension and learn how to physically align your body to maximize strength.

You should learn how to deal with competitive resistance, force transfer, and varying degrees of pressure and speeds to which you must respond. These features will benefit you by training your musculoskeletal system while simultaneously developing your proprioceptive, vestibular, and interoceptive senses in both a dynamic personal sense and a relational sense to your opponent.

When training in a sufficiently high-energy martial art with competitive and cooperative elements, you have an opportunity to learn and develop both your autonomic and somatic nervous systems. Recall that the somatic branch of the nervous system is responsible for your intentional movements. The autonomic nervous system governs things like heart rate and breathing, but it also affects your muscle tension. Exerting somatic control of breathing, learning to be aware of tension for maximal effect, keeping proper posture, and controlling vision at varying levels of intensity helps train the autonomic nervous system for highly improved outcomes.

As your nervous system experiences various levels of sympathetic arousal, you can learn to better adapt to resistance by improving the alignment and gradients of pressure needed for best results. You can learn muscle efficiency through controlling varying levels of tension. Over time, gross motor and refined skill development will result in improved adaptability. To enhance this further, the sensory stimulation involved in responding to physical pressure will uniquely develop your nervous system. The use of pressure will develop touch sensors and improve the bi-directionality of information from the peripheral nervous system to the central nervous system. Training will eventually improve pressure-based reaction and awareness.

156

Your Fight tool training should include timing and distance control. For both of these features to be present, a variety of different speeds of training are important. Full-speed training is not the only speed that should be used, but it *cannot* be neglected. Many martial arts schools fail to include full-speed training in their regimen with regard to partner work. As a "safe practice," they often practice at a maximum speed of 50 to 75 percent. Full-speed training will enhance your optic capacity and thus your visual awareness and reaction time. It will fine-tune your nervous system. Safety should not be abandoned, but neither should full-speed training. An effective martial art that uses effective training methods can find the necessary balance to include both safety and full-speed training.

The training should include both competitive and cooperative elements. If there are only competitive elements, the learning curve and depth will diminish, because developing a skill requires repetition of the same movements. In competitive training, you rarely repeat a sequence consistently enough to be able to reproduce it under high pressure. Along similar lines, if you practice with only cooperative elements, your ability to understand and integrate timing, pressure, and adaptability will never come to full fruition. A balance must be struck.

As a teacher, I witness many martial arts students over-emphasize one of the two contexts. Those who are overly competitive lack refinement in their movements. They also tend to exert far more energy than would otherwise be needed. They generally rely on out-muscling an opponent rather than finding structural unity to maximize their strength. On the other hand, those who over-emphasize cooperative training or neglect partner work altogether struggle a great deal when faced with the physical demands of a resisting opponent.[2] Therefore, to gain the greatest results from your Fight tool, it must include both competitive and cooperative elements. A great deal is learned from both types of training.

Although time spent doing repetitions by yourself should certainly be included in your training regimen, the relational element of a Fight tool is a critical feature. Bottom line: You need training partners. Only by training with partners is it possible to develop real-time response and adaptation. Moreover, working with another individual will teach you to foster trust in yourself and others. There are neurochemical and hormonal benefits to this. Training in an effective martial art while managing the inherent risks associated with that training has the potential to build deep bonds between people. That you literally put your safety in another's hands is both the value and the hazard in martial arts.

So be wise when choosing a style and school. If you discover that the culture is shaped by those who abuse trust, or if there are no clear rules in the training arena, my advice is to leave immediately and not return.

The Emotional and Mental Requirements

One of the greatest values of using the Fight tool as a survival stress training tool is that it necessarily contains a strong emotional component. There are quite literally threatening consequences when you fail, although these consequences should not be construed as always including injury. From time to time, failing may result in injury. The goal is to develop sufficient control to limit damage and to train with partners who share this same goal. Remember, a strongly *perceived* threat is sufficient to fulfill the emotional requirement.

This is what separates fighting from most dance. In the previous paragraphs, it would be easy to substitute dancing for fighting in so many places: developing gross and refined movement, controlling tension and pressure, developing greater adaptability, using relational elements, maintaining solo practice, establishing reaction time and distance control, and so on. I love to dance. Dance is primal, emotional, and cognitive, tapping into ancient brain centers and higher-order brain regions alike. However, dance usually lacks the threat element necessary to be a survival stress tool. Furthermore, even when a threat is present, it is not intentional; rather, it is a byproduct of the risk assumed in certain movements. This is the primary difference between martial arts and dance. Intentional threat makes all the difference, and it is why I advocate the use of fight training as a tool.

Intentional threat fosters a high emotional and mental threshold that allows us to effectively address avoiding the freeze. This is absolutely essential in good martial arts training. The other day, as I taught a group of roughly thirty women the essentials of self-defense, one of my students was struggling to voice a question. Looking at her, I could almost see the fear that gripped her as she hesitated. Her emotional state gave me a clue, and I later learned that my read was correct: She had experienced a difficult trauma in her life. A man had attacked her suddenly and without warning, and she had frozen when it happened, to her own detriment. The guilt that she had from that response still weighed on her heavily, even as she stood, proactive, training in my school that day. This woman's question was simple: How do I avoid the freeze? It's a common question in my self-defense workshops, from men and women alike.

How do I avoid the freeze? To be clear, the ability to exist in a heightened state of stillness, wherein we can be silent to avoid detection, is an asset in the right circumstances. Additionally, thermoconditioning—sometimes referred to later in this book as the 'Freeze' survival stress tool—is a welcome state that strengthens the mind and body. Neither should be confused with the unwelcome freeze of non-response when we need action for survival.

The negative freeze can occur for a variety of reasons. It can happen when we are surprised by a threatening animal, such as a snake or a bear. It can happen when a loud sound disrupts our neural processing. And it can also happen in the midst of a fight; a combatant can be "stunned" upon encountering the unexpected, such as a fake attack quickly followed by a true, alternate attack from a different angle. At its core, the freeze is a result of the body and brain being temporarily overwhelmed. Once this is understood, proper steps can be taken to train the system to avoid this unwanted state[3]

Three Steps to Avoiding the Negative Freeze via Martial Arts

The three steps are: understanding posture and alignment, relaxing your vision and curtailing information, and connecting to your breath. No matter your skill level, understanding and incorporating these three steps can allow you to maximize your potential in skill development at any given time.

A good martial art, as well as the facility where it's taught and the trainers who teach it, should ideally incorporate physical, mental, and emotional skill development to maximize your abilities and minimize your chance of being overwhelmed. There are many skills a good martial art will teach you, and developing those will allow you to grow in confidence and efficacy over the period you train. However, your ability to use those skills in the moment when you need them is built on the following three steps.

First Step: Ensure Proper Posture and Alignment

It's remarkable how something as simple as posture influences the mind and body's natural ability, willingness, and confidence—conscious and subconscious alike—to respond. Physically, there are clear reasons for this, but I am talking about from the emotional perspective. How you hold your head; where your weight is distributed in relation to your hips, feet, and arms; and how bent your knees are all tremendously influence your emotional state.

Our nervous systems are tied into our legs, neck, spinal alignment, weight distribution, and head placement. Just sinking a little bit into your legs by bending your knees can shift your emotions rapidly. The natural athletic posture of bent knees ties into our physicality in a way that few other things do. When standing, shifting your weight slightly forward and maintaining balance gives you the ability to adapt in a hundred different ways. When crouching, keeping your weight fifty-fifty offers phenomenal adaptability, and your mind and brain know that on every level.[4] And when you do not have an athletically inclined posture capable of immediately adapting, your mind and brain know that too. The simple experiment described below will allow you to tap into this concept and test it for yourself.

Grab a friend. Stand ten feet away from one another. Don't smile or laugh, but also don't be menacing or *act* in any way. Simply maintain constant eye contact with each other. One person stands with palms out, arms open, locked knees, straight legs, feet shoulder width, weight slightly on the heels without losing balance, and chin up. The other person stands with bent, natural knees and good shoulder posture, then walks forward slowly while maintaining eye contact. Both of you should notice how you feel as the distance shrinks. When you are roughly one foot apart, stop. Don't touch one another. Check in and see what the experience was like for each of you. Then reverse roles and repeat.

For the next part of the experiment, the stationary person should put their hands in a neutral posture at their chest, bring their feet slightly closer together, bend their knees, shift their weight slightly forward, and lower their chin. Once they have assumed this position, the other person should do the same walking experiment, maintaining eye contact and walking slowly enough that each has time to register the effect. Both individuals will find a staggering emotional difference between the two halves of this experiment.

I have done this experiment hundreds of times. It is interesting to do it with people you know and already trust. When done well with a serious tone, it is impactful. However, it is something else entirely to do it in a room full of people you have just met. It may still be a safe environment (such as a self-defense class), but the simple fact that you don't know the other person magnifies the effect dramatically. The exercise can give you a glimpse of how you might react emotionally to an aggressor on the street. It also reminds us how important it is to maintain good physical posture when addressing conflict or potential conflict.

Second Step: Retrain Visual Cues and Curtail the Information You are Consciously Attempting to Process

Learning to avoid distraction, in addition to knowing how and where to focus, can greatly improve your ability to respond effectively and avoid the hesitation that can lead to freezing. Training your mind to let go of unnecessary thoughts is essential.

The eye captures information and sends it to other parts of the nervous system at a speed that is unrecognizable to the conscious mind except in hindsight. As you work to reduce the visual load of information you are trying to process, you free yourself to act.

When faced with an opponent, distracting yourself with unnecessary thoughts, focusing your eyes on the wrong location, or trying to see too much causes great hesitation, and with hesitation comes a host of challenges. In Tsun Jo, I train my students to approach, or close on, their opponents based on specific rules, distance being one, and shoulder alignment being another. Intentionally keeping only a few variables in play can help students limit their concentration to avoid distraction. When hesitation arises due to a student trying to analyze too much information, or if the student's worry over possible negative consequences (i.e., imagined harm) takes hold, it almost inevitably results in poor performance, exposure, postural breakdown, and other associated problems. As a student becomes more proficient at keeping his or her mind focused in a particular way, the rules of eyesight focus, shoulder alignment, distance, weight distribution, and so on are eventually integrated into one. This is where a student can simply act, exhibiting the aforementioned practice of *mushin* or 'empty mind'—there develops a much faster connection between the survival brain and the body. Everything becomes linked; information is processed without unnecessary filtering, such as imagined harm; and hesitation is removed. The result is a high percentage of success in both defending and counterattacking. The perhaps ironic thing about the concept of *mushin* is that, while it is referred to as 'empty mind,' it can be best understood as the thoughtless fullness of presence. It is not that the mind is turned off and therefore 'empty.' Rather, the mind is unfettered to operate without interruption or interference from the labored conscious attention that humans so often try to interject—at great peril, I might add. In other words, we must rest in a state of consciousness, prepared to simply act.

The time to apply imagination and thoughtfulness is before or after training or a confrontation. That way, thoughtfulness can help us reflect on how well we did, and imagination can help us examine different ways of doing things. In a broader sense, imagination and reflection can assist us in developing strategies or movements, inventing and reinventing ideas, creating cohesion with others through shared beliefs, planning for the future, and evaluating the past in order to repeat success or make necessary changes. When it comes to the moment of engagement, however, it is critical that the imagination is not left to run wild. In fact, when dealing with the *now,* it is best to leave out imagination entirely.

The human optic nerve can capture an incredible amount of information.[5] Estimates for a 120-degree view suggest the equivalent of a 576-megapixel camera. For comparison, my iPhone X has a twelve-megapixel camera. Of course, the eye does not work exactly like a photo camera. It is more like a video camera with a processor, our brain, that both files and filters the tremendous amount of information captured at any moment.

On various levels of consciousness, we are aware of and influenced by the information our eyes capture. However, we are only able to fully process an extremely limited portion of that information. And while we can and should train to improve our processing bandwidth, it's equally or more important to recognize that the brain tracks a great deal of information on a subconscious level. Therefore, creating and following certain rulesets that take advantage of this fact can be of far greater utility than becoming bogged down in the consciously processed information stream.

The rules that guide training at my martial arts school help students engage in the now by simplifying the information they are trying to capture before they respond. For instance, students learn the rules of reaction time in relation to distance: the time it takes for the eye to capture visual information and your body to provide a response. Understanding these rules helps a student understand certain limits, which enables the brain to operate more freely and therefore better. Also, clarifying and practicing this concept can significantly reduce the surprise element that often leads to impaired performance and nervous system freeze. Basic principles and exercises for this rule can be learned in a single training session. Then, it is a matter of repetition to achieve consistency and eventually mastery.

Working at a variety of speeds, including full speed, allows students to become increasingly comfortable in the distress caused by rapidly moving objects and bodies and resistance without becoming overwhelmed. Visual and contact training inform the brain to make necessary adjustments and refine its ability to capture more useful information.

The final piece of the second step is the mindset during engagements. Just affirming that you are ready, willing, and able translates to empowerment and fuels positive emotional intensity; it counters anxiety-riddled anticipation belabored by a questioning insecurity. Training a student to have a resolute mindset that operates on acceptance rather than denial or uncertainty greatly contributes to his or her brain and body's support of the engagement. The mindset heavily influences one's willingness to rise to the occasion.

Your ability to maximize performance in the moment rests, in large part, upon your willingness to practice full acceptance. By accepting the ultimate outcome of the interaction, whatever it may be, you will greatly improve percentages of success over time. You will more easily maximize your field of vision, operate in a psychological mindset that supports you, and better control your emotional state. All of this will send proper signals to the nervous system and help to ensure that you don't freeze.

Third Step: Control the breath

Breathing, though autonomic by default, offers unique and direct access to the nervous system when consciously applied. By developing improved awareness, we can better steer our nervous systems toward a desired result, simply by where and what emphasis we place on our breath. Breathing properly can control our responses and ensure sustained energy. Breathing improperly can rapidly contribute to a feeling of being overwhelmed and simultaneously leave us out of breath and defeated. The body and mind can be directed by how we breathe from the beginning of a confrontation through its end. Our breath will either support a useful response or undermine it.

When we are scared, surprised, or overwhelmed, the initial reaction is frequently to take a large breath of air and hold it. Very often this response is followed by rapid breaths, sometimes shallow, sometimes deep, but all of which increase the activation of the sympathetic nervous system stress response. The body is preparing for action by pulling in, or trying to pull in, more oxygen to fuel the metabolic process that will need to take place.

In order to balance this breath response, stress hormones rapidly increase and the heart is kicked into high action.

The heart and the breath are inextricably linked, always attempting to balance one another. When the breath speeds up, so does the heart. This helps to ensure that air volume and blood flow volume remain in a proper relationship. Vasoconstriction and vasodilation of the vessels support this relationship and control oxygen and blood flow, so as not to waste either one. Matching oxygen intake with heartbeat and blood flow is essential to maximizing performance. Though this is largely an autonomic function, as we deliberately exert control of inhalation or exhalation, it creates bi-directional influence.

Now, recall that we discussed heart rate variability. Each time we breathe in, our heart rate speeds up due to sympathetic nervous stimulation. Each time we breathe out, our heart rate slows down due to parasympathetic nerve stimulation. The difference is heart-rate variability and it is dictated largely by autonomic function. With every heartbeat, heartrate variability affects general health and performance.

In terms of influencing heart function over a period of time, how we breathe can help control the speed of the heartbeat and the overall arousal state. For example, by controlling the length and depth of inhales versus exhales, we can steer the nervous system toward a more energetic, aroused state or a calmer state.

The simplest way to think about optimal breathing is that you want to make sure your breath remains flowing. Controlling depth and speed while exerting emphasis on either the inhale or exhale can manifest powerful results.

Holding your breath—unless it is part of intentional training exercises or used during a period of prescribed recovery—is deleterious with regard to your ability to respond effectively. Learning to be aware of this tendency and working to *let go* by exhaling can allow for the beginning of control. One example of this is catching yourself if you are unintentionally breathing fast and lengthening your exhales to help you bring your breath and nervous system back under control. When you breathe out, the vagus nerve is stimulated. This nerve ties into the hypothalamus, the master of hormonal function and a central piece in the HPA axis discussed earlier in this book. In a very simple sense, this extra stimulation of the vagus nerve through longer exhales triggers the hypothalamus to perceive that you are ok; this edges you away from any over-aroused state that can lead to freeze.

For a deeper discussion of breath, along with multiple breathing exercises to help develop optimal oxygen flow, heartbeat control, and mindset practices when faced with a variety of conditions, please visit my website at mattsoule.com.[6]

Managing Risks

The optimized risk feature of the Fight survival stress tool should limit impacts to the head and reduce the high cost of injury. The point is to train and develop yourself, not to become incapacitated or brain damaged.

When I mention martial arts training, high stress, and testable truths, many people automatically assume mixed martial arts (MMA) to be the likely candidate. However, like the other styles, it depends on the training and the facility. Even though MMA has grown extremely popular in recent times, it is *not* a style I typically recommend.

No-holds-barred fighting organizations have attempted to address questions surrounding effectiveness. In many respects, the result has been a wakeup call for the martial arts world. While not everything can be tested in a ring, a great deal can, and a number of truths have been demonstrated by various practitioners.

Personally, as a martial artist, I have always tried to gravitate toward the truth. For me, there are features that are essential for a fighting system to work on a consistently high-percentage basis. These features are minimizing damage taken, distance control, timing (both speed and reaction time), functional strength (including power and alignment), pressure, and adaptability. If a martial art fails to meet, understand, and incorporate these aspects, its likelihood of successful outcomes diminishes tremendously.

Additionally, without these features, the timespan over which you will be able to train in a style drops. For example, if a martial art or training does not *minimize damage taken*, you are more likely to be injured regularly. This will be a detriment to both your desire and your ability to train, and it can have even more serious consequences. If you suffer brain damage, not only will you be unable to train, you will likely have a significant health issue for the rest of your life.

So why not MMA?

Since its inception in 1993, MMA has developed into arguably the fastest-growing sport in the world. According to a *Forbes* article published in 2018, there may be as many as 260 million fans worldwide. After opening its first gym in 2009, UFC opened 150 gyms worldwide in the eight years leading up to the article.

It may be popular, but the training varies greatly, and often the risks outweigh the rewards. Although MMA can incorporate many combinations of styles, the most common combination is boxing, Thai kickboxing (or muay thai), and Brazilian jiu-jitsu, and the first two are often more dangerous than they are worth. Or, to put it another way, they don't meet the necessary standards to serve as a survival stress tool.

Boxing, for example, I would label as *a hit and be hit sport*. As a spectator, I have watched hundreds if not thousands of boxing matches. I appreciate many aspects of the sport. However, from a training and longevity point of view, it has extremely restricted value. Boxing's limited defensive moves and its reliance on close-range eyesight reaction capability makes this a brutal sport, and its participants take a great deal of damage—winners and losers alike. If you are a business executive, a doctor, a lawyer, an engineer, an artist, or

167

frankly anything other than a professional boxer, I highly discourage this as your training. Beyond my own boxing training experience—intentionally limited, I might add—I've reached this stance after watching so many practitioners take consistent and repetitive strikes to the head, *regardless of skill level*. In the following section, I will address traumatic brain injury (TBI) and its implications.

For now, let's turn to the next common MMA component, which is kickboxing. Muay thai training can vary greatly. There are gyms that might be great to train in, but overall the training itself can be quite damaging, as this is another *hit and be hit sport*. My advice, should you decide to study this art, is to tread slowly and examine your local gym carefully. Many practitioners experience a great deal of harm to the nervous system, whether from repetitive strikes to the head, severely damaged nerves in the legs and arms, or any number of other issues. This pattern largely stems from high-contact training while remaining in the power pocket.[7]

At the other extreme, some gyms—especially large chains—advertise boxing or kickboxing devoid of partner work. However, doing only bag work or solo work to practice these arts does not fulfill the Fight requirement of a survival stress tool. My goal is not to undervalue solo training, but rather to illustrate the difference and unique benefits of using a Fight tool as a survival stress tool. Partner interaction, for example, is critical to develop the mindset, confront the deepest primal fears, and develop the physical prowess essential for such a tool. The goal is finding a martial art that meets the Fight tool threshold while mitigating the risk of nervous system damage.

Fighting and good fight training tap into the most primal center of a human being. There are very, very few pursuits that when practiced, bring to the fore our primal machinery and confront our deepest fears of physical threat. If a martial art is practiced in the proper context, the true confidence that emerges is the result of two skills: an ability to protect yourself, and a level of physical control that allows you to purposefully come within a whisper of hurting another without stepping over that line. Possessing this razor-sharp edge of control allows you to truly know that you can inflict great damage when needed beyond the training room. This empowerment is transferable across multiple unrelated domains in a way that other training is not. It is my firm opinion that the outlined specific attributes of martial arts training are absolutely necessary if you want to master the stress response. This prescribed training provides tremendous opportunity to practice staying calm under threat, train the nervous system to adapt rapidly, and cultivate internal and external awareness beyond conscious attention.

Traumatic Brain Injury

TBI stands for traumatic brain injury. Over the last decade, a plethora of data has emerged as TBI evidence has grown across a great number of sports and activities. TBI is incredibly common in boxing, MMA, and American football, but it is also associated with soccer, basketball, equestrian sports, water sports, skiing, snowboarding, and many other pastimes. According to the *Journal of Neurosurgery*, between 2003 and 2012 there were over 4,000 sports related-incidents of TBI.

TBI can include life-changing results that deeply and negatively impact those injured. Personality changes, increased aggression, depression, and impaired social functioning are some of the most prevalent symptoms among those suffering from TBI.[8]

When utilizing a Fight survival stress tool such as martial arts, risk of all injuries, including TBI, need to be optimized, but they should not be eliminated. Learning the proper way to assess and manage risk not only helps to develop better decision-making abilities, it is also a key feature of mastering the stress response.

Having been involved in many sports and several different martial arts over the years, I have experienced a broad set of attitudes upheld by various coaches and teachers. If you plan to train in a martial art that includes partner exercises involving contact, which I believe to be critical, be prepared to ask intelligent questions such as, *what is your policy around head contact?* The answer can give you a good idea about the type of facility you are considering. A coach who blows off that type of question for any reason is not to be trusted. Furthermore, instructions like *hit only as hard as you want to be hit* can be a dangerous policy. It is not altogether wrong, but tread carefully with this one.

The policy at my martial arts school is that beginners have zero head contact and furthermore must not strike within six inches of their partner's head. This is mostly in consideration of the fact that new students do not yet have the control needed to get any closer. As students become intermediate and advanced, training partners are expected to demonstrate full control and make only light, if any, head contact, even when going full speed. Advanced practitioners are permitted to request that their partners attack them at full speed and strength, but these students are capable of defending against an extremely wide range of attacks. The martial art I teach, Tsun Jo, is built on integrated strikes and deflections, a type of active, adaptive blocking. Because of this, practitioners of Tsun Jo become very skilled at simultaneously defending and counterattacking using the forearms, knees, and shins as shields.[9] Moreover, Tsun Jo includes a great deal of high-pressure sticking, which trains the nervous system to track and respond to high-level resistance under pressure.[10] My school emphasizes full control of an opponent even when he is trying to hit us, and we incorporate significant submission grappling, both standing and on the ground. In all cases, we emphasize control and observe the head contact policy.

Everyone is responsible to ensure safety. We foster strong bonds of trust so that we can attack and train at full speed while greatly limiting the likelihood of significant head impact. I am proud to say that while I have taught thousands of students, and the teachers before me taught thousands more, we have had an extremely low injury rate. Simultaneously, we have trained very skilled martial artists. So, if you walk into a gym, academy, dojo, or school and the instructor tells you that you need to accept being hit, my personal advice is to either leave or completely and intentionally accept the full risks that come with that philosophy.

A Couple of Recommendations on Choosing a Martial Art

If you have examined the physical, emotional, and mental requirements as well as the supporting elements needed to tap into the survival machinery and you are still uncertain on how to proceed, my suggestion is to begin with a martial art that includes quality submission grappling.

Many martial artists these days choose to focus solely on submission grappling. While this style is not without its risks, intentional head contact is *not* a common one, as it is not usually a feature of styles such as Brazilian jiu-jitsu. I have attended many submission grappling academies that either do not include head contact in their practice curriculum or reserve it for specialized training.[11]

While I prefer an art that includes kicking, striking, and grappling, I believe submission grappling to be one of the best arts to develop the Fight survival tool while managing the risks associated with martial arts training. It is by no means the only one, but as a general category I can speak confidently and very highly of its utility and results in Fight survival tool training.

Regardless of what art you choose, my advice is find a facility that builds trust among training partners and respects the human body, both in terms of pushing practitioners to be better and balancing the goals of long-term training. If the school has a high injury rate, you likely want to look elsewhere. Choose carefully which attitudes will truly serve you. Submission grappling schools can exhibit an unwillingness to tap or a disregard for ear health.[12] Many practitioners suffer from cauliflower ear, which can impair ear function and increase overall health risks. Many practitioners and coaches find this is acceptable—sometimes even deem it desirable. To me it is neither. Although I have some permanent ear damage, I have tried to be mindful of using ear protection and promoting healing when the damage has occurred. In any case, you must choose what is acceptable to you. If you wish to master the stress response, a truly high-functioning nervous system is required. Injuries, infections, and damage will hold you back.

Two Tips

1. If you like the facility where you train but feel a little uncomfortable putting on ear protection due to societal norms there, practice being comfortable with the uncomfortable. It is an important developmental step in your ability to master the stress response.

2. Learn to tell a good joke. My favorite line when I began training with Brazilian jiu-jitsu guys who revered cauliflower ear as a badge of honor was, "My wife said that if I get any uglier, she will divorce me." The guys all laughed and we kept training. This attitude never interfered with my ability to build trust and train hard. You don't have to do what you are unwilling to do for fear that you might not be accepted. Stand strong and hold to your values. You will be respected.

FREEZE

THE SURVIVAL STRESS tool as outlined in this section focuses on Freeze. In the last chapter, we discussed freeze in terms of nervous system overload, such as panicking or shutting down. But here, we will discuss a new type of Freeze: an environmental acute stress tool that lets us tap into one of our most powerful connections to our ourselves. This positive Freeze uses short exposures to frigid temperatures that allows us to train and improve the vascular system, bolster the immune system, reduce muscular tension, and reset the nervous system; balance hormones; reach flow states; and face fears. The extreme temperature of the cold automatically shifts the physical for a myriad benefits as we will learn in detail, but Freeze training also offers an incredible opportunity to foster mental and emotional resilience while teaching us full acceptance. This has profound implications when we confront the many things we cannot change in daily life. The training offers a way to address needed emotional resolution, find stillness amidst excessive stimulation, reinterpret the environment and adapt.

In recent years, thermogenic training has become increasingly popular and for good reason. The term *thermogenic* simply refers to temperature training. Both cold training and its counterpart, heat training (such as sauna use), offer a myriad of health benefits. Although much of the discussion of this tool will focus on cold training and its unique characteristics and benefits, heat training offers many distinctive benefits as well. I will touch briefly on some of those, and I will address questions regarding how to train when integrating these two modalities to get the most out of each.

Using thermogenic training helps reset body systems; offers repair and recovery for cells; protects telomeres in your DNA; improves vascular performance; re-balances neurotransmitter activity, improving mood and emotion; boosts immune function; and reduces all-cause mortality, contributing to maximized longevity. And if that is not enough, the Freeze training tool offers psychological benefits as we learn to face fears, develop deeper layers of consciousness, and reconnect to our inner nature and the nature that surrounds us.

One of the keys to life is the ability to be comfortable with discomfort, to know when there is no sense in trying to change that which you cannot change. You simply must learn to accept circumstances for what they are and adapt. You must learn when and how to fight, but you should also learn when to let go. This profound shift offers great insight in life and is a key to ultimately mastering the stress response.

Whenever I talk about thermogenic training, many ask about heat. Heat can also be a wonderful training tool. Intense exercise, thermogenic training such as hot yoga, sauna use, and other heat training modalities can be of great benefit. In these conditions, heat shock proteins unleash in your body to perform many actions similar to those performed by cold shock proteins, including regenerating synapses, offering cellular recovery and repair, and reducing inflammation. Regular use of a sauna has been linked to significant reductions in heart- and cardiovascular-related diseases and deaths, as well as to significant reductions in all-cause mortality.[13]

Thermogenic training, both the cold and heat aspects, is a high-value stress tool for health and well-being. I regularly train at a Russian-style *banya*, which has a wonderful sauna that typically sits above 240°F, and the dry, intense heat is a great compliment to the cold plunge. This combination is what is known as contrast therapy. It is an increasingly popular combination borrowed from many parts of the world, especially the Scandinavian countries, Russia, and Japan.

When doing contrast therapy, try starting with cold and ending with cold. Starting with cold requires extra focus, which bolsters the psychological and emotional benefits as well as the cardiovascular system. Ending with cold closes the skin pores, trapping the skin's natural oils, while leaving you feeling refreshed.

Give yourself a little bit of time between the heat training and the cold training exposures. After the cold, give your body a few minutes to heat itself up while waiting in ambient temperature conditions. After the heat, do the same to cool down. Allowing your body to do a bit of the work between contrast sessions will help you finish each metabolic process before going on to the other.

Although there are a few exceptions, one of the best benefits of cold training that is not commonly present in heat training is the fear factor.[14] I have certainly met people who do not like the heat, but I have never met a person who fears acute doses of the heat. If you meet this description, you are the rare exception.

Cold training presents you with the rare opportunity to face the fears that humans tend to associate with cold. This is one of the chief reasons that I suggest cold training by itself; it offers a mental and emotional challenge with its own unique benefits. It is also the reason that I have chosen the cold, or freeze, as the survival stress tool for this book.

The Cold

When I lived in New York City in the mid-2000s, I absolutely dreaded walking outside in winter, even with a coat on. My hands, feet, and face would hurt, my legs would ache, and I couldn't wait to get inside. The wind would lash around each building in the cityscape, adding to the frigid onslaught. When I left New York, I vowed to never again live in a place that was windy and cold.

When I moved to the Pacific Northwest, with its relatively mild winters, I thought I would be all set. There is little wind, and the temperature rarely drops below 40°F. And after a few months, I did indeed notice that I had somewhat acclimated to the cooler overall temperatures. But while I got cold less easily some of the time, there were still problems. I found that the dampness and almost constantly cool temperatures would seep into my bones even at 50°F, and certainly when the barometer dipped lower. I resigned myself to being the guy who would wear long johns for nine months of the year and always have a hat and gloves nearby. When summer came, I would still wear my nice thick socks to bed.

Then, from 2013 to 2015, I found myself caught up in a new

problem. It was a stressful time for me, as I was going through a divorce. Physical outlets—such as martial arts training, strength training, running, hill sprints, and so on—all have the potential to cause hormetic stress, *the good stress, in the body.* Traditionally I have always used physical stress to release emotional and psychological stress. But during those years, even my *normal* training was causing me to meet or exceed my stress threshold daily. When I exerted myself the way I wanted to, I was not recovering. Small injuries turned into larger injuries. Constant and extended pain often resulted. I found it virtually impossible to find the right balance. My inflammation was out of control. And yet, when I tried to lessen my exercise output, my emotional stress levels surged.

In early 2013, John Beall and I had a conversation about cold as a modality to address health issues. He had been casually following the now-famous Wim Hof for several years, mostly through Wim's incredible physical feats, such as ascending to the Mount Everest "death zone" wearing only shorts and shoes. This and other extreme feats intrigued John, who has always been keenly interested in maximizing human potential. Both John and I were intrigued by what Wim could do and how he was pushing the human body, mind, and spirit. And moreover, Wim was willing to test his claims by subjecting them to scientific scrutiny. This was incredibly inspiring, and Wim became a centerpiece of our conversations.

Wim has done many interesting things that push a variety of boundaries, but there is one accomplishment that stands out. In 2011/2012, Wim participated in a scientific study wherein he was injected with an endotoxin of *Escherichia coli* (*E. coli*) and successfully influenced his autonomic nervous system to practically eliminate all symptoms from the injection.[15] Prior to this experiment, science did not have evidence that this was possible. Wim was also able to induce significant, documented shifts in his inflammatory response during the *E. coli* experiment. Results from the experiment indicated that those beneficial shifts were effective for the next six days.

This evidence revealed possibilities in my own life and pushed me to learn everything I could about inflammation. As I educated myself, I started to realize how many of my seemingly unrelated activities contributed to my problems. Being an entrepreneur and raising a family on my solo income, I needed to work very long hours when I first took over the martial arts school to make it sustainable. As a martial artist highly dedicated to developing my art and craft, I had been consistently overtraining since I took the school over in 2010.

In late 2012, I broke my hand, the first major injury I had had in many years. It was partly a freak accident of mistiming a defense against a training partner's kick, and partly from a lack of focus and being tired. I trained through this injury, having a cast on my right hand, and simply focused on everything I could do with my left hand. I never let my body rest.

So much training was beneficial for my nervous system development in certain ways, but it was detrimental to my body's recovery process and health. Although my hand healed in six weeks and was relatively normal, residual pain remained in my hand and wrist for years.

Maintaining a no-matter-what training attitude, pushing my body's threshold to maximum capacity every day without the rest necessary to recover, started to add up. Small tweaks from practicing different choke holds or armbars slowly turned from understandable mild soreness into chronic inflammation that wouldn't go away for weeks or months.

At that point in my life, I didn't really understand the full role of inflammation. From years of sports and pushing my body with little consequence, I had the impression that I would always be able to do that. Anytime I was in pain, a day or two later all was good. I knew, in very general terms, that inflammation was associated with soreness or pain and increased swelling and blood flow after a hard workout or to an injured area. If the pain was really bad, I could put a bag of ice on it or take ibuprofen. That was it, and that was about as far as my interest in the subject went. In other words, I didn't really *know* about inflammation.

At the time, an increasing number of articles were being written discussing inflammation and connecting it to any number of problems and diseases. According to the National Center for Biotechnology Information, an incredible number of lifestyle diseases are linked to inflammation in some way.[16] This fact was unfolding right before my eyes. It was no longer just about visible redness and swelling at the site of an injury: It was about a body breaking down at the result of unheeded and unending signals from my nervous system.

By late 2013, I had chronic inflammation throughout my body. The primary pain centers that were affecting me day and night were in my right jaw and neck at the C5/C6 area of the spine. Pain from what seemed like the trigeminal nerve felt like talons lacerating my lower jaw, cheek, and forehead.[17] I also was experiencing intermittent sciatica, a kind of nerve pain, that traveled from my lower back to my groin, knees, and toes on my right leg. This further inflamed my pelvic area, legs, and feet. As the inflammatory process continued, I suffered from persistent bacterial infections, which further inflamed my jaw and face.

The host of injuries I experienced over that three-year period provoked me to learn everything I could about inflammation and nerve pain. I tried to understand the difference between the two, to comprehend how pain sensors and signals function and what I could possibly do to improve the problems. I spent thousands of dollars on unsuccessful medical treatments that offered little if any respite. Neither painkillers nor alcohol worked; the slight and temporary reprieve only made the next bout worse. I needed something else.

A Path Forward

John and I continued to discuss Wim Hof and the cold, the latter of which, it seemed, could curb inflammation. Furthermore, the cold seemed to offer additional psychological benefits. Everything John was reading at the time supported that cold training was a great modality to promote health and well-being.

We kept returning to the long traditions of cold training and martial arts folklore: Ueshiba, the founder of aikido, who would meditate under freezing-cold waterfalls for his health; Rickson Gracie, a famous Brazilian jiu-jitsu practitioner, and his training methods that included meditating in cold streams and rivers; and of course, Wim Hof, with his seemingly insane endurance for ice exposure and cold water immersion.

Not fully understanding my own potential, Rickson's, Ueshiba's, and especially Wim's feats looked all but impossible to me. I tried to read Wim Hof's book, *The Way of the Iceman.* I tried to wrap my head around the breathing techniques. I tried to practice the visualization and take cold showers. I tried, but I struggled to succeed. I was the guy who couldn't sleep without thick socks on, even in the heat of summer. How would I manage to acclimate to the cold? *Let's face it,* I thought, *I am just not built like that.*

Things are Changing

In August 2015 I got an email from John titled "Things are changing." I opened the email to find a link to Wim Hof's new documentary.[18] Life at the time was still quite overwhelming. By then, I was representing myself in my divorce, lawyers no longer being affordable, and we were just about to go to trial. Nevertheless, I watched the documentary that day and was fascinated and inspired.

Watching the video clued me in to what *the breathing should look like.* While the full method was still elusive, and the cold was touch and go, I began to mess around with the breathing I had seen in the documentary. I spent that fall just getting by, working constantly, trying to make it through. I was in pain most days; emotionally taxed, I relied on my mindset to guide me from moment to moment and did my best to maintain a positive attitude. I reread the works of the Stoics, did short journaling, and trained as hard as I could, albeit far below my desired level. I used any useful tool or distraction I could manage.

When I finalized my divorce in December 2015, I drove down the street blaring Nina Simone's *Feeling Good.* With the car windows down, I belted out the lyrics at top volume. With open road ahead, I felt I could focus on gathering up the fractured pieces of my life. The next couple of months would prove to be some of the most revealing I have ever experienced.

Searching on the Internet, I found Wim's first ten-week online course. I signed up with a friend and started practicing WHM. When tackling any new habit that requires commitment and consistency, having accountability is very useful. Online courses don't inherently provide accountability, so having a friend I was accountable to was helpful.

The first episode of the course laid the groundwork for the method. When I actually *learned* the breathing method for the first time, I finally understood what I was supposed to do.[19] Sitting in a comfortable, meditation-like position, I began to breathe. When I did my first retention (a breath hold that happens on the exhale), which lasted about 45 seconds, I found it difficult to breath that much. My mouth got a little dry and my relatively weak diaphragm had to work extra hard. I was relying too much on the upper chest for breathing—thoracic and clavicular breathing—as I tried to keep up.

Even though I struggled to keep pace, I felt pretty good after that first retention and went into the next round of breathing. During the second retention, I extended my breath hold to more than ninety seconds. I felt a tingling and light sensation. During the final round, the rapid breaths outlined by the protocol became easier, almost as if my physiology was more willing to accept what I was doing. I breathed vigorously for those thirty breaths, feeling a deeper connection among my breath, body, and mind. Concentrating on the final three breaths, I took in huge amounts of air, and when I let the last one go, I felt free and elated. To my deep surprise, I had held my breath for more than two minutes and felt great. I'd floated through space and time in those two minutes. When it was finally time to breathe again, I took my recovery breath and felt supercharged.

Next, it was time for the cold shower. Although I was feeling great from the breathing, I was excited yet nervous about this step. The protocol was to start off with a warm shower, proceed to twenty to thirty seconds of cold shower, and finally return to warm. I got in the warm shower and, with a bit of reluctance, flipped the dial to cold. The water bit, but not nearly as much as during my previous experiences with cold water. It was funny and tolerable. I yelped now and again, the high-pitched tone ringing throughout the apartment. A few curses were also let loose, but they were paired with a big smile. After thirty seconds, I flipped the dial back to a warmer setting for a minute or so and then got out. I felt alive and refreshed. My body was a mix of pleasure, relief, and excitement. I finally had a glimpse of the connection between the cold and breathing.

Steadily, I practiced daily, and it got easier and easier. Every day, I found I had more energy than the day before. I was noticing changes in many parts of my life, not just physically but emotionally. My divorce had resulted in financial challenges and a less-than-ideal parenting plan, but this new method was providing an unexpected emotional outlet. I was highly motivated to continue.

Each day, I was able to manage my life better. As the next few weeks went by, the WHM course called for increasingly cold exposures. I could feel my body changing and adapting to this new norm. Whenever I had to do the cold showers, they weren't easy, but I got enough enjoyment, clear pain reduction, and general happiness from the protocols that it encouraged me to keep going.

By the time I was in week five, I was telling whoever would listen that I had found something incredible. So when I saw that there was an advanced training module for the first class of US instructors coming up in April, I knew I had to be part of it. I signed up immediately and continued to practice every day.[20]

The weeks and months went by. As I progressed in my training, more and more people would send me articles or other relevant information. My uncle, for example, would regularly send me information on the Blackfeet Nation, a North American tribe. In winter, the buffalo-runners used extremity training of the hands to improve dexterity for hunting. They would rub their hands with sand and snow so that they could go without gloves in cold weather, improving their accuracy. I also read a book called *Blackfeet Indians* by Frank Bird Linderman. An author and ethnographer, Linderman lived among the Salish and Blackfeet tribes in the late nineteenth century. His book recounts common practices among the tribes. Virtually every morning at dawn, Linderman would witness the men and boys submerging themselves in the icy streams. Winter was not an exception to the practice.

I expanded my reading list, learning about the purposes of various cold practices and looking for additional insight.[21] There is the practice of *Shugendō,* as part of which Japanese monks in lightweight robes strengthen their spiritual power by dutifully stepping under frigid waterfalls before ascending a mountain.[22] Or there is the practice of *misogi,* a part of Shinto religious rituals that involves cleansing and purifying the body and spirit by stepping under sacred but cold waterfalls or rivers. To prepare for the cold immersion, it is common to engage in *furitama,* fist and body clenches, and sometimes deep breathing.[23] To rewarm the body after the cold exposure, light activity or calisthenics are performed. The founder of aikido, Morihei Ueshiba, was known to practice *misogi* regularly for health, spirit, and vitality.

The further I progressed in WHM, the less abstract such practices seemed. Each layer of learning turned to another, and then another, as I explored the different methodologies of cold as a beneficial practice. Every day revealed new and positive changes. I thought the process would soon plateau, but so far this has not been the case. Today, as I continue to daily WHM practice, I also continue to see positive changes in and a deeper connection between my mind and body.

This process has been like watching a baby grow into a teenager, then into an adult: Each day something is different, although it is often difficult to pinpoint each specific change from day to day. But if you compare the present incarnation to that of a year ago, the differences are clear.

The changes were clearest during the custody battle for my daughter that ensued two years after I had been practicing. Like a divorce, a custody battle is emotionally, financially, mentally, and physically exhausting: a colossal stressor. Yet, with the tools I needed now firmly established, I was able to navigate the process with calm, focus, and perseverance, a major juxtaposition to the me of just a few years earlier. The new baseline of what I could handle had shifted.

Looking back over the years of daily practice, I realize that I have grown beyond anything I could have imagined. The foundational structure that this practice has provided has changed every area of my life. My old perspective—that I could not be like the warriors of folklore or the Wim Hofs of the mountains and ice—was far from the truth. It was in me and it is in you too, regardless of your background and starting point.

Understanding Limits in Order to Break Them

In the course of my training to become a WHM instructor, I met a number of incredible individuals from all types of advanced body disciplines. As part of our certification, we were required to present our personal stories within the context of the WHM. Virtually every story had truly compelling elements, many of which brought us to tears or amazed us. It was a powerful experience to say the least.

One person I met was David, a certified kettlebell instructor and competing strongman living in Nashville, Tennessee. A strongman, as the title suggests, is someone who performs incredible feats of strength: I witnessed him bend sixteen penny nails, rip through decks of cards, and bend horseshoes. And although he wasn't unique in his ability to impress in that group of outstanding individuals, he regularly gathered a crowd as he displayed his skillset.

When it was David's turn to tell his story, it was immediately apparent that he was a great teacher. His thoughts on defining and breaking limits rang the gong of truth, creating a resonance that vibrated inside me. I had used David's approach to limits most of my life, but it had been on an intuitive level. I am forever thankful to him for articulating this tool so well, as it has allowed me to use it as a teaching guide ever since.

David expressed his thoughts using the following example. Say you have the ability to bench-press fifty pounds. If so, then trying to bench-press double that amount is reckless and will almost certainly lead to injury. Such an attempt not only won't increase your limit, it will likely make it go down, perhaps by a lot due to injury to yourself. But if instead, you gradually increase your limit to reach your goal of 100 pounds, it will be only a matter of time and practice before you achieve this.

Constraints on growth really boil down to time and training methods, because human potential is not fixed. We keep improving. However, many of us get impatient and rush to improve faster than we can. Having a mindset that incorporates training as a lifestyle approach and has clear and reasonable short- and long-term goals will foster the best outcomes and lead to the greatest results. If you are unsure of your process, truthfully answer some clear questions:

> *Is cost of improving certain metrics worth bearing? What are the opportunity costs of my training approach? What am I losing out on as I progress toward my goal? Does my short- or long-term goal come at the cost of my health?*

These questions can and should be applied to whatever training you pursue. And when it comes to the contents of this book, these questions can be a guideline to cold training that is tailored to your personal approach.

When starting out in cold training, you may have no concept of your own baseline. When you don't know your current limits, it is important to understand the variables likely to contribute to risk and safety. Much of the recorded information on cold risk and safety is related to accidental falls into cold water, although this is changing rapidly thanks to practitioners of cold training. Supplemental research compiled through military programs can also lend insight to some useful boundaries.

Three Primary Concerns for Cold Water Immersion

There are three primary concerns with regard to cold water immersion: cold water shock, incapacitation due to cold, and hypothermia.

First Concern: Initial Reaction

Our initial reaction to the cold, known as the cold shock response, commonly lasts for one to three minutes. Whether the immersion is accidental or intentional, this response is part of an initial entry into cold water until habituation takes place. That being said, even those habituated to the cold often experience this initial reaction, albeit generally to a much smaller degree and for a shorter length of time.

Fortunately, there is an easy way to overcome this concern. My advice to cold water practitioners, especially new(er) practitioners, is to enter the cold water with calm and intention, rather than jumping in. The initial cold shock response can cause involuntary gasping and hyperventilation. If water is inhaled, it increases the chance of drowning.[24]

The other reason to enter the cold with calm and intention is to benefit from mental focus. To use cold water immersion as a training tool to master the stress response is to learn to avoid panic as you meet intense discomfort. Stepping into the cold water slowly and intentionally allows you to control your mindset as your body physiologically adapts to the cold stress. Practicing in this way yields tremendous psychological benefits and will help you recalibrate your responses to other stressors in your life. It offers you a healthy way to practice expressing your new reactions to stressful circumstances, meeting them with calm, focus, attention, and presence while your physical body experiences a hormonal stress boost.

Second Concern: Reduced Muscle Capacity and Dexterity

Reduced muscle capacity and dexterity occurs over the course of a short immersion in cold water. Depending on water temperature and other factors like wind and precipitation, body mass, and surface area exposed, impaired muscle and nerve function can occur within a very short time. This is especially important to understand if you plan to be in a natural, uncontrolled setting to do your cold immersion.

The US military has conducted studies and published information on how long it is advisable for soldiers to be in cold water. These studies have covered a variety of temperatures and immersion depths, but even in water as warm as 50 to 54°F, it only takes the average soldier five minutes to begin experiencing deficits. This is because body cooling begins to happen after the first three minutes or so of immersion in cold water. Hypothermia, which we will cover in depth shortly, is defined as a core body temperature of less than 95°F. The US Army has calculated that muscle and nerve impairment begins to occur, limiting manual responsiveness, at 95.9°F, a temperature just above initial hypothermia.

In Seattle, we have not only a number of cold lakes and rivers nearby, we also have a cold part of the Pacific Ocean. I spend a substantial amount of time traveling the Pacific Northwest to experience the variety of cold training opportunities in gorgeous natural settings. Virtually all the cold training workshops I teach are done in nature rather than in ice baths. So again, when in an uncontrolled setting, being mindful of the speed at which your muscles and nerves can begin to experience diminished capacity is quite important.

My martial arts teacher and friend John Beall experienced this dangerous decline while in a bathtub in the early days of his own cold training. Granted, he had been in approximately 47°F water for close to forty minutes, *but* he was following the recommendation of a neuroscientist's blog. In my personal opinion, John was not significantly habituated to cold. He had successfully completed the preparatory protocols advised by the neuroscientist, but the result was a near-death experience. After sitting immersed in the cold water for that length of time, John was virtually unable to remove himself from the tub, and there was no one nearby to assist him. By sheer force of will, he managed to pull himself from the water and survive.

I mention John's story for a couple of reasons. There exists conflicting information with regard to intentional cold water immersion for training purposes. The incongruity generally pertains to how long you *can* or *should* stay in the cold to gain benefits and elicit particular responses in the body, including cold acclimatization.

Some also assume that if they are good swimmers, many of the rules do not apply to them. This results in unnecessary risks and sub-optimal training results. The primary dangers posed by intentional cold immersion are the first two listed above: cold shock response and incapacitation due to cold immersion, both of which can affect good and bad swimmers alike.

It is also worth noting that a substantial number of victims who fall into cold water die due to drowning, although these are generally *accidental* cold water immersions. The National Water Safety Congress advises the one-ten-one survival principle: one minute to take control of your breathing, ten minutes to use your muscles for meaningful movement without exhausting yourself, and one hour before hypothermia and loss of consciousness.[25]

Cold shock begins immediately upon entry into cold water and can last approximately one to three minutes. Incapacitation commonly takes around five to fifteen minutes, although it can occur faster. Hypothermia typically won't set in for thirty minutes or more. Again, these estimates are based off of accidental cold water immersions, but they are still worth paying attention to *because they also define cold water as less than 70°F*. That temperature is much higher than that used by cold immersion practitioners. In order to induce cold thermogenesis for training purposes, the water must be no more than 64°F, and temperatures in the 30s or 40s are usually preferred.

So if you are new to cold immersion, don't assume that just because you are a good swimmer, you will be capable of defying these rules somehow. Professor Michael Tipton of the Institute of Naval Medicine in England states that fifty-five percent of open-water drowning deaths happen within approximately nine feet of safety.[26] Further, forty-two percent are even closer, within six and a half feet of safety. The research also shows two-thirds of the victims were thought to be good swimmers.

Cold habituation through consistent training will improve your ability to swim in cold waters and tolerate low temperatures for extended periods of time. However, it is essential to have clear ideas about managing the risks as you habituate. The length of time that different individuals can safely sustain low temperatures in cold water varies greatly. This is largely why the US Army has what may seem like comfortable training limits for its soldiers, such as five minutes in 50°F water. There will always be discussion about training methods to improve outcomes, but as far as safe starting limits for this survival stress tool, it is wise to heed these warnings and approach your training with thoughtfulness and patience.

Third Concern: Hypothermia

As mentioned, hypothermia does not set in right away, but as a cold immersion practitioner, you must certainly be aware of it. According to the US Search and Rescue Task Force, expected survival time for those who fall into water at or below 32°F is somewhere between fifteen and forty-five minutes. The thirty-minute difference is largely due to individual characteristics: body mass, body surface area, type of clothing, and *emotional* response. In other words, do they panic or make extraneous, unhelpful movements that lead to further decline and poor decisions? If so, exhaustion or unconsciousness can occur in fewer than fifteen minutes.

In contrast, an individual who falls into 40 to 50°F water is expected to survive for one to three hours. This is a substantial increase. The timeline to exhaustion is estimated to range between thirty and sixty minutes.[27] As before, these numbers are for accidental exposures; for our purposes, we can even assume that the individuals are not cold acclimatized.

In the event of an accidental cold water immersion, it is reasonable to assume that the victim is fully clothed. This is because many of these types of accidents occur when people are boating, fishing, or hunting. Others who suffer accidental cold water immersion may be cross-country skiing, snowmobiling, or pursuing other winter sports that typically involve clothing.

I mention this because clothing can help trap heat in the short term and help the body conserve its own heat. When cold-seekers expose ourselves to freezing temperatures, we often do so with little or no clothing. But with patience and consistency of practice, the small assistance of clothing will be unnecessary as you progress ever closer to mastering the stress response.

Heat Exchange Principles

It is helpful to understand how the body functions under cold stress conditions. In order to do that, let us start with heat exchange principles. Although that may sound counterintuitive, cold is better understood through heat conservation or heat loss. Heat is exchanged through four primary mechanisms: conduction, convection, radiation, and evaporation.

Conduction heat loss happens when two objects with different surface temperatures come into contact, like when you sleep on a cold floor. The floor is colder and it pulls the heat out of you.

Convection heat loss is caused by the movement of cold water or air. Your body maintains an insulative layer of heat on the skin's surface to protect you; the movement of cold water or air reduces that layer. This will make a large difference when standing still in a river versus doing so in a lake. It also matters when you train on a windy day and *especially* once you get out of the water and you are still wet. The combined effect of being wet and having wind present can be very challenging and potentially lead to frostbite if you are not careful. Final note here, although wind and flowing water both cause convection heat loss, heat loss from water is twenty to twenty-five times greater than it is from air.

Radiation heat loss occurs when surrounding objects have lower surface temperatures than you do. If, on the other hand, the objects around you have higher surface temperatures, you will gain heat. This is true of surrounding rocks, for example, but it is also true of the sun. A clear, sunny day, even when the air temperature is quite cold, offers significant heat contribution to help warm your body, because this type of heat exchange is independent of air temperature. I have explored many frigid lakes in various weather conditions and I'll tell you, the difference between a sunny day and an overcast one when you are dipping into the cold water is staggering. The rewarming period can be significantly reduced due to this mechanism as well.

And finally, evaporation occurs primarily from sweating, although to a lesser extent it can also be from respiration. It can also occur because you are still wet after emerging from a cold lake or river. Therefore, it is usually important to get dry relatively quickly to help protect you from evaporative heat loss.

Unique Aspects of the HPA Axis, Blood Shunting and Hormones Due to Cold Stress

The next thing to understand is how our bodies respond to cold conditions. The thermoregulatory system's response is governed primarily by the now-familiar HPA axis, which is integral to the stress response.[28] As the hypothalamus receives sensory information about temperature, its circuitry signals the body to make the necessary adjustments to maintain homeostasis, the goal being a stable core body temperature. As you initiate cold exposure, either voluntarily or involuntarily, vasoconstriction, or the narrowing of vessels near the extremities, redirects blood to conserve heat around the core. Vasoconstriction in the hands and feet can start when skin temperature falls just a few degrees, and the strongest effects are felt when skin temperature drops below 88°F. Skin temperature fluctuates rapidly during cold water immersion, easily dropping to the 60s or below within just a couple of minutes; skin temperatures on the fingers drop even lower.

Once a person has been submerged for several minutes, another phenomenon begins to take shape: cold induced vasodilation (CIVD). This is a protective mechanism for the fingers, nose, ears, toes, and cheeks. CIVD is not a constant dilation but rather a periodic oscillation between constriction and dilation in an effort to optimize prioritizing demands under cold conditions. CIVD improves with training but in a new practitioner, this mechanism is limited, and often causing feet and hands to become and remain quite uncomfortable or numb for extended periods, even after getting out of the cold. Fortunately, your body will acclimate over time using this mechanism.

The vasoconstriction process of blood being redirected from the extremities and gathered in the core is called a blood shunt. This happens quite rapidly in the early stages of cold immersion. As it occurs, glucose is primed and pumped from the liver to find its target receptors in the heart and other organs, thereby increasing the metabolic activity of your cells. Heat production results from this type of increased metabolic activity.

During prolonged exposure to cold, however, fat oxidation becomes a larger driver of heat production. This has profound implications for the seasoned practitioner's ability to develop highly beneficial tissue known as brown adipose tissue (BAT) or brown fat.

BAT is specialized body tissue made up of a dense collection of mitochondria that produce energy directly in the form of heat. Remember that mitochondria are the energy workers of the cell. In the case of BAT, more and more mitochondria are produced in densely packed areas, where they burn fat for energy. In contrast to white fat, which serves as the body's energy storage, BAT is a highly metabolic fuel burner. White fat can, over time, be converted to brown fat, a process known as beiging.[29] Consistent and regular cold exposure assists in this process.

The neurochemical and hormonal stress response under cold conditions is governed, in large part, by norepinephrine and dopamine. At water temperatures of around 40°F, a steep spike of norepinephrine occurs in the body and brain, as much as 200 to 300 percent above baseline in as few as 20 seconds.[30] Dopamine has been demonstrated to increase substantially under similar conditions. This makes sense, as dopamine acts as a precursor to synthesizing norepinephrine.

We learned in earlier chapters that norepinephrine is released from the area of the brainstem called the locus coeruleus and from the adrenal medulla located just above the kidneys. The job of norepinephrine is to activate the adrenergic receptors of the sympathetic nervous system. In other words, it helps activate the stress response.

In the case of cold exposure, norepinephrine signals both the blood shunt and thermogenesis, or heat production. However, norepinephrine does not work alone, but in combination with epinephrine. Whereas norepinephrine primarily works on vasoconstriction to reroute blood, epinephrine helps dilate the core's vascular network in muscles and the liver to help ensure proper blood flow around the vital organs.

Other stress hormones that initially release under cold stress conditions, such as ACTH and cortisol, will lessen over the course of training. The seasoned practitioner experiences declines in these hormones while maintaining the positive effects of norepinephrine and dopamine release.

Cold immersion's profound effects on inflammation also have direct implications for serotonin, since inflammation has been shown to inhibit the release of seratonin. Furthermore, the body's natural pain killers—such as anandamide, an endocannabinoid, and endorphins—are released during cold immersion.

Researchers such as Steven Kotler, author of *Rise of the Superman*, and others have identified six neurochemicals that, when present at the same time in the body, can produce what is known as a flow state. Although additional research is needed, evidence exists that these six chemicals are present during ice bath training, especially when the practice is done in groups and preceded by breath exercises. From my personal experience as both a practitioner and a teacher, cold water group immersions are an excellent source of flow state.

How Much Cold Do I Need for Its Benefits?

You very likely do not need as much cold as you think, and more is not always better. As discussed, studies have demonstrated benefits and positive responses after cold water immersion at 40°F for as few as 20 seconds. Other studies have shown the beneficial effects of cold showers. One study tracked participants who took cold showers in the winter for thirty consecutive days. The showers lasted thirty, sixty, or ninety seconds, depending on the test group. With few exceptions, all three groups reported more energy and fewer sick/leave days from work. And we have already discussed the endotoxin study in which Wim Hof shifted his pro-inflammatory markers down and anti-inflammatory markers up, while also stirring the white blood cells to be primed and active, all with one two-minute ice bath.[31] The benefits of cold therapies have been demonstrated across a wide range of variables, often at far shorter durations of exposure than one might expect. If you begin with the mindset that small amounts of cold can be beneficial, you are starting with the best mentality to foster a lifelong practice. *Learning the art of gradual, less intense daily exposures is the key to consistent practice over a long arc.*

When I started cold training, I took cold showers, sometimes as short as twenty seconds. Because I began my regular cold training using WHM, I started with the breathing protocols intended to manage the cold, which proved to be an invaluable resource. The breathing preparation was a useful enough tool that I was encouraged to keep moving forward. The low bar of twenty seconds was more than manageable, inspiring success. I took these small daily wins and built on them, slowly extending my times. Within just a few weeks, I had successfully progressed from twenty seconds to ten minutes.

What I found compelling about the ten-minute cold shower was that in the days and weeks following that first experience, my body pushed itself to a new norm. I really felt a boost in my ability to handle and tolerate cold. I am grateful that I did not start off with a ten-minute shower or fifteen-minute ice bath, as I have seen others do. It is not that you cannot do that, but the experience limits practitioners' long-term desire to train. Many have negative experiences, which discourages consistent practice, without which the full benefits will not be forthcoming.

The Mistakes I Made and the Changes I'd Suggest to Others

For the first several months when I began cold training, I took *only* cold showers any time I showered. I perceived that this was necessary in order to maintain the practice, and I got totally accustomed to it. Beyond that, the cold gave me such tremendous energy that I even started to forego sleep and rest. Over the years, I have modified the cold-only shower policy to include sometimes hot and cold. I also vary how long I stay in the cold shower, letting my body and mind guide me by staying aware of my stress and health on any given day. And most importantly, I get plenty of sleep to rest and recover. I can confidently report that I am much happier and healthier for it.

What I didn't adequately take into account early in my training was that the cold is a *stressor*. Yes, when used appropriately, it is a hormetic stress and induces a beneficial stress response. But it is a stress nonetheless, and to forget that runs counter to the end goal maximizing the benefits of this survival stress tool.

In recent years there has been a great deal of talk about stress, everything from "stress lowers the immune system"—which it absolutely can—to "stress is only bad if it's perceived that way." This paraphrased comment is from Kelly McConigal, PhD, whose research led to a popular TED Talk regarding how perception of stress is the most important factor in whether it positively or negatively impacts the body. As she astutely points out, perceiving stress to be a *good* or *bad* thing changes how the autonomic nervous system directs blood flow, what neurochemical composition the system manifests, and how open or closed blood vessels remain. When stress is perceived as *good*, the body has improved blood flow, less work for the heart, and a more beneficial hormone composition. Bottomline: Having a positive outlook on independent stress response events can be the difference between the stress being beneficial or harmful.

However, the ability to sustain a positive outlook each time you encounter stress, year after year, is a challenge and needs a careful approach. Training and daily practice are the tools we can use to support our ability to rise to such occasions. We must be able not only to deal with and respond to the total aggregate of stress—physical, mental, emotional, environmental, and so on—we also need to recover from the stress in our lives. We must create the space necessary for quality downtime and the recovery that is needed.

If we choose to train artfully—by which I mean to train consistently while keeping aggregate stress levels moderated relative to capacity as tolerance for stress grows—survival stress tools such as the cold are the most efficient and effective tools available. Using these tools, we can recalibrate stress, modulate stress, and equally as important, *improve the rest and recovery time* we need to operate optimally. Successfully balancing cumulative stress and recovery plays a substantial role in meeting both the individual and aggregate stress challenges in our lives.

Using the cold survival stress tool can offer wonderful benefits along the path to mastering the stress response. Or, if used incorrectly, it can create another challenge in our already stress-inundated lives. I have received many questions and comments, from newer and trained practitioners alike, who have cited issues with getting sick on the days immediately following intense cold exposures. All too often, these individuals assume that you must do fifteen minutes in an ice bath to benefit. When I respond that two minutes can be highly beneficial—*even for a trained practitioner*—I have been met with surprise and skepticism.

Ultimately, each of us can decide how we want to maximize the cold stress tool in our lives, but understanding its components is the key to longevity, health, and vitality. Getting sick after doing a cold exposure is a pretty clear indication that you are overdoing it. I am not suggesting that you never do ten or fifteen minutes in cold water, or that you shouldn't work toward extended lengths of time to challenge yourself personally. I am a huge advocate of personal challenge and pushing limits. But balancing those desires with other priorities such as health, recovery, fitness, and consciousness development is equally important.

I have confronted a variety of stressors in my life in the last seven years. Weathering a difficult divorce, adapting to a single-father lifestyle, dealing with the emotional fallout of losing a close business associate, figuring out how to plug a large business gap while continuing to manage and grow that business, an unexpected custody battle: The list goes on and on. But I am not unique in this experience. I'm sure that you have your own list, and it might be twice as long as mine. Life is challenging and filled with stress.

What I learned during this stressful time has allowed me to climb to new heights in recent years. Survival stress tools let us maximize rapid adaptability, neural plasticity, and recovery under the most difficult of conditions. But due to their intensity, the duration must be limited, and you must take into account the cumulative stress in your life as you approach your training. A healthy person with fewer responsibilities is likely to be able to train more often and longer—especially early on—than someone who bears tremendous responsibility and faces significant stressors daily. Optimal doesn't look the same for these individuals, yet both can achieve exceptional results.

As you train, prepare for optimal change. The simplest advice is to train while prioritizing the recovery mindset. If you do so, you will improve faster because you will be able to train more frequently. Frequency is the key to the biggest and deepest gains in skill development, but there must be balance. For many of us, a daily ten-minute ice bath is unlikely to be sustainable or useful. But a daily cold shower and a weekly ice bath, for example, can work miracles.

As you are able to train more frequently, you will also develop greater depth in your training. Working under a model of recovery, you will avoid unnecessary setbacks and increase the nervous system's ability to handle stress of any kind. No longer will you be beset by overload: You will stand strong in the midst of the environmental chaos.

Training using the recovery state as the model takes an active and mindful approach. Focusing this way keeps the beneficial neural messaging intact. It avoids the perils of constantly stressing your body by trying to outweigh bad stress with good stress. It eludes the pitfalls of overtraining, burnout, and possible early-onset andropause, all of which can discourage or even prevent further effort.

The cold is an exceptional tool. It is also an incredibly strong one that demands respect. Build slowly so that your foundation is solid. Then, when you decide to shoulder a significant load in the form of a personal challenge, you will rise to that challenge, remain intact, and be all the better for it.

Freeze Training, Muscle Strengthening, Performance and Recovery

Cold training studies with regard to improvements in human strength, mitochondrial biogenesis, stable muscle glycogen re-synthesis rates even with reduced blood flow, and enhanced gene expression have demonstrated the wide potential offered by cold training. Furthermore, additional studies with animals have shown oxidative stress improvements as well as improved edema and in-flammatory responses. However, studies have also noted muscle strength limitations, hypertrophy limitations, endurance limita-tions, and delayed recovery times associated with cold training.

How can such discrepancies exist?

How you train and under what conditions can make all the dif-ference. Although future research could offer more insights into optimal routines, let's dig into some of the themes for each group of studies, as well as use reason to understand why some of the apparent conflicts may exist. I will also share some of my own ex-periences and those of my students.

In many of the studies I have reviewed with an eye to perfor-mance, I have noticed that lower temperatures (i.e., less than ap-proximately 44°F) tend to correlate with positive outcomes.[32] These studies generally used ten- to twenty-minute total time exposures.

Studies that used temperatures of more than approximately 50°F for similar time frames tended to produce more mixed results; some results were positive, but more were negative. Clearly, although the difference between 44 and 50°F may not sound like a lot, that is not the case. Experientially, I will tell you that it is a huge difference. Lower temperatures (i.e., 45°F or lower), in my experience, consis-tently produce better results for strength, endurance, and recovery times, especially when paired with shorter sessions of multiple reps that total ten to twenty minutes.

In all fairness, I train for efficiency, endurance, and functional strength. I don't train for hypertrophy, so I cannot really speak to that topic. However, one of my students consistently cold trains and trains for hypertrophy, and he has had highly positive results. There is no way to review the alternative for individuals, so such examples are purely anecdotal and very limited. I still believe they are worth noting, as the available research looks very similar to my experience, small and informal though it may be. I consistently train in 33 to 45°F water, and I tend to do rounds of anywhere from two to ten minutes, usually three to five rounds per session.

When cold should be applied is also a question, and the research here is not so clear. I could not find consistencies to support one timing method or another. In my personal experience, however, it is best to do your cold training separately from your workouts. At minimum, give yourself a couple of hours after exercising before any cold immersion. The reason I advise this is to harness the benefits of your body's inflammatory process, which triggers with workouts. The inflammation recruits blood and nutrients to begin beneficial repair of your tissues, and that takes time. Let that process work for you. Then, after a few hours, do some cold training to get the cold benefits. Experiment with the timing of what works best for you.

My personal routine typically involves doing cold training in the mornings. Most of my workouts and intense physical activities occur in the afternoons and evenings. After a hard workout, I usually take a warm/hot shower with only the slightest bit of cold—often less than sixty seconds. Then the following morning, I do deep cold training, temperatures and duration as described above.

In addition to overall improvements in life quality, this reasoned approach has trained my body to recover incredibly fast. A tweak or small injury of any kind is gone the following day. More substantial injuries to my neck or shoulders heal, with very few exceptions, in a day or two. This holds true as long as my routines remain consistent. The exceptions are during periods when my cold schedule is inconsistent, usually due to travel or work-related interruptions. But these exceptions are, fortunately and intentionally, infrequent. The rule dominates.

Furthermore, my strength has increased, most noticeably in activities like rock climbing or submission grappling activities. I encourage you to use this guidance to experiment with cold as a highly valuable training tool for strength, and to use cold training to connect your nervous system and condition your vascular system. All of this is integral to mastering the stress response.

The Balance of Intensity and Duration

The two primary factors for intentional cold stress exposure are duration (time) and intensity (temperature). As a guiding principle for health, strength, and resilience, the colder the exposure, the less time you should be in the cold. This is true not just for surviving but for thriving.

Temperatures of less than 64°F are needed to trigger non-shivering cold-induced thermogenesis.[33] So, assuming your water is below that temperature, it is a matter of optimizing duration, frequency, and recovery. However, as mentioned, there is also evidence that lower temperatures produce better results.

There are three simple rules to determine the proper combination of duration and intensity, referred to as a dose. Because timelines shift from day to day due to cumulative stress demands, the following three rules can be a great guide to keep you moving in the right direction.

Cold Indicators

1) How long can you remain focused?

Before you get into a cold immersion, be aware of your present state. Did you get good sleep? Have you eaten recently? What emotional, psychological, or physical challenges are you dealing with? No need to harp on these things; just be aware that they all contribute. A day when you are dealing with an inordinate amount of stress is likely not the best time to attempt a personal record.

The vast majority of days, show up to the cold with an open mind and pay attention. You can know how long to stay by how long you can remain focused. Rather than guessing in advance or setting yourself up to meet a predetermined time, learn to pay attention and listen to your body. Doing so can also help you avoid the pitfall of trying to force an exposure through sheer will. That's often a good way to get injured or worse. There may be a time for that type of action, but it should be reserved for infrequent, very intentional occasions.

Another thing to be aware of while in the cold water is strong perceptual changes. I have had the opportunity to see how even highly conditioned practitioners can experience perceptual changes. It can happen relatively quickly after entering the cold and can sneak up on people. Many report that once they have been in the cold plunge for about five minutes, they feel like they could stay in there forever, or rather, for an unknown, extended period; they feel no pressure to get out of the cold stress. However, many also report that around the seven- to ten-minute mark, their vision begins to change, becoming glassy or slightly blurry. That is their body letting them know that they should get out of the plunge, but it is the *only* indicator. They do not feel unwell or cold. One associate of mine, a long-term practitioner, told me he'd once stayed in the plunge for thirteen to fifteen minutes. He was unsure about the exact time because when he looked at the clock, he found that while he could make out the hands, he didn't quite know what they meant. By all other accounts he felt great, but he figured he should get out. It was the right call.

Although such stories are anecdotal, I feel the information is worth noting for a few reasons. One is the fact that the same numbers keep coming up, for example, the fact that once people pass the five-minute mark, many feel no pressure to get out of the cold. The other is that more and more frequently, people around the world are gathering in groups to do cold exposures in freezing temperatures for more than five minutes. While I am clearly an advocate for the practice, many of these people are unconditioned or only moderately conditioned to cold, and are therefore unaware that the cold exposure itself is only half of the exercise. You still must warm up and recover. Furthermore, when in a group of people, especially one having fun, it is easy to lose focus and awareness and suffer negative consequences as a result. The goals of the practice are to build up your strength, gain the myriad health benefits, and become more resilient and more connected. Breaking the body down too far by staying in too-cold water for too long will not result in those gains.

For these reasons, start with how long you can remain focused in the cold, and remember that you must recover from the cold exposure. To use an appropriate metaphor, to undergo the cold exposure is only the climb up the mountain—you still must descend safely.

2) How fast can you recover?

As you are learning, growing, and challenging yourself with this practice, you should also use your recovery to guide you. For those who are new to cold training, a cold exposure in freezing temperatures often results in numb hands and feet that remain so for as long as an hour after emerging. In rare cases, it may last a bit longer. These effects subside with practice and safe exposures over time.

All practitioners should use recovery time as an indicator of both safety and progress. A good goal for full recovery is ten to fifteen minutes without an exogenous heat source and without an adverse afterdrop experience, a topic I cover in detail later in this chapter.

If you are new to cold exposure, I recommend starting with a maximum two-minute exposure, assuming the water is at or below 45°F. Such an exposure is challenging enough and will give you great benefits. As you get comfortable with that and you begin to recover faster, you can safely move to the next step: increasing the reps.

Rather than extending exposure times—which becomes easier to do but not necessarily to recover from—it is far better to limit the times and increase the reps. Continue using two-minute cold exposures, but do more of them in a single session. Between each rep of two minutes, warm up with light activity and focus. This approach is far more informative of your body's ability to handle more cold time than is a single, longer session. It allows you to check in frequently. If you are able to do three sets of two minutes and feel good, you can very likely do six minutes in a single session and feel good. Using the two-minute rep mark will build you up much faster to doing extended times safely. It is also a useful mental hurdle in training yourself to meet stress over and over, while shifting your perception and overcoming the presented challenges.

3) How do you feel throughout the hours and days following the exposure?

The minutes, hours, and days following a cold exposure provide a good measure of whether you are receiving optimal benefits. Remember, stress put on the body that acts as a catalyst for positive changes is hormetic stress. Stress that breaks the body down and leaves it vulnerable is chronic and leads to distress, illness, and injury.

Let's draw an analogy using wind and how it acts upon trees. Wind is a stressor for trees. In order for a tree to develop strong roots, it needs to have some wind. But too much wind, such as a hurricane or tornado, no longer provides beneficial stress: It simply rips the tree from the ground.

We could make the argument that a few trees survive such storms, and that they benefit from having come through so much stress intact. While this may be true, such trees are few and far between, and there are other factors in play besides the strength of the tree.

Individuals, like trees, have different capacities to handle total stress at different times. When I first began to subject myself to cold, I was very unconditioned and struggled a great deal. Just a small amount of cold stress was a substantial challenge. Considering how many other stressors I had in my life at that time, it would not have been useful to pile on large quantities of cold stress. Instead, taking a gradual and consistent approach allowed me to soar. Now, having taught thousands of students, I recognize how similar my experience was to those of so many others. And in contrast, I easily understand why so many have struggled in their attempts to build this practice.

When you remain in cold water for a reasonable length of time, a beneficial stress response ensues. When you get out of the cold, you should feel energized and elated, because large amounts of hormones and neurotransmitters are driving this chemical joy train. But if you get out and feel a deep ache and disorienting chill, you have gone too far. Both responses can range in intensity, so pay attention to the first feeling. It is your initial indicator to determine the appropriate dose of cold.

The next indicator is how you feel between one and four hours later. Do you still feel energized? If so, excellent; you did the right amount. If you feel tired, cold, or worse yet, exhausted with an aching chill that will not go away, you definitely used too long of an exposure and need extra recovery time. Mistakes will happen, so take a warm shower and rest. Next time, back off and do less.

The exception to these guidelines is when you intentionally set out to do an intense cold exposure and push yourself to your limits. When you do this, just make sure you give yourself plenty of rest and recovery time afterward, and always be mindful of your safety.

The last indicator for this section is how you feel the next day. Did you wake up ready to tackle the day after a great night of sleep and recovery? Well done! Your cold training is serving you as intended. If, on the other hand, you have residual fatigue, have a cold injury such as frostbite, numb toes, or fingers, or wake up sick, *you did way too much.* Get plenty of rest and recovery. It may be a bit difficult to come back from this setback. You might struggle to resume your practice. However, if you recognize it as a mistake, you can pick yourself up and begin again, except that this time you will be much more aware. Use this experience as the extremely important lesson that it is.

Cold Injuries

I find that cold injuries happen because individuals override the messages they receive from their bodies, usually for one of two primary reasons. The first reason is that individuals don't want to break up a practice group; an individual may say, "I didn't want to get out of the cold. The group was staying together." This kind of thinking violates the principles of proper cold training and can have significant consequences. Even when you are training in a group, you must always look after your own safety by paying close attention to how your body is responding to the stress. If you are unclear on the messages your body is sending you, get out and try again later.

The second most common reason that individuals ignore the messages from their bodies is that they are being overly competitive. Whether you are competing with yourself or others, doing so against the backdrop of life-threatening stress tools, like the cold, is generally a terrible idea. If you choose to compete in this setting, be prepared to accept the consequences.

One simple message our bodies often give us to indicate that we have been in too long is that we begin to shiver *while in* the cold water. Say you get into the cold and get past the initial shock. You've gained your breath, and you are breathing slowly and in a controlled manner. You are staying focused. Then, after some time has passed, you begin to shiver or shake. You find that you cannot control the urge to shiver. If this happens, get out of the cold. Shivering is one of your body's mechanisms to warm up and that is fine; in fact, it can be useful, as it can aid in the production of hormones and proteins that assist your body in creating BAT and improving metabolic function.[34] But if you go from controlled to shivering *in the water*, that is a certain indicator to get out. Your body is telling you that you have had enough. Ignoring this message is a bad idea.

Is it best to get my head in the cold water?

Dunking the head is great in cold training, and once you're conditioned, you greatly reduce the risks associated with jumping into cold water. However, I recommend starting slow and gradually building up a conditioned response to the cold.

The best way to train the head at the beginning is gradually and consistently. For example, say you are getting into a 40°F ice bath. This is a controlled setting, which is good for practicing new skills. You intend to do a cold exposure of no more than two minutes.

To begin, get in slowly and intentionally, submerging yourself up to your neck. Avoid getting your face and head wet on entry. About halfway through the cold exposure, with intention and focus, dunk your face and head. This will trigger the mammalian diving reflex, which includes activating the vagus nerve to slow down your heart rate and increasing vasoconstriction in the peripheral shell of your body.

Oxygen metabolism becomes highly efficient during this reflex. What is important to note, and what is sometimes misunderstood by those practicing, is that once your head pops back up from the water, the sympathetic response is triggered again. Take a moment to regain full control by breathing slowly and focusing on long exhales. This will allow you to get back to a parasympathetic/sympathetic balance and conserve your energy. Once you have made the transition, *then* get out of the ice bath. Abiding by this recommendation will prepare you to steadily increase your cold exposure safely and consistently. It will also offer the highest level of cognitive and emotional control benefits available from head dunking.

Safety in Different Types of Cold Exposure

The practical implementation of cold exposure can vary. Doing a hike in snowy weather in limited clothing, or walking around your neighborhood on a blustery winter day while dressed for summer can be a fun way to alter your training.

Some of you may decide to go to your local cryochamber. A cryochamber is essentially a refrigerated box that allows for full exposure or a tank that allows for head-out exposure. Common cryochamber air temperatures get down to -150°F, with some as low as -240°F.

In all cases, basic safety should be observed.

Safety considerations for cold air training differ somewhat from those for cold water training. Since most circumstances allow you to be in cold air safely for much longer than in cold water, be mindful of whether the environment is controlled or uncontrolled.

A controlled environment is something like a cryochamber.

Those who run the facility will limit how long you can be in the cold environment (usually a maximum of around three minutes). If you ever find yourself at this kind of facility and have the opportunity to use this equipment alone, DO NOT do so; solo use is the biggest risk with this kind of equipment . Beyond that, there is very little risk, providing the cryochamber is used as intended.[35]

The majority of cold air exposure training occurs in uncontrolled settings, which always present added risk. It is important to take a few precautionary measures whenever you go about this type of exercise in an uncontrolled setting.

1.   Have warm clothing with you as a backup. This is very important if you are in the mountains, but obviously far less so if you are walking around your neighborhood. I typically stash warm things in a backpack when I head to the mountains. That way, if things start to go sideways, it is easy to adapt and put on clothing as needed.

2.   Any time you're out in nature, whether or not you're training, bring a friend. If you do plan to get into cold water, it's a good idea to stagger your training, especially if you are new to cold training or the conditions are difficult.

3.   Take into account all the variables when determining how long you can be safely outdoors in cold weather. This length of time varies greatly. As you develop your safe range, keep a few things in mind: your existing cold conditioning; how much clothing you have on, including type of footwear; and the altitude of the area. Altitude affects available oxygen, which plays a key role in the body's ability to produce energy efficiently; lowered oxygen levels due to altitude can significantly change how much heat your body can generate. Also, note if there is wind and if so, how fast it is moving, and finally whether it is humid, or worse, raining. Many of these variables also apply to cold water training once you emerge, because you will be rewarming yourself in an uncontrolled air environment.

Water Versus Air

Water has a feature called the heat-specific density. Because a water molecule is very dense, changing its temperature requires a relatively large amount of energy. Once changed, however, it will hold that energy for a longer period because of that density.

In contrast, an air molecule has a relatively low density. This is why it is difficult to keep an empty room heated or cooled. Almost as fast as you heat it up or cool it down, the temperature will equalize to the surrounding temperature. Having objects in a room changes this scenario, because the items, being denser than air, absorb the heat in the room and hold it for a longer period. The relative lack of objects to retain heat is one reason why a desert can fluctuate in temperature so much.

For cold training, it is helpful to understand this physics concept, at least in general terms. It will help you determine what training tools you might want to purchase, depending on where you are in the world and the space and natural elements available to you. It will also help you assess risk when going outdoors. Finally, in an indoor setting, it will guide you in determining how much ice you need in order to lower the temperature of water.

In water, you will lose heat twenty-five times faster than in air of the same temperature. This is why you can be in 32°F water for only minutes but stand outside in such a temperature for hours. It is also why you can sit in a 240°F sauna for fifteen to thirty minutes, but submerging yourself in 240°F would result in horrific burns.

So, if you decide to go on a shirtless snow hike, remember that humidity, precipitation, and wind all contribute to risk. Wind by itself is challenging, but pair it with precipitation or humidity and you're at risk for frostbite. I have dealt with some pretty gnarly wind in very cold temperatures for hours, but because the air was dry, it was manageable. If you want to practice in wet conditions, don a thin, waterproof shell that will allow you to stay dry(er). Just be mindful of the added risk any time water is present.

Training at Home

From a practical standpoint, there are a number of good options for training in cold water at home: a bathtub, an above-ground pool, a converted hot tub, a large trashcan, a galvanized metal stock tank, or a collapsible single- or multi-person rubber unit. The biggest concern is how to cool your water most efficiently. The answer really comes down to how often you will be training with the cold and how much space you have to dedicate to it.

If you have the space and you plan on training frequently, many people use a converted freezer. The advantages to this are they come in various sizes, you can control the exact temperature of the water, they are economical,[36] and they are easy to convert and maintain.[37] The disadvantage of this option is that freezers are not designed to be cold water immersion tubs. So, to convert one is a do-it-yourself DIY job that carries risk.

If you choose to take the freezer route, a note of CAUTION: DO NOT get in the tub while it is plugged into the wall. Furthermore, if you train using this option, you do so at YOUR OWN RISK. So, be mindful and deliberate with your actions. Keep yourself safe.

A second option, if you have the money and space, is one of the newly designed cold tubs recently on the market. There are downsides to this option, one of which is cost: Manufacturers are charging roughly $4,000 to $6,000, so they are relatively expensive for the average practitioner. Furthermore, due to the filtration system in these tubs, temperatures will not be close to freezing, and adding ice to the water damages the tub's parts. However, the upsides are that the tubs are well-designed and attractive, and they keep water cold. Not, as mentioned, around freezing, but they can achieve temperatures of approximately 42°F, which can still offer good training opportunities. As mentioned, I do a significant amount of training at a local *banya* that has a cold plunge of around 45°F. A colder temperature is not an absolute requirement to benefit significantly from this practice. The art is largely about consistency rather than intensity once you get cold enough.

If you live in an apartment, a condo, or a house that simply doesn't have room to add one of these tubs, you may choose one of the other listed options above. If you live in cold temperatures, you may just set a collapsible tub filled with water outside overnight. If you don't live in a cold area, or if it is too warm in your area in the summer months, you will need ice.

How Much Ice Do You Really Need?

This is where heat-specific density comes into play again. Water coming out of faucets all over the world varies greatly in temperature. In my home state of Washington, tap water typically varies between the 40s and 60s or even higher, depending on the time of year. As I have traveled the world, I have regularly used a laser temperature reader to test the water.[38] Even in winter, many places regularly have tap water in the 50s or 60s.

So let's assume the temperature of your tap water is around 60°F. With a large bathtub or galvanized stock tank (100 gallons), adding roughly ninety pounds of ice will get the water down into the 40s (in my experience). When water from the tap is already cold, say around 47°F, just fifty or sixty pounds of ice will get the water close to 39°F, and adding ninety pounds will get it very close to 33°F.

These guidelines are estimates based on my own experience rather than any exact science. The point is, it takes a lot more ice than people commonly think to get the water as cold as it should be for training. Remember though, ice baths can easily be reserved for once a week, assuming you have a sufficiently cold shower to do more frequent training.

How to Avoid Afterdrop

Afterdrop is when your core body temperature continues cooling even as you are rewarming from hypothermia. A core body temperature below 95°F is considered hypothermic. Afterdrop can occur after an extended ice bath or other deep cold exposure. Recall that when you get into the cold, your body goes through a series of physiological responses to protect itself. This survival mechanism includes vasoconstriction, primarily in the extremities, so that blood can circulate around the vital organs near the midsection of the body as well as the head. When you begin to rewarm after that cold exposure, the cold blood in the extremities begins recirculating and mixing with the warm blood from the core. When this happens too quickly, it can further lower the core body temperature. This can be very uncomfortable, causing violent shivers or, if severe enough, leading to loss of consciousness. Therefore, be careful to avoid pushing your body to hypothermic conditions.

Even if your core body temperature has not been lowered dramatically, it is still important to rewarm slowly and deliberately after a cold exposure. If you don't, you may experience a deep-sinking cold feeling even after rewarming, and that may result in a negative association with the cold.

Depending on the duration and temperature of the cold exposure, the time it takes for your body to heat up naturally will vary. Remain focused and do light activity such as walking, low-energy hiking, or other simple movements to assist your body in heating back up. Get dry immediately after the cold exposure, but avoid putting on a great deal of clothing right away. Thick layers of clothing can signal the hypothalamus to increase the rate of vascular dilation, further increasing the speed at which the warm and cold blood mix in your body. Instead, don layers slowly as you remain focused on performing light activity. For these same reasons, avoid jumping into a hot shower right away. If you need assistance to warm up, start with a warm shower and gradually increase the temperature.

Extending Times and Challenging Yourself

As you become more accustomed to cold exposures, you can safely increase your time even as you begin to use lower temperatures. You will be more aware of how your body and mind respond under different conditions. Plus, you will have acclimatized and be producing more BAT, a physiological mechanism that will support your ability to train.

The fact is, we do not know the limits on human potential. To account for this, I have chosen to outline numerous pertinent variables that must be accounted for when assessing risk, and to provide examples that illustrate the benefits of a range of times. Hopefully, all of this can help point you in the right direction when investigating cold exposure as a practice to help master the stress response.

We have covered a great deal of safety information, including expected survival times in different temperatures of water and evidence of impacted function after certain amounts of time in water. But the fact is, how you train makes all the difference, and an individual's ability to safely withstand extraordinary circumstances is largely dependent on that training.

Wim Hof, for example, has withstood being submerged in ice for nearly two hours. Lewis Pugh has swum in negative-temperature waters for more than twenty-three minutes. Lynne Cox swam the 43°F Bering Strait for more than two hours. These individuals are only three of many, many more who have achieved extraordinary cold feats.

Each year, thousands of relatively unconditioned individuals endure sub-zero hikes, braving blisteringly cold conditions in just shorts and hiking boots. I have personally led throngs of practitioners—new and experienced alike—through ice, frigid waters, and snow. When it comes to human beings, there is much that is similar among groups and a great deal that varies among individuals. Human potential is unknown and we keep pushing its boundaries. Using the indicators and guidelines outlined in this book, I wish you all the best in finding a suitable method for your cold practice, one that allows you to explore your own potential using the valuable survival stress tool of the cold: the Freeze.

FAST

T HE SURVIVAL STRESS tool Fast refers to going without food for specific time periods. Used in the correct manner, this becomes a different type of environmental acute stress tool that physically helps us optimize our bodies through hormone and gene expression and vastly improves senses and sense awareness while contributing to our longevity.

This tool is unique in that it requires us to mentally and emotionally confront the stress of scarcity and overcome the fear of having to go without. The liberation that we can experience in using this tool allows us to put otherwise wasted energy into tackling the next challenge, despite the feeling that we don't have enough. It also allows us to also appreciate what we have when we do have it. Daily gratitude of this kind coupled with satiating experiences enable us to tackle new heights by learning to do more with less.

As here are a great number of fasting types, rules, and guidelines, I will narrow them down for the Fast survival tool. For the purposes of this book, the tool has two parts: one is time-restricted eating on a regular day-to-day basis, and the other is prolonged fasting. Time-restricted eating involves training your body to *comfortably* eat only within a specific window of time, usually lasting five to twelve hours. Prolonged fasting, on the other hand, is going without food for more than twenty-four hours.[39]

As a lifelong athlete, I have tried and been advised to eat a variety of diets, mostly in an effort to improve my performance in a particular pursuit. The need to balance carbohydrates, protein, and fat, eat to gain or lose weight, eat to build muscle, or any number of other goals always drew primary consideration. These diets have included countless variants over the years, everything from eating five small meals or more per day to eating one large meal and two others of medium size.

Regardless of the diet, I always found going without food for any extended period to be incredibly challenging. Because my daily training and activity level has usually expended a great number of calories, I have always made sure to have protein bars or peanut butter to spoon into my mouth between sizable meals throughout the day. This was the *required* norm, or so I thought.

Fortunately, I have never had a metabolic issue. However, fourteen hours with minimal food intake would make my blood sugar unstable, sending me into a "hangry" crash. So the thought of a full fast for any extended period was cause for concern. *I am an athlete*, I thought. *I must have fuel for my body.* This idea is not altogether wrong, of course. However, the need to eat incessantly, even to fuel an athlete's body, is deeply flawed.

It is only within the most recent seventy years or so that more affluent cultures have had an overabundant food supply. Food abundance started out as a desire to tackle food scarcity. New institutions created after WWII, such as the United Nations and various international food programs, focused on ending world hunger.[40] Part of that effort came in the form of new technologies for farming, government subsidies around certain farming practices, and improved distribution.

Each subsequent decade added its part. The Green Revolution of the 1950s and 1960s resulted in significant technological changes, including irrigation improvements and chemical fertilizers, that tailored farming to focus on high-yield cereals, wheats, and rices. The 1960s also saw the introduction of factory-farmed animals in various industrialized nations. Born out of agricultural policies that included subsidies to farmers for increased production, this approach sought to shore up food security. Likewise, the Food and Agriculture Act of 1977 in the United States established higher prices and income protections for farmers in an effort to ensure abundance for consumers. Throughout subsequent decades, policies have continued to encourage and promote wide-scale food production in an effort to stem hunger.[41]

These policies, which have allowed us to steadily reduce world hunger, have created other problems. Especially in the United States, but increasingly throughout industrialized nations, obesity has become a concerning epidemic. According to the CDC, obesity affected more than 30 percent of the adult population in the United States in 1999 and more than 42 percent in 2018.[42] Also in the United States, among children aged two to nineteen years, nearly one in five is obese.

To a far lesser extent, but still relevant to the use of fasting as a survival stress tool, we need to be aware of the other side of the proverbial eating coin: bulimia nervosa and anorexia nervosa. Both disorders cause significant distress and lead to serious health problems, including possible death.

Bulimia nervosa is a disorder that involves binge eating followed by purging. Types of purging primarily include vomiting or excessive use of laxatives and diuretics. However, they can also include excessive exercise and fasting. Anorexia nervosa is a disorder characterized by persistent and chronic under-eating. It is often paired with body dysmorphia, a mental health disorder causing perceived flaws in appearance. Because both bulimia and anorexia are mental conditions arising from an unhealthy relationship to food, I mention them here. In both conditions, a sense of one being *out of control* is present.

As you begin to train using the fasting tool, being mindful in your approach is essential so as not to deregulate your system and suffer negative consequences. If you are just beginning to learn about fasting and are not used to restricted times for eating, be patient. A gradual approach is key to avoiding unnecessary stress on your nervous system and all its bi-directional parts, triggering potential adverse responses.

I have encountered students who have reported problems with the fasting tool, either due to impatience or misunderstandings about fasting protocols. I have seen students experience unintentional weight gain, sleep problems, decreased recovery time, and impaired immune function—all signs of the body's *distress*.

My students are far from the only people to have gone down this road and experienced adverse reactions. Please remember that fasting is a stress tool, which means that a poor approach will lead to problems rather than benefits. Fasting should not be used carelessly or lightly. Be patient and train your nervous system and body over time, so that they adapt in a positive way. Fasting as a survival stress tool is a means of optimizing overall health and functionality while confronting the emotional and psychological challenges of scarcity. It is a powerful tool, so being patient in your approach is critical. This process is about creating an optimized lifestyle, *not* diet advice.

Not too long ago, Harvard Heath Publishing cited a 2017 article about research published in *JAMA Internal Medicine* that studied three groups of people: intermittent fasters, a type of fasting that in this case occurred on alternate days; fasters restricting daily calories, which is more or less what most traditional diets advocate; and a group continuing to eat their typical diet. After one year, the traditional diet group and the intermittent fasters ended up in more or less the same situation. Both had lost weight, but neither showed a significant advantage over the other in terms of weight loss. Based on this evidence, one could conclude that fasting and a traditional diet plan produce similar results.

Reading about this kind of research, one may also assume that restricting calories daily would be much easier than stressing the body by fasting on alternate days. Personally, I'm likely to agree with this assumption. Fasting is not easy. It is uncomfortable. Furthermore, there can be a psychological tendency to eat less healthful foods during non-fasting periods, because our bodies have extra cravings induced by the stress of fasting. The willpower needed during the fasting periods may not last if not carefully managed during the non-fasting times.

Beyond weight loss though, fasting has a number of advantages over a traditional diet plan, including autophagy, increased stem cell production, and more sensitive insulin receptors. Think beyond weight loss. Though weight optimization tends to be a central goal, it is better to let it be a byproduct of an optimally functioning system.

There are a number of different fasting techniques and protocols.[43] I do not recommend alternating day fasts, especially for

215

those just starting out. Rather, I suggest taking more time to deliberately retrain your body to eat within a shorter period of time.

Restricting the time window during which you eat is the first step I would encourage as you begin training your fasting tool. The goal is to retrain the body to eat only within a five- to twelve-hour window. This alone has a myriad of benefits, as it helps to rebalance two essential hormones, ghrelin and leptin. Shortening the time window also aids in re-sensitizing insulin receptors, improving sleep quality, and improving tissue repair

Why? All chemical messengers—including ghrelin, leptin, and insulin—have purposes in the body, but not all can be prioritized simultaneously, nor should they be. You are a complex system with many competing needs. Recall that your sympathetic nervous system, the one involved in action-oriented states, prioritizes increased blood flow to organs, muscles, and parts of the brain associated with sensory processing, all to meet perceived external demands. Part of this response requires inhibiting other parts of the body to ensure the best allocation of resources where they are needed. On the other hand, optimally digesting food, which includes the production of certain enzymes, primarily occurs in a more resting state overseen by the parasympathetic nervous system.[44]

Virtually all kinds of receptors in the brain and body become desensitized under constant bombardment, and insulin is no exception. Insulin's job is basically to signal cells to take up sugars (carbohydrates) to be used as energy. When a sufficient supply of sugars is already present in a cell, insulin signals the liver to store the sugar there in another form, called glycogen. Having to constantly digest food while awake and in the earlier hours of sleep is sure to cause overstimulation of insulin receptors.

The time of day when eating occurs has also been shown to contribute to health. Eating late into the evening, when the body is attempting to prepare us for sleep, forces metabolic allocation to give way to the priority of sleep.

When the body prepares for sleep, the pineal gland in the brain[45] increases its production of melatonin, which signals the body to prepare for sleep.[46] One effect is that the body begins decreasing its core temperature, receiving its instructions from the suprachiasmatic nucleus located in the hypothalamus.

The body's natural rhythm, or circadian rhythm, governs the sleep-wake cycle. Body temperature decreasing in the evening and increasing in the morning is part of this rhythm. But digestion is an activity that *raises* body temperature. Eating something light has less of an effect, but it still impacts the body's systems and how they must respond to that input. And if you are eating foods high in calories and sugar, as many desserts are, the effect is far greater. Rather than going through the intricate process of extracting valuable nutrients for energy, the body prioritizes sleep function and sends the message to store the caloric energy for later. This is not a signal that supports optimal sleep or optimal energy production and allocation.

If we want to be optimal, we must support the body and brain's natural desire to find its proper rhythm. This starts with eating on a more restricted schedule, because it will allow the body to prioritize functions properly without the interference of other processes.

A Guide to Begin Remolding Your Time Window of Eating

Step 1: Set a Time Window

Start by narrowing your window for eating to ten to twelve hours a day for two weeks straight, and plan the hour blocks within which you will eat your meals. Any drink other than black coffee, tea without sugar or cream, or water counts as eating.

If at all possible, be consistent from day to day. For example, if you typically get up at seven o'clock in the morning, consider eating between eight in the morning and eight at night for the first five days. Then, narrow the window by one hour, closing the window at seven in the evening, for the next five days. For the final four days of those first two weeks, try reducing the timeframe to ten hours, from nine in the morning to seven in the evening.

Be sure to be consistent throughout the entire fourteen-day

period. Get rid of the idea of "cheat days" or other half-hearted commitments, as they will not serve you. If a twelve-hour eating timeframe causes your body excess stress, such as difficulty sleeping or concentrating, don't reduce the window further immediately. Wait until you have had two to three days of consistently feeling adapted to this new normal, and you no longer feel stressed.

Any time you make a change like this, it will take your body at least a couple of days to adapt. The goal of time-restricted eating is to gradually build a habit that further supports you to be healthy, and eventually to fast healthfully and safely.

When beginning a new habit, the initial period requires the most effort. There is only so much willpower we can exert in a given day. If you spend all or most of your energy trying to decide, then re-deciding, then questioning your decision to rationalize how you might make a different decision tomorrow, you will quickly give up. Commitment offers you the freedom from the stress that comes with making the same decision over and over, or if you prefer, not making a decision at all. If you decide to take this on, then do it. Be committed. With this type of resolve, you will find your new habit feels far less difficult and far less intrusive. Instead of experiencing the stress of decision fatigue, you will rise—surprisingly effortlessly—to meet your goal.

That said, if you do make a mistake, don't punish yourself into giving up. That will not serve you either. Be accepting of your failure and immediately try again. Your goal is to create momentum and make this a habit.

By staying focused and committed, you can *become* this new lifestyle. This is not just something you *do* but something you *are*. You are a time-restricted eater now. Make the commitment and follow through. Make the decision *before* you begin. That way, if you run into difficulties, you can remind yourself that the decision is already made. YOU DON'T NEED TO MAKE IT AGAIN. I realize I am emphasizing this point greatly, but I do so because I have encountered many students who struggle with this concept. If you have to make the decision every day, you are bound to fail and eventually give up, likely before you get very far.

This advice is not exclusive to time-restricted eating. Commitment is a life fundamental. In a world of curated and virtually infinite choices, we are easily lured into half-commitments. But if you really want to know if something is going to work for you, or if you have decided that you want to build a particular skill, then commitment will be the deciding factor. You can and should be strategic in your efforts, but you should never be uncommitted.

Make a Plan

As part of step one, make a plan for these first two weeks before you begin. Consider what could throw you off. For example, if a friend, partner, or colleague invites you to have drinks one evening, will you go? If this is a common thing in your work or social life, the time window for when you eat (and drink) needs to take this type of thing into consideration.

Anything of benefit takes commitment, and often sacrifice is part of that. Finding balance in whatever sacrifices you make, in conjunction with your other responsibilities, commitments, and desires, will serve the overall quality of your life. It is not necessary to sacrifice everything, nor to abandon enjoyment of food in your life, for the sake of your new time-restricted eating lifestyle. But certain sacrifices will be necessary, especially at the beginning, and likely until you are fully entrenched in your new routine.

You might consider setting a boundary that you need at least forty-eight hours' notice to meet for dinner or drinks that would otherwise be outside of your newly established time window. If, say, your new time window lasts from seven to seven, and dinner or drinks is scheduled for eight at night, then not eating until ten in the morning that day can be a prudent way to stay committed to your new routine and still socialize.

It is, however, a good idea to limit how often you change the routine. Disruption is useful for breaking bad habits or a monotonous routine that fails to fully engage you, but momentum is critical to keeping good habits going in your life. Your body and brain operate on rhythm and habit. Disrupting *good* habits can increase your likelihood of faltering and breaking your momentum. Our systems form habits regardless of conscious input. Be intentional in and aware of your routines. Be mindful of your disruptions. Build good habits.

Step 2: Reduce the Time Window

After two weeks of ten to twelve hours, decrease the eating window to eight to ten hours, and maintain this schedule for another two weeks. Take your time and go slowly at first. This is very helpful for longevity. Recall the human negativity bias: for every one negative experience, we need five positive experiences to compensate. It will do you no good to rush your habit formation.

Another benefit of retraining your body without rushing is that it reduces the unnecessary stress associated with the change. Your goal is to receive the benefits of time-restricted eating while minimizing the potential chronic-like stress that would be induced by an erratic reduced eating window. Once again, consistency is the key here.

Step 3: Firm Up the Eight-Hour Window and Shift to Maintenance mode

Once you are down to eight hours, take the next two weeks and firm up that window. By now, you should have a solid routine. You have been patient and reinforced a good habit. The eight-hour window is inevitable.

Once you have achieved a consistent eight-hour time-restricted window, my advice at that point is to choose maintenance. You can now pay closer attention to *what* you are eating and how it is making you feel. Do you feel more energy throughout the day? Are you getting sufficient nutrient density in your meals? You can answer these questions largely by seeing how you feel thirty minutes and four hours after your meals. If you find you are getting extremely hungry between meals in the eating window, or that you are experiencing added stress during the non-eating periods, take a look at what you are eating. Are you giving yourself enough calories? Are you filling up on mostly carbohydrates and simple sugars? If so, it may be time to revisit your diet to ensure sufficient nutrient density. Once you get to eight hours, feel free to fine-tune and experiment with the exact window that works best for you. Do you feel better restricting your intake to a single meal? That may sound extreme but many find this ideal. Others swear by the five-hour window. This is where the art of the individual must experiment and explore to determine optimal balance.

Here are three helpful questions to help you stay on track and not push yourself to the point of adverse results. Before using the answers to these questions, be sure you have established consistency in your eight-hours or less eating window.

1. Are you having trouble eating enough in the period afforded to you, experiencing low energy throughout the day, or craving coffee or other caffeinated beverages?

2. Are you experiencing increased anxiety?

3. Are you having trouble sleeping?

If the answer to any of the above is yes, I do not suggest shrinking the time in which you are eating. These are all signs that you are already experiencing a high stress load. This is not necessarily indicative of your eating schedule alone; stress is cumulative, so what you eat is only one contributing factor to stress load. Nevertheless, it is important to manage all contributions to your overall stress profile.

If you struggled to get from step two to step three, you may need to take a careful look at what you are eating. For example, if your diet is heavy in carbohydrates, you may struggle to reduce your eating window. Consider more fats and proteins.

After substantial and consistent success using time-restricted eating as a foundation, you can move on to include fasting.

Step 4: Extended Fasting

Eating as a principle can be viewed through two lenses: one, eat to fuel activity, or two, eat to replenish diminished fuel stores.

Any motivation beyond these reasons is eating for the sake of eating, which often ends with damage and poor fuel partitioning. Both eating to fuel activity and eating to replenish diminished stores are predicated on using the fuel you are giving to your body. If you wish to be optimal, understanding this principle is critical.

Chronically over- or under-fueling the body is detrimental to its performance, as well as to your physical, emotional, and mental health. *Fasting*, by contrast, is short-term under-nourishment. As humans, we are more than capable of surviving without food for extended periods of time, three weeks or more with the caveat that sufficient water is available.

During eating periods, protein and carbohydrates are absorbed into the blood, supplying the gastrointestinal tract before moving on to the liver, which makes the necessary energy allocation decisions before the blood returns to the heart. If you happen to eat protein in excess of what you need the remaining amount is often converted to either carbohydrate or fat. This is a process called glycogenolysis. In a typical eating cycle, sufficient exogenous glucose is supplied to your body and brain by the fruits, vegetables, and other carbohydrates you eat.[47]

Fat, when you eat it, does not follow this pathway. Instead, fat is absorbed into the lymph, after which it is typically stored for later energy use.

The essential thing to understand is that when you eat, energy is either immediately used (rare) or stored in the liver, muscles, and fat cells throughout the body. The two primary hormones driving this activity, insulin and glucagon, are produced by the pancreas.

However, the other hormones in this process are norepinephrine and epinephrine, which are produced by the adrenal medulla and travel by way of sympathetic nerves signaling the liver and adipose tissue. Through this hormone signaling, primary blood glucose levels are generated from the liver. This is especially important with regard to the stress response. If food was recently eaten, the body's signals trigger the liver to produce glucose via the glycogenolysis pathway. If food has not been recently eaten, the liver makes new glucose on its own, a process called gluconeogenesis.

During prolonged fasting, the liver, and to a lesser extent the kidneys, can produce sufficient glucose for the body to function up to a point. If necessary, the liver will rely on gluconeogenesis, which can supply approximately 180 grams of glucose per day, roughly equivalent to 720 kcal. The energy output of an individual is commonly 1,500 to 3,000 kcal per day, so 720 kcal is an insufficient supply of glucose. As a result, most of that glucose is allocated to the brain. The other organs and tissues in the body shift from relying on glucose to relying mostly on fat.

When there is insufficient glucose, the liver takes fat and makes it into ketones. Ketones, during a prolonged fast, are a critical compound to assist the body and brain in functioning. They become a central energy source used by many tissues. The brain also can and does use ketones during prolonged fasting.

During the first days of a fast, the body begins to alter what fuel it conserves and what fuel it utilizes to operate. As the body shifts to a greater reliance on ketones, this results in much less breakdown of protein. Because the gluconeogenesis pathway requires fewer amino acids, protein stores in the body will last longer. It also means that our bodies can withstand extended fasts without incurring tissue damage or disruption.

The human body becomes hyper-efficient during the fasting period, as it goes through this process of conservation. Even after several days of fasting, the glucose in the body is lessened only by a small amount. And after a *month*, the reduction is only 25 percent.[48] This allows our bodies to preserve lean muscle mass.

Let that all sit for a minute. How incredible is that process?

Let's reiterate and simplify: Our total body energy stores allow us to survive for many weeks without experiencing significantly adverse effects.[49]

The goal of fasting in our context, however, is not to use it to simply *survive*, but to use fasting's benefits to *thrive*.[50]

How often and how long you want to fast varies substantially by individual. However, it is critical to remember, first and foremost, that fasting is a stress. When done properly, it is a highly beneficial stress. So do it properly—don't overdo it.

At the beginning, as you are learning how your body reacts to fasting while dealing with your other responsibilities, I encourage you to create a schedule for the first three months. What initially kept me from starting these protocols was concern that I might not be able to do my job if I fasted. I often work six or seven days per week, for at least a few hours each day. I am often highly physical, doing martial arts or leading groups of people into cold settings in mountains, lakes, and rivers. This work is very rewarding, but it also requires a substantial amount of mental and emotional invest-ment in addition to the physical demands.

When it finally occurred to me that what was stopping me was simple fear, it made my decision to move forward much easier. I am grateful for it, as it turned out to be an incredibly impactful way to do work around fear and discomfort. As soon as I showed up to do the work, I discovered surprise after surprise, all of which turned out to be insightful and edifying. It became abundantly clear how necessary fasting was as a tool to master the stress response.

Beyond the physical benefits of fasting, which are plentiful, you can learn to confront the fear of being without food, one of life's basic needs. You can deal with fear of scarcity. You can practice being comfortable with discomfort. You can tap the deep reservoirs of empowerment inside you and reveal with clarity the messages of your nervous system.

Plan Your Fast

Sample Fast Schedule

Month 1

I recommend starting with twenty-four-hour fasts. This is due not only to evidence of extended fasting benefits starting at the twenty-four-hour mark, but because twenty-four-hour fasts are excellent resets for the body that don't require substantial stress.[51] They also provide a lower barrier of entry to establish fasting routines that can reasonably fit inside your life.

Over the course of the first month of your three-month routine, commit to fasting for twenty-four hours between one and three times. Pick the day(s) on your calendar in advance. Don't over-plan; just pick the day(s) and move forward.

Start off with a twenty-four-hour fast that includes water or coffee/tea only (no cream, no sugar). I typically prefer to do this from Saturday to Sunday, although Thursday to Friday is not uncommon either. For the timeframe, I like to have an early dinner around four or five o'clock, and then break the fast the following day at the same time.

I usually plan my fast around a day when I know I can start with exercise first thing in the morning. I also make sure I won't have any social commitments on the evening I begin the fast. One of my favorite ways to connect to people is to share an extended meal with food, drinks, and laughter. So, taking extra care that my fasting does not interfere with my social life really goes a long way to helping me focus on what I am doing. I eat my dinner early and take it easy that night. It is not difficult to go to bed since I have eaten several hours earlier. When I get up in the morning, I drink a glass of water, sometimes a black coffee, and start my breathing exercises. Following this, I go for a walk or begin other exercise.

As you get to know your body and how you respond during a fast, you may modify these routines. However, if you are new to this, I encourage you to begin with light exercise such as walking when you wake up. Walk between one and two miles. This will help you transition your nervous system into more of a sympathetic, or action-oriented, state. This is a big help in terms of how your body responds. Remember, being in a more sympathetic state inhibits food digestion to prioritize more action-oriented behaviors. Getting moving and having something to do also helps to keep you focused.

Just lying on the couch in a resting state only makes things harder, but you also shouldn't overdo it. Work to train your body to handle more action-oriented behaviors over time. If you need to rest, rest. Drink plenty of water without overdoing it. Add just a little salt to the water to help to maintain cell balance and prevent dehydration.

Eat a normal meal before going into the fast and when you break the fast. It is not necessary to binge eat in fear of the upcoming restrictive period, nor is it helpful to do so post-fast. Having a clear mindset around this and looking forward to the fast as a beneficial thing is very helpful and not to be underrated.

After the twenty-four-hour fast period, resume your normal time-restricted eating pattern. For example, if you typically eat from ten in the morning until six in the evening, eat your last pre-fast meal at around 5:30 p.m. on Saturday (so you are done by six), then resume eating Sunday evening at that same time, ensuring a full twenty-four hours. When you wake up Monday morning, be prepared to do light activity, drink water, and re-establish your ten to six routine to get back on your normal eating schedule. This will help with your rhythmicity and maintaining good structure.

Month 2

During a fasting state of more than twenty-four hours, the glucose supplied by the body cannot meet the needs of an individual. In response, the body begins to favor the fat metabolic pathway to produce the necessary fuel to function. The result is the production of ketones, which acts as the alternative fuel for the body and brain.

Having healthy fats as part of your typical diet, with the possible supplementation of coconut oils, medium chain triglycerides (MCT oils), and other similar compounds, can help trigger the ketone transition more robustly. Be careful to not overdo supplementation oils, since doing so can often cause diarrhea.

During the second month of your three-month fasting progression, again aim for one to three fasts. However, try extending *just one* of the twenty-four-hour fasts to forty-eight hours. Use the same guidelines as above, except start on Friday evening instead of Saturday evening. This only needs to be done one time during the month.

There is no need to change your diet before or after the forty-eight-hour fast. Staying connected to your body by listening to it should help guide you on what will work best. For me, high fat and protein and limited carbohydrates tend to be best most of the time.

Month 3

You have now built a solid foundation. This month, try a fast for seventy-two hours. Instead of starting Friday evening, start Thursday evening, and break the fast Sunday evening as usual.

It is only necessary to do a seventy-two-hour fast once in the entire three month period. Be patient and find consistency using a combination of time-restricted eating and twenty-four, forty-eight, and seventy-two-hour fasts, so that you can steadily build your body up without over-stressing it or experiencing setbacks. Even if you manage only one twenty-four-hour fast in month one, one forty-eight-hour fast in month two, and one seventy-two-hour fast in month three, you rocked it! More is not always better.

Regardless of the length of the fast, there is no need to plan exactly what you will eat to break your fast. Simply eat whatever is in your diet. However, have the meals planned and ready to avoid turning to junk food. I have made this mistake in the past as you will soon hear.

During the fasting period, your body does a lot of cleanup work. It kills off damaged cells, enhances intestinal stem cell functionality, and re-sensitizes hormone receptors. However, a great deal of fasting benefits also come when you break the fast, *after the stress*. In this more resting stage, your body can safely prioritize rebuilding and repairing rather than conserving. It is through both the stress *and* the recovery that your systems optimize. So it is good to feed your body healthful, good tasting, nutrient-dense food. Your body, brain, and mind will thank you.

Finally, with regard to food preparation, there is magic in preparing and cooking the break-the-fast meal yourself. Take the time to smell all the ingredients, the spices, and the aromas as you prepare it. It can be delightfully intoxicating. Don't rush to make this meal. Take your time and enjoy the whole process!

Below, I have included the journal from my first two-and-a-half-day fast. I have done many more since that first attempt, yet I still find that many of my initial discoveries continue to hold true. You may find it funny and interesting, as it is basically unedited.

My First Fast - A Diary

Day 1

Day 1 flew by. It was more or less easy. I did extra rounds of breathing (3 or 4 total sets for the day with DMT-like release).[52] Gauged how I felt throughout the day. Was dragging a little in the afternoon until I went rock climbing. I climbed well and felt great after. Packed a dinner because I prepared myself for a 24 hour fast. When I went to the school though and wrestling began, I was alright. Taught and wrestled. I was still doing fine so I kept the fast going. When I finished teaching the 7:30 Tsun Jo class, I still felt ok. I was hungry but not crazy. I stayed up til 11p and had a little trouble sleeping. I was hungry. Finally fell asleep hard and didn't wake until my alarm, which is unusual that I would make it that long.[53]

Day 2

Woke up hungry this morning but hanging in there. Had coffee with XCT oil in it. Coffee was ok but didn't taste as good as with my usual cream. Did my breathing, packed a lunch just in case. I taught two classes this morning and did great. Exercised and did half-hearted heavy bag work. No problems at all. Then student's mom came in with burgers for students after their lesson and I almost lost it. Pulled it back together though and kept the fast going. Got home. My brain is strangely quiet and at peace even though a storm is surging in the belly. I'm hungry today. Trying not to think about it too much though. Staying hydrated with a pinch of Himalayan salt in a glass of water. I've been drinking a lot of water. Just in the last hour is the first time I've felt even slightly dehydrated, which is why I tried the salt.

Each time I do my breathing there's an intense response. With very little effort (3-4 rounds last one with pressure/ inhalation) I get a good DMT-like release.

Orgasms are super intense as well.

Trying to relax and conserve energy before I go back to teach tonight, so I'm watching the news (a special on Vice). It's

228

about a democratic candidate, a woman named Katie who is running for Congress in California. The report shows her training new staff to go knock on doors for her grassroots campaign and the camera pans to show donuts for the staff. I swear I could fucking smell the donuts through the television. That was incredibly bizarre.

Kept strong through the day, went and taught classes. Private lessons (two) were review and sparring. Then I taught the advanced class. We were sticking and trapping, primarily high-pressure 2-on-1. I got home. It smelled like deliciousness. I just went to my bedroom while e and x ate.[54] During our family brain / body exercise discussion (buddha brain), I felt calm and relaxed. Just tired and a bit hungry, mostly tired. After reading to e to put her to bed, I tried to sleep. My body was stressing. I couldn't go to sleep. I got an hour or so of rest but not sleep. Then I couldn't even rest. Came out to the living room to try tv as a distraction.

I also read a bit about fasting to help stay focused. I did some breathing then tried to go back to bed. Still no way. I had to eat. I came out to the kitchen and ate the salad I had made 3 days ago along with leftover pizza and the elk ribs made earlier in the week. Eating the salad, it tasted incredible. I could also differentiate every ingredient, each taste in the salad. It was wild. And even though it was a few days old, it tasted so good. All the food did in fact. Finally I digested for an hour and then went to bed at 2:15a. Woke up this morning at 6a to go teach a lesson to Chris. Had to fight to not cancel it.

Reflections

This was my first extended fast (longer than twenty-four hours). It debunked my inaccurate expectations about how my body would respond. My initial concern that I wouldn't have sufficient energy to do my job as a martial arts instructor was completely overturned. Not only did I have enough energy to do my job—which is highly physically, mentally, and emotionally demanding—but that week happened to be sparring week. Sparring is intense and demands an especially high level of action and output. I also kept up with my typical routine of rock climbing, office work, family obligations, and sex with my partner. In other words, with the exception of eating, I hardly changed a thing in my typical schedule.

One thing I relied on extensively, however, was extra breathing protocols and meditation. I found this to be critical in remaining focused throughout, especially when I would start to lose willpower. The heightened sensitivity of the fast tied me into unique perceptions during meditation that I had not otherwise experienced. Most notable was the fine subtlety with which I could detect individual smells. And as mentioned in my diary, upon breaking my fast, I could distinguish each flavor on a level previously foreign to me. It was remarkable.

Masturbating during the fast felt unusually good, but sex with my partner was beyond incredible. I had altogether heightened sensitivity, and when combined with breathing exercises and intimacy meditation focused on my partner, the results were staggering. In the words of my partner, it was an *out-of-the-vagina experience*. That description made me laugh for days, but it was altogether too accurate to describe our sexual experience. Even though she was not fasting, through our combined intimacy, breathing protocols, and focused meditation, we were able to connect on a truly profound level. My personal experience included every bit of her level of orgasmic pleasure. We shared in delight during that otherwise stress-provoking period.

I walked away from the experience with new eyes. It would have been easy for me to chase the bliss I found in the fast. But experience with other survival stress tools helped me reign in the desire to overdo it. Instead, I proceeded with exploratory caution. I knew I had tapped into something incredibly useful and profound, but it was a powerful stressor and as such, it demanded respect.

Over the course of the last three years, I have done a number of extended fasts ranging from twenty-four to eighty hours. For me, this has proven highly valuable and sufficient. I haven't felt the need to fast beyond the eighty-hour mark, although I'm quite confident I am capable of doing it and even sustaining a reasonably high level of activity during the fast. Though I have read of people who recommend five, seven, or even ten days of fasting, I haven't pursued these recommendations.

The biggest reason I haven't gone beyond an eighty-hour period is simply that I have not seen a reason to do so. I do not have an underlying condition that would warrant it, such as a need to lose weight, and the benefits I have received from my existing fasting protocols have been substantial. I have not seen a reason to further stress my body. Although the exact frequency of fasting for any individual is a combination of science and art, one thing I am certain of is that more is not always better.

Whether you abide by my exact timeline or modify it to develop your own, taking a careful and deliberate approach, building a strong foundation, and tapping into the deepest recesses of your body and mind will allow you to navigate the path that is right for you.

What About Juice Fasts or Waterless Fasts?

I do not recommend juice fasts for several reasons, most notably a lack of good evidence that a juice fast offers the same benefits as a water-only fast. There is some evidence that a juice fast may increase nitric oxide production and beneficially alter the gut biome.[55] However, there is a dearth of substantive evidence to support many of the claims. Furthermore, reducing ingested glucose to reduce circulating insulin and re-sensitize insulin receptors is one of the primary goals in fasting, and *feeding your body simple sugars is the exact opposite of this.* Drinking juice during a fast interferes with your body's ability to transition to a fat-burning engine that increasingly relies on ketones.

In addition, once you have made the transition to rely largely on ketones, you are likely to find that fasting is much more manageable in terms of how it feels, mentally, physically, and emotionally. My students, friends, and colleagues who are on regular keto diets (or carnivore diets) report far fewer difficulties with extended fasts. Those on more carb-based diets report greater struggles during the first forty-eight hours. This is not a coincidence. I recognize that these last comments about *how it feels* are purely subjective and anecdotal. However, I hope a better understanding of what happens during the transition to fasting can help you clarify why this correlation may exist. I encourage you to evaluate this for yourself and make your own determination.

Waterless or dry fasting involves eliminating all consumption for a period of time. I refrain from recommending it because of the increased risks associated with it and the lack of substantive evidence. In principle, I can understand the possible utility of waterless fasting. I look at it in terms of dosage. Dose, as previously mentioned, is a combination of duration and intensity. In this case, the method is extremely intense. Since the individual eliminates all water and food, the time would necessarily shrink to ensure a beneficial "dose" of fasting.

I am not convinced at this time, however, that waterless fasting offers sufficient benefits that cannot be derived from water-only fasting. I may be persuaded in the future if further evidence comes forward, but for now there is not enough of it.

Finally, in terms of risk management, I believe water-only fasting to be superior. If you do decide to undergo a waterless fast for health or religious purposes, I would advise observing a very limited fast, or doing it under the direct supervision of a medical professional to ensure safety.

Final Notes on Fasting

Fasting has been *en vogue* in recent years and as a result, there have been a fair number of scientific studies on its effects. More studies will likely be forthcoming that may help us tailor certain fasting protocols. However, we all behave differently as individuals, even if we average out on paper. Experiment with what timeframe works best for you. Prioritize the routine and work to minimize chronic adverse effects.

We want to create acute stress by using fasting as a survival stress tool. I believe that typically, this is best accomplished over a one- to three-day period (as proposed above). There will be exceptions to the rule, but what we don't want is a chronic stress-inducing practice. Regularly eating too few calories in a given day keeps your body in an elevated stress state, increasing the likelihood of heart disease and other organ damage, impairing sleep quality, and impeding repair and recovery.

My personal time-restricted eating windows typically fluctuate by four to eight hours. For periods of several weeks my time windows will be consistently five hours; then they'll change to seven hours for another several weeks, and so on. The change typically accompanies some other alteration in my life. I try to listen to my body carefully and balance my routines as needed.

For extended fasts, I typically start around three in the afternoon and break them around that same time. I have found this works best for my personal schedule; since I teach martial arts primarily in the evenings, my biological rhythms are shifted slightly later. My morning routine involves a series of breathing exercises. This is sufficient to get my metabolism up and running, rather than relying on breakfast in the morning. Using a high metabolic breathing method to support both your time-restricted eating plan and fasting schedule can be highly beneficial.[56]

What I have described with my morning routine is an example of stacking stress tools. As you work to stack stress tools in your life, be mindful. Work with your body over time to develop a keen awareness of how your body reacts under different circumstances. Today, I have trained my body to the point where it can safely be pushed in any number of ways—but I did not start here. Furthermore, things change over both the long and short term. I always listen to my body, and if I need to change course—eat at a different time for one day, do less exercise, sleep more—I do that. Being committed doesn't mean ignoring clear signs from your body that it *needs* something. Wanting something is different. Wanting can be overridden with determination, grit, and focus. Denying your body what it needs, however, will inevitably lead to poor health and catastrophe. Check in with yourself frequently. Don't fool yourself into thinking that what you want is what you need or vice versa.

If you find yourself lightheaded, feeling weak, or feeling dizzy or disoriented while fasting, these are dangerous signs: *seek medical attention.* Always respect the power of the tool to serve you when properly used or injure you when improperly used.

Fasting is a great survival stress tool that can add incredible benefits to our lives if used well. To paraphrase Dr. Peter Atia, who specializes in longevity, fasting is the only tool that has demonstrated an organism's ability to live longer. It is also a key component to mastering the stress response while helping you achieve a longer, higher-quality life.

F^CK

Y ES. THE FUCK survival stress tool is real. It refers to those acts that join people together in the deepest bonds of the human experience. Training with Fuck appropriately allows us to use it as an a separate relational acute stress tool that improves immune function, physically strengthens us, and refines coordination. It has the cardiovascular health benefits of lowering blood pressure and hypertension and reducing the risk of heart disease and stroke. It offers headache relief, lowers the chance of prostate cancer in men, and is associated with the reduction of all-cause mortality. In women, it strengthens the pelvic floor, improves vaginal lubrication production, protects against endometriosis and incontinence in later life, and assists bladder control. It helps relieve menstrual and premenstrual cramps and reduces other pain.

The Fuck tool improves cooperation, communication, and creativity. It can help us learn to cultivate and harness both desire and passion. Unlike of the relational tool of Fight, which is founded on advantage, Fuck is founded on the intricacy of physical, verbal, and emotional coordination that helps a union reach the highest peaks of mutual gain. We discover the right balance of sacrifice and support to achieve these ends. We learn to engage in the work necessary so that who we choose is positively reflected in who we are. It teaches us better alignment who we think we are and who we actually are. We learn the balance and importance of both separateness and togetherness, whether the partner is for an evening, a season, or a lifetime.

Now, you might be asking yourself, why did I choose to choose the word fuck?

Fuck has a long oral history and an uncertain written origin. It has evolved so that it can be used on any number of fronts in daily life. Thanks to the word's ability to morph grammatically, it can function as a verb (both transitive and intransitive), adjective, noun, or adverb. For our purposes, I will focus on the verb form and its sexually connotative meaning.

Due to fuck's ubiquitous and amorphous history, I feel justified in taking creative license by expanding its definition yet further. Rather than restrict the word to a more typical meaning—a casual encounter devoid of feelings, or the mere fact of carnal knowledge—I use fuck to represent the full range of consensual sex between individuals: from a lust-filled one night stand to the deepest intimacy usually reserved for long-term couples. I want fuck to encompass our erotic desires and help us learn to confront our fears and insecurities in the sexual domain. I want you to get excited just thinking about the term and what it implies without making it cheap. Can fuck accomplish this end? I think it can.

People the world over have used this traditionally explicative term to mean all sorts of things. With varied intonation and context, it can propagate a thousand shades of meaning, even within just the sexual realm. This chameleonic quality is the primary reason I chose fuck. That, and for obvious alliterative purposes, of course.

Whether it is a physical expression of love, a way to make children, or simply an intimate encounter, to fuck, in this book, refers to an unmistakable act of bonding between humans. Understanding its role in the stress response is where we will begin.

Recall the HPA axis discussed in an earlier chapter. It is the central circuitry through which the body sends the messages that govern the stress response. Sex stress is also partially directed by the HPA axis.[57] However, it is the hypothalamic-pituitary-gonadal (HPG) axis that principally directs sex hormones and the stress response associated with sexual encounters. The HPG axis is the neural endocrine circuit of the gonads. The gonads include ovaries for females and testes for males.

Both sets of circuitry influence the sex hormones vital for many bodily functions that contribute to overall health, growth, and well-being. When the gonads are stimulated, they secrete steroid hormones, usually just termed sex hormones. The principle sex hormone in males is testosterone.[58] The principle sex hormones in females are estradiol (a type of estrogen) and progesterone. Males also produce small quantities of estrogen and females produce small amounts of testosterone, but these amounts are typically very small in relation to the primary sex hormone(s) of the gender in question.

Men and Testosterone

Testosterone has many important functions in men. As the HPG circuitry stimulates the production of testosterone, testosterone in turn messages the hypothalamus, which triggers decreased amounts of that as well as other sex hormones. Testosterone is necessary for sperm production and maintenance. It maintains function for accessory reproductive organs. It is involved in bone growth and protein synthesis for muscles. It influences behavior like aggression and competitiveness. This list is not extensive, but you can quickly garner that testosterone plays an important role.

Therefore, low testosterone in men can greatly alter quality of life. Low testosterone can be caused by a number of conditions, including endocrine disfunction, brain damage, and other reasons. Men with insufficient testosterone report a lack of energy, irritability, cognitive decline, listlessness, depression, and lack of desire. These men also commonly experience one or more of the following: loss of muscle, brittle bones, low libido, impotence, small testicles, and larger breasts.

When their testosterone is increased, these men report feelings of life-satisfaction and desire, not just for sex, but for many of life's pursuits. This has led a great number of men to pursue exogenous testosterone in the form of prescription medications. According to an article published in the *International Journal of Environmental Research and Public Health*, prescription testosterone sales jumped from $18 million in 1988 to more than $2 billion in 2013.[59]

Although most prescriptions are for aging men, the decline of naturally produced testosterone in men of all ages during the last 100 years is staggering. A study published in *The Journal of Endocrinology & Metabolism* found a significant decline in base testosterone levels between 1987 and 2004 among more than 1,500 randomly selected men aged forty-five to seventy-nine.[60] And unfortunately, this trend continues today, as it has likely done since at least the 1920s. Our dads had a leg up on you and me, but our grandads had a leg up on them.

Before running off to purchase exogenous testosterone, which has had mixed results, let us take a look at natural methods that boost the body's ability to create it endogenously.

Does Nature Play Cruel Jokes?

If we look at some of the more well-documented causes of impaired testosterone, two of the first that pop up are excessive alcohol intake and obesity.

The Fight, Fast, and Freeze survival stress tools and guidance can assist in both weight optimization and stimulating the brain to form good habits around exercise, as well as neurochemical drive and satisfaction. Alcohol, for its part, affects many of the same brain receptors that our survival stress tools tap into during training. That means that incorporating survival stress tools into daily life can help cut down on alcohol consumption. What is more, instead of relying on alcohol—which is unfortunately toxic to the human body in that it damages the liver, negatively impacts the blood, and narrows the wiring of our brains—we can experience *better overall* effects through training while simultaneously increasing brain growth and adaptation.

I am not saying never drink alcohol. I would be a hypocrite. I believe in balancing individual life quality. For me, this means enjoying a glass of wine with a nice dinner or a good whisky with a friend. I'm sure you have your preferences, too. We just want to make sure that we are not hijacking our brains for the cheap thrill too often.

In earlier chapters, we learned that vasopressin is associated with fear as well as attachment. When we experience high levels of fear, vasopressin is present in the brain in large quantities, impairing testosterone production. Instead of tapping in the courage we need to overcome this neurochemical shift, many of us tend to reach for liquid courage. Alcohol reduces vasopressin levels, thereby reducing the fear we may feel when seeking a mate, taking a chance, or initiating intimate contact. For those of us who try to use alcohol as liquid courage, whether to fight or find a date, hopefully the information in this book will help us face discomfort and prevail without such "help."

If we look at what *increases* testosterone, proximity and availability of sexual partners is high on the list. Not too surprising. But there is another, more surprising influential factor: stress. Testosterone levels are linked to those of the other stress response hormones: dopamine, epinephrine, and norepinephrine. In this case, stress is good and necessary in that it drives us to take risks, find a partner, and initiate, and engage in sex, However, a balance needs to be inherent to this response. Nature provides this balance in a number of ways, one of which is vasopressin.[61] Upon orgasm, vasopressin increases to very high quantities, impeding testosterone and facilitating attachment. Vasopressin levels also tend to increase generally in long-term relationships, fulfilling a similar function. This can be great if the individual knows what's happening, but if he is unaware of why his testosterone is decreasing, it can also be deleterious.

The aware individual can take the steps necessary to strike a balance between healthy activities that promote testosterone and enjoying the meaningful and stable intimate relationships encouraged by vasopressin. The unsuspecting person, however, may feel that their vitality has been stripped away for reasons unknown. In such situations, the individual may incorrectly blame the relationship or partner. This inaccurate assessment can result in fear of commitment or resentment toward a partner.

Therefore, what's critical to remember is that primary sex hormones need to operate within a balance for a man to be healthy, just like the rest of the body and brain.[62] We need testosterone and healthy ways to produce it naturally. However, to offset the *drive* of testosterone and facilitate attachment to a partner or child, the body also needs vasopressin. It also needs serotonin, oxytocin, and healthy nitric oxide, all of which have calming, vasodilating, and satiating effects; a return to a rest and relaxation state is another major balance. In other words, higher testosterone can help us climb a mountain, work hard to get a top-paying job, start a business, or find a mate, but once we have accomplished our goals, we should feel peace and experience rest; neither side independently offers complete fulfillment.

Women and Hormones

Estrogen, progesterone, and (to a much lesser, but still very important, degree) androgens such as testosterone are the primary sex hormones for females. In a complex monthly cycle, these and other sex hormones circulate through a woman's body. This is an autonomic function initiated by the hypothalamus. As a woman approaches monthly ovulation, estrogen increases sharply, peaking and then rapidly declining right before ovulation. Progesterone, meanwhile, mostly increases right after ovulation, temporarily rising above circulating estrogen before falling again.

Estrogen and progesterone have many important functions in the female body. Just to name a few, estrogen stimulates growth of the female reproductive organs and glands, contributes to bone growth, and protects against osteoporosis. It also has vascular effects. Progesterone also has many functions, two of which are to help prepare the endometrium for implantation of an embryo and to induce cervical mucus, which can assist a male's sperm in reaching the uterus. And finally androgens, such as testosterone, play an important role in skeletal muscle health and sex drive for women.

Unfortunately, trends in women's hormonal disruption are no better than men's. Studies conducted over the last forty-plus years have linked abnormal balances of females sex hormones, primarily estrogen, to increases in problems like breast cancer.[63]

The significant mood swings, mood disorders, and depression associated with fluctuating estrogen levels—especially disruptions to normal levels—have resulted in females seeking hormone replacement therapy as well. And like men, they are doing so at a rapidly increasing rate. If these men and women were simply optimizing their bodies through the advances of modern technology and medicines, I would be more on board. But far more often, they are reacting to the negative disruption of base levels in humans over the previous decades.

Whatever your sexual orientation, finding balance within your body systems and mind is critical to mastering the stress response and engaging in life's greatest pleasures. Participating in a deeply bonding activity and sharing close intimacy with a partner is a great way to express healthy neurochemical and hormonal ends and find proper balance. The challenge we face is finding the space and time to develop the deep connections that foster physical, emotional, and mental health. We also need ways to break through existing barriers so that we can have better conversations, a clearer understanding of our partners, and thus more sex positive results.

The Anatomy of Sexual Pleasure

Like all of us, I have made mistakes with sexual encounters. For instance, there have been times when, as a sexual prospect was evolving over the course of an evening, my nervousness provoked me to drink far more than I should have, and the result was suboptimal sex when the encounter came to fruition. The obvious lesson learned was that a lack of refined motor control and awareness rarely contributes to the best outcomes. At other times, I have made the mistake of thinking that one partner is just like another. After developing certain techniques with one partner that allowed us to experience great sexual heights together, I expected these combinations to be universal. That presumption was shattered with the following partner.

I have also experienced unexpected successes by being willing to say yes in the moment. The first time I tied a partner up—at her request, of course—I did so with my own shirt while in a car. I couldn't have been more aroused, elated, and scared, but I accepted the risk of the unknown, and it turned out to be a wonderful experience.

However, for many years, my mistakes and successes followed no particular pattern. Neither could be predicted with any consistency because I was not engaging in sexual endeavors with clarity. Sometimes I was successful in arousing my partner; other times, the experience felt disjointed and I felt that I had failed. Rarely did I receive any helpful feedback even when I mustered the courage to ask. The verbal communication was often sparse and generally fell into one of two categories:"Oh, my god that was fucking great," or words of praise paired with body language that signaled dissatisfaction. My ability to read my partner's nonverbal cues was limited, as was my overall experience—not just my sexual experience, but my knowledge of how to break through the communication barriers around sex. Most of us have been in similar positions, especially early in relationships or when conversations rarely or never take place. It is hard to develop perspective when we don't really know what we don't know. It takes a great deal of courage to actually tell our partners the truth, and moreover, we need to be able to articulate that truth to ourselves as well.

As the years have passed and my experience has grown, these waters have become much easier to navigate. My partner's verbal and nonverbal cues are increasingly clear, not only because I have learned how to listen to her, but also because I have much greater awareness of my own body and mind. One of my biggest early breakthroughs was simply admitting to myself that I didn't really understand certain things about me or my partner. This included even basics such as anatomy. In my early years, I thought I understood a lot more than I actually did. Looking back, I see that I fooled myself terribly, partly for ego's sake but also from simple misunderstandings. But admitting to myself that there was a lot that I didn't know led to curiosity and a desire to change that. Since early conversations did not often lead to great insights, I would try to read about techniques and give them a try. Being willing to fail even as I tried to remain a compassionate and passionate lover allowed for small steps forward. It helped me practice control, patience, and timing rather than always focusing on distractions, insecurities, or ego. This turned out to be helpful beyond the encounters themselves, as conversations with friends and partners about sex became easier *and* more informative. I started to realize that part of the communication problem was simple ignorance on *all* sides, not necessarily a lack of desire stemming solely from insecurities or taboos.

Another discovery came while talking with a friend of mine. She and I got on the topic of oral sex. When I mentioned that I struggled to get consistently great results, she told me she had the same problem on the other side. We laughed at our common challenge, and then she gave me a great article that she and her friends had found very informative. That simple article broke down a few clear dos and don'ts when it came to performing oral sex on a female. It was better than any book I had read on tantra or any other sexual advice I had come across up to that point. I very much wish that I could offer credit where credit is due, but the author and name of the article are long gone, lost in the recesses of my memory. Nevertheless I can still summarize the content.

The article talked about four progressions. *First*: Lightly stimulate the clitoral area (nonspecific) and allow enough time for your partner to warm up before moving to the next stage. *Second*: Start with your tongue at the highest point on the outside of the clitoris (i.e., the clitoral hood), and only go underneath the hood once the arousal state is sufficiently high. Basically, don't touch the actual glans clitoris until the rest of the area is aroused. *Third*: As your partner nears orgasm, delicately insert one or two fingers into her vagina, palm up, and make a gentle *come here* motion with your fingers. All of this was to access the "g-spot," or area that connects to the clitoral structure from the inside, while minding good pressure. *Last*: Directly after orgasm has occurred, very gently hold the clitoris in your mouth and don't move. If you do all the steps right, the author added, you will have a partner for life, begging you to service her.

When I read this, it wasn't just the techniques or the step-by-step instruction that was so illuminating—though I appreciated those details. The magic was that she seemed to offer insights to certain principles of great sex, even if she didn't express them explicitly. At the time, I mostly digested the techniques, but as those specifics were internalized and adapted to different partners' preferences, principles emerged that put so much of my past into perspective. I finally understood why at certain points my partners had been deeply aroused or why there had been a shift that had required the arousal state to be rebuilt. Now that I understand so much more about the stress response, specifically as it relates to sex, the principles and broader applications are as clear as a freshly cleaned mirror.

Here is the takeaway. If you are unsure about where to start or need a shake up to your routine, read up on this or that technique. It can be informative and help you expand your creativity. But understand that specific techniques are often only applicable to certain partners, unless those techniques are adapted to preferences while guided by underlying principles, specifically those outlined below. All are based on the assumption that you are having informed, ongoing conversations with your partner(s) as you learn and better integrate these concepts. The following steps can lead to epochal change in your sexual experiences.

Step 1
Know your erogenous zones, both yours and those of your partner.

Step 2
Have an understanding of the nervous system as it relates to sex.

Step 3
Own the three pillars of great sex.

Step 4
Integrate the above with breath for maximized control, awareness, and peak orgasms.

Step 5
Explore consciousness and eventually master the sexual stress response.

Erogenous Zones

As I went about codifying information for the Fuck tool, I interviewed Dr. Ariadna Uriarte, a neuropsychologist and sexologist. She was instrumental in helping to deliver quality insights for this and related sections. As Dr. Uriarte points out, "Every individual has an exclusive topography of pleasure that can change throughout a person's life." So taking the opportunity to explore yourself and your partner to discover what he or she enjoys and being adventurous enough to try new things creates both positive reinforcement and a powerful aphrodisiac. This pairing engages the best of our neurobiological systems for excellent outcomes.

There are three overarching groups of erogenous zones that are part of the sexual response: the initiating zones, the proximal zones, and the primal zones. When it comes to erogenous zones, there is wide variation and inconsistency in the literature, so these descriptions are my own, informed by experience, research, and my interviews with Dr. Uriarte.

In brief, the initiating zones are often the first we engage as we flirt or begin the sexual response. The proximal zones move closer to the genitals and have more obvious sensitivity. The primal zones refer to the genitals and pubis in both sexes, as well as the prostate in men.

Initiating Erogenous Zones

Initiating zones are areas of the body that offer increased sensitivity and reception to initial touching and caressing, which stimulates the sexual response. These areas include the hair, the mouth and tongue, the armpits, the backs of the arms, fingers and hands, the belly button, the legs, the hips, and the back, especially the spinal erectors. Here is a fun side tip: The area between the shoulders tends to be especially responsive in women, whereas the sacrum area tends to be sensitive in men.

Other body parts to make this list are the eyelids, the ears, and the neck. The eyelids have many parasympathetic nerves that can be aroused by a gentle kiss. The ears respond to the sensuous engagement of the lobe, the pinna, and the back of the ear. Meanwhile, the neck can be a site of vulnerability or intense excitement: Although stimulation of this part of the body is certainly good, you can think about the neck more in terms of nonverbal communication and psycho-emotional implications. For the person receiving the touch, it registers as a sensation of trust; for the person giving, it signifies tenderness and possession.

All of these zones have the potential to offer an invitation into the sexual stress response. Another tip: Always check with your partner for best results, as no description is 100 percent accurate for all people.

Proximal Erogenous Zones

Proximal zones include the breasts, nipples, pubis, and perineum, all of which have a significant number of nerve endings that are sensitive to manual stimulation that furthers the sexual stress response. The gluts or buttocks are also on this list, not only for its receptors to touch, but also for the message it sends. For example, if we are flirting, we might graze hands, but touching or grabbing a person's ass is quite another thing. Finally, I also include feet in this zone because some people's feet are reportedly as sensitive as genitals.

Building bi-directional nerve pathways between the breasts and the genitals, the nipples and the genitals, the perineum and the genitals, and so on, is a relatively easily conditioned response that can augment orgasm. Some report the ability to induce orgasm simply by stimulating these areas (without touching the genitals), though this has not been established under scientific observation.

Primal Erogenous Zones

Is this where we get to measure size? Sure, why not? Male and female genitalia are actually remarkably similar in size.[64] Among males, however, the majority of the genitalia is on the outside, while it is on the inside among females; this includes much of the clitoral structure. I hope that this fact serves as a powerful equalizer in the size discussion. Meanwhile, we can move on to some important similarities and differences between the two genders to highlight means of sexual pleasure.

Meanwhile, we can move on to some important similarities and differences between the two genders to highlight means of sexual pleasure. The primal zones make up the areas most sensitive and responsive to sexual arousal and orgasm. In women, this includes what is known as the vulvar erotic pyramid. In men, this includes the penis, the testicles, and the prostate. Both women and men have highly sensitive areas, and the degree of excitement induced often determines the amount of pressure the nerves can sustain. If the clitoris experiences too much pressure too early in the sexual response, for example, the receptors can block the signal, resulting in pain or numbness. On the other hand, light stimulation, especially near the beginning, can foster increased blood flow and receptivity, increasing both the sexual response and the desire to have greater degrees of pressure.

Let's dive deeper.

The five components regarded as the vulvar erotic pyramid are: the clitoris, the bulbs of vestibule, the labia minora, the urethra, and the distal portion of the vagina.[65]

Most women orgasm through stimulation of the vulvar erotic pyramid. According to my interview with Dr. Ariadna Uriate, some women have reported being able to achieve orgasm through massage of the pubis alone, but this is not the norm.[66] The clitoris, bulbs of the vestibule, and labia minora all contain erectile tissue that swells with blood upon arousal. While the distal portions of the vagina and urethra don't have erectile tissue, all five structures have great sensory innervation, with a multitude of receptors highly sensitive to touch and vibration.

During our conversation, Dr. Uriarte also discussed the so-called "G-spot," a zone inside the vagina that is receptive to sexual stimulation. In 1944, German physician Ernest Grafenberg described an "erogenous sensation zone" located on the surface of the anterior wall of the vagina, below the urethra, exactly where the urethral glands are.[67] Over the subsequent decades, debate has ensued on whether the G-spot even exists, and if so, exactly what it is.

In 2009, French researchers Odile Buisson and Pierre Foldés, a gynecologist and surgeon, respectively, posed an interesting hypothesis: that the G-spot is an area of the vagina where the internal portions of the clitoris can be contacted through the roots of the clitoris and the bulbs of the vestibule. Using ultrasound, they showed that when the clitoris is erect, the bulbs of the vestibule are very close to the vagina; this could explain the clitoris's increased sensitivity. This hypothesis is currently the most accepted, although other studies continue to observe a greater sensitivity in the anterior wall of the vagina than in the posterior, suggesting that there are more nerve endings in the former.

As we explore our partners' anatomies, it is essential to be mindful of what areas are sensitive and receptive if we wish to create a positive stress response of heightened eroticism. If too much pressure is delivered to particular receptors before they have sufficient blood flow, this will reduce, impair, or even eliminate their receptivity. Positive stress breathing and varied, stimulating touches, allowing nerves to reload, can simultaneously accelerate the sexual stress response and reduce the irritation or blockage of nerve endings in erogenous zones. Rhythm, timing, pressure, and repetition all play critical roles in engaging the female anatomy, lifting her to higher expressions of erotic pleasure.

Men's sexual pleasure is driven by the prostate, the penis, the testicles, and the pubis.

Unlike a woman's clitoris, which exists only for sexual pleasure, the male's penis has multiple functions, including urination and ejaculation. Nevertheless, the penis has a multitude of nerve endings that are responsive to pressure and vibration and is a major site for erotic pleasure.

The prostate, located at the base of the bladder, is the other main sexual organ for a man. The perineum, the area between the anus and the testicles in men or the anus and the vulva in women, is a zone of great erogenous pleasure for both sexes, but in men this pleasure is particularly intense due to the perineum's proximity to the prostate. Prior to the availability of 5-phosphodiesterase inhibitor drugs (commercialized under the name of Viagra), erectile dysfunction was treated with a wide variety of cognitive-behavioral strategies. Prostate stimulation can be so intense that many sexologists considered it to be an infallible method to combat erectile dysfunction.

Only men have a prostate,[68] and it can be accessed two different ways: by caressing and massaging the surrounding areas, or by anal penetration.[69] Both methods have the potential to generate a great deal of pleasure, since the inside of the prostate has numerous nerve endings connected to the pleasure centers of the brain.

The Nervous System and Sex

The peripheral nervous system comprises both sympathetic and parasympathetic nerves, both of which innervate our primary sexual organs, the genitals. As we become sexually aroused, the peripheral nervous system directs blood flow to the genital area, where the genitals become erect. A stress response begins to take shape.

In men, an otherwise flaccid penis becomes rigid. This is a vascular response, via which blood fills up three cylindrical compartments that run the length of the penis. The engorged organ is a result of neural inputs to small arteries, which initiate the process and ensure that the veins of the penis remain passively compressed. Autonomic neurons release nitric oxide, a potent vasodilator. It is the high brain centers that direct these pathways, so thoughts, emotions, visualizations, and sensations all play a key role in this process. This largely parasympathetic response must be harnessed, however, with the necessary sympathetic innervation of ejaculation upon orgasm. In other words, erection requires the *inhibition* of the sympathetic nerves to the small arteries of the penis, and ejaculation requires the *stimulation* of different nerves. Upon orgasm, skeletal muscle contractions occur throughout the body, accompanied by increased heart rate and higher blood pressure. Once an orgasm is complete, deep relaxation takes place.

In women, much of the same physiological phenomena take

place. In her case, muscular and vascular contraction increase with sexual excitement; breasts swell, and nipples become erect. The woman's clitoris fills with blood, giving it an erection of its own. Her vaginal epithelium also swells while secreting lubricant.

As in a man, this largely parasympathetic behavior requires sympathetic innervation during orgasm. The intense pleasure of firing nerves, increased blood pressure and heart rate, and rhythmic contraction of the vagina and uterus are sympathetic stimulatory responses.

The physiology of sex and orgasm is reliant on a carefully tailored response of the nervous system. The response, as it conducts its symphony, relies on stress—but *not chronic stress*. Chronic stress dramatically impairs the instruments, the notes, and the song.

When coordinated well, the sexual stress response helps to blend all of our body systems, as each contributes to the bi-directional feedback loops. Our arousal state is influenced by sensory inputs that are folded into the loops. Skin throughout the body has an average of approximately 1,000 nerve endings per square inch, which serve as conduits to heighten our sensory experiences. In the primal zones, the number of nerve endings is vastly greater. The sounds one makes or does not make contribute to a heightened state of excitement. Smells and pheromones we release add to the rhythm and song. Taste supports our sexuality. Visual images of the mind bounce between all this. These bi-directional signals in the brain modulate arousal and play a key role in our sexual stress response.

William Masters and Virginia Johnson, through their extensive studies in the mid-twentieth century, identified four stages of the sexual response; sequentially, they are excitation, plateau (heightened pleasure, full arousal but not yet orgasm), orgasm, and resolution (the period directly after orgasm). Years later, Helen Singer Kaplan, PhD, a leading sex therapist, introduced a new concept in the cycle of sexual response: desire. She proposed a triphasic model consisting of only desire, excitement, and orgasm. Dr. Kaplan felt that this model better served her clients on a practical level, as the terms "plateau" and "resolution" could be elusive or confusing, whereas desire, excitement, and orgasm were clear. Today, many doctors, therapists, and sexologists endorse a hybrid model of the sexual response that includes all five stages (desire, excitement, plateau, orgasm and resolution), but not necessarily in a linear progression. Rather, these stages are seen as points along a track that can be traveled either direction, and some stages can be reversed, skipped, or repeated. In other words, desire doesn't always precede excitation—sometimes it follows. Plateau may move backward to excitation and then jump to orgasm. Resolution may reignite excitement, and so on. Understanding that a linear progression is not necessary for the sexual response can help clarify expectations, create space for patience, and allow us to gravitate toward engaging in these stages with varying degrees and intensities.

The Three Pillars of Great Sex

It is important to understand that at the most fundamental level, there are three guiding pillars of great sex: timing, rhythm, and pressure. Supporting these three pillars are the practical considerations of proper hygiene.

The pillar of timing includes initiating the right degree of touch at the right time so that the nervous system responds in a way that augments the sexual response. You or your partner may enjoy rough sex and aggressive grips or touches, but when applied to a proximal or primal area too early in the sexual response, such techniques can elicit resistance, unwelcome pain, numbness, or many other adverse reactions. If we are untempered in our advances, we limit the pleasure, excitement, and duration of the sexual response, leaving us with a disjointed experience. Mistiming between partners is all too common. To take an easy example among heterosexual couples, consider a man who tries to rush his female partner through various stages. Rather than creating a receptive partner, he finds (sometimes confusing) resistance. When the man becomes aware of this mistake, he sometimes makes an alternate error by trying to tiptoe through the stages. In that case, he fails to create sufficient arousal, again due to a lack of precise timing. Because every individual moves through the sexual stages at different speeds, responding

251

to various intensities along the arousal continuum, we must learn to really listen to what our partners are saying, both verbally and nonverbally. This is essential in eliciting greater sexual arousal responses. The trust and connection that a good "listener" can foster form the foundation on which sexual heights can truly be explored. Having both the element of security and enough willingness to be adventurous requires trust. Timing is one of the key principles to support that end, and with it, a deep bond of connection.

Rhythm is the second pillar. In order to have good rhythm, we need good timing. Rhythm speaks to timing expressed as a continuity among the when, the where, and for how long. Let's use the analogy of a full-body massage. Imagine you are receiving a massage. The masseuse squeezes your shoulders once and it feels great, squeezes a second time and it feels even better, initiating a desire for a third squeeze. Instead, the masseuse squeezes your leg. You feel the experience was a little disjointed, but the leg squeeze still felt good, so you try to stay engaged. But while you're waiting for a second squeeze on the leg, the masseuse starts rubbing your arm. It takes you a moment to mentally and physically transition and just as you do so, the masseuse goes right back to squeezing your shoulders. You may have liked every touch individually, but because this massage lacked rhythm and continuity, it would surely fail to meet the requirements of a satisfactory experience.

Sticking to the massage analogy, let's instead assume that the masseuse starts rubbing and squeezing your shoulders. It feels great. The squeezing and rubbing continue at the exact same pace and pressure, as if guided by a metronome. How long before this touch would be unwelcome? At some point, the receptors shut off or send a different signal, leaving you numb or irritated. Proper rhythm requires enough consistency in a repetitive motion to stimulate the receptors, yet enough variation so that the receptors *stay* receptive. Rhythm also takes sufficient continuity, so that all the various areas stimulated feel linked, despite any transitions. Practicing and exhibiting good rhythm harnesses the nervous system and guides the sexual stress response for positive results.

The third pillar is pressure. Pressure changes everything. Though this is true mentally, emotionally, and physically, let's focus on physical pressure. Apply hundreds of thousands of pounds per square inch to the right carbon constituents and you have a diamond. Apply a fraction of that pressure when you hold a teacup and it will shatter. If you want to go to outer space, you need to exert millions of pounds of pressure over a particular area to create sufficient velocity to escape earth's gravitational pull. The amount of pressure appropriate to a situation could not be more varied.

The human body thrives on physical pressure experienced in the right amount, at the right time, on a proper rhythm. The pressure appropriate in sex just prior to orgasm is vastly greater than at the beginning of an encounter: Use significant pressure at the beginning and the result is likely to be akin to the teacup shattering. On the flip side, only using a light touch as the sexual stress response increases will very likely leave your partner unable to rocket skyward. Our skin nerve receptors respond vastly differently depending on when, where, and to what degree stimulation occurs. As noted, there are an average of approximately 1,000 skin receptors per square inch throughout the body. However, in the primal erogenous zones, there can be *hundreds of thousands* of receptors.

With regard to pressure, one of the easiest ways to understand ideal receptivity is through its relationship to blood flow. With more blood flow, typically more pressure can be exerted on that area to stimulate excitatory reception. While ultimately, varying degrees of pressure need to be exerted at different times to give nerves the opportunity to reload and remain positively receptive, the following statement is an extremely useful guide: If you start by exerting light pressure, then increase it as more blood flows to the various body parts you want to arouse, you'll engage the sexual stress response with a dynamic and useful entrainment-like ability. This general precept is one of the main reasons augmenting your sexual response with breath work can have such powerful results. Very simply, proper breath work can increase blood flow, serving to prime your body, augment the link between mind and body, or peak your orgasm to the highest level. More details will be covered in the Breathe survival stress tool section.

One note of caution: Pressure misunderstandings directly after orgasm can result in overstimulation, irritation and/or pain for either gender. Even with significant blood flow in the primal zones, the guide above does not typically hold true directly after orgasm.

A woman's resolution tends to be of shorter duration than a man's, and she is therefore able to return to one of the other phases more quickly. When the sexual stress response is properly harnessed, a woman can return for another period of excitement, desire, and/or orgasm after a brief interlude. Men, meanwhile, typically need more time after an orgasm before desire, excitement, or the ability to orgasm returns. Each sex respecting the others' natural timeline differences can enhance longer and better sexual experiences. Take, for example, a female receiving oral sex. If, following the female's orgasm from her partner's oral stimulation, the male moves directly into intercourse with virtually no pause, it can cause unwelcome dissonance. On the other handan interlude, even one as brief as one minute, can help her return to the excitement phase and engage with her (likely) very excited partner. Optimal timing is based on each individual and the interplay between you both. Take opportunities to communicate and reach ever higher together.

Though the resolution period differs substantially between men and women, both sexes tend to be extremely sensitive directly after orgasm. Continuing to stimulate the nerves using significant pressure, especially coupled with movement of virtually any kind, is almost always undesirable. However, a light or moderate connective pressure that does not involve movement can have wonderful effects and assist with a more ideal resolution period. How much pressure will vary by person, so check in with your partner and experiment to see what works best for you both.

Integration

Integrating all three along with the breath is the key to mastery of the sexual stress response. As we work to integrate all of the above, we should operate with the understanding that timing, rhythm, and pressure will overlay the five phases of sexual arousal, and that breath can play an essential role in facilitating blood flow, connection between partners, and peak orgasms.

A Few Simple Ways to Include the Breath

Consider priming your sexual experiences with breathing techniques. These can be something as simple as synchronized breathing to link up with your partner and shift your focus, or something more involved, such as high-metabolic breathing combined with breath holds to increase blood flow while inducing a positive stress response. This can serve as foreplay or a warm-up for the nervous system, because breathing in this manner can shift how the skin receptors respond, fostering greater degrees of sensory awareness *and* control. Peak orgasms can be harnessed with well-timed breath holds preceded by oxygen loading through relatively rapid but controlled breathing rhythms. The results can simulate an autoerotic asphyxia-like response without the dangers typically inherent to that practice.

Or consider joining high-metabolic breathing with long, active exhales while performing de-binding exercises.[70] This combination can quickly alter the muscular tension throughout your body, increasing blood flow, mobility, and perceived vulnerability. Add placing your hands on the personal erogenous zones of your choosing to amplify the effects.

Try holding hands or placing each other's hands on your hearts while using stress breathing techniques; this can greatly heighten sexual tension *and* foster intimacy.

Use extended eye contact while remaining silent; it will allow you to really look at your partner and bond with them. If you combine this with breathing exercises, it works to form deeper bonds quickly.

Alternate breathing and breath holds with your partner while you lie in a connected position. This type of breath sharing feeds a strong emotional connection.

On mattsoule.com, I offer a series of videos to guide you, with simple-to-learn breathing techniques that will assist in fostering a deeper connection between you and your partner. I also include examples with detailed visual instructions.

Consciousness and the Mastery of the Sexual Stress Response

In the 1990s, the singer Sting, perhaps best known for his time with The Police, confirmed a rumor about his ability to have sex for seven or eight consecutive hours. After that, his name became virtually synonymous with tantric sex, a spiritual yogic practice that connects practitioners on a profound level. Although in an interview nearly twenty years later, Sting clarified to host James Lipton the actual time in bed and jokingly added that those seven or eight hours would include dinner and a movie, the practice he was alluding to was altogether accurate.

The spiritual practice of tantric sex has gained increasing prominence in recent years, largely due to people like Sting, Woody Harrelson, and other celebrities touting its benefits. The search term 'tantric sex' on Google brings up more than 54 million hits, including articles on heathline.com, mensjournal.com, and thousands of other publications.

What is Tantric Sex and Does it Have to Be Tantra?

The term tantra simply refers to a system or a practice. According to the Oxford Dictionary, tantra is "an adherence to the doctrines or principles of the tantras, involving mantras, meditation, yoga and ritual." The tantra tradition is not just about sex but is largely a practice of spirituality.

The primarily sexual reputation that tantra has earned in the West was started by a yogi who is largely credited with bringing yoga and tantra to Western culture: Pierre Bernard. The details of Pierre Bernard's life are muddled and somewhat questionable. For example, he may have changed his name several times, and he was arrested for kidnapping (although not convicted) after two teenage girls charged him with assault. He mixed with New York City's elites in the first several decades of the twentieth century, teaching his sexualized yogic practices. Eventually, he was lawfully barred from offering his teachings due to their overtly sexual nature. He was, in short, pretty scandalous.

Reading this, it would be easy to dismiss tantric practices as hokey yoga stuff introduced to the West by a questionable figure—which Bernard most certainly was. But a closer examination of the core principles of tantra helps to uncover why it resounds so strongly. If we strip away any dogma, at its heart, tantra is a combination of embodied consciousness, movement, and breathing exercises, all firmly rooted in active practice. Such exercises are, of course, not exclusive to tantra, and they are well within our conscious directive capacity and can help us to express ourselves in highly meaningful ways.

The combination of embodied consciousness, movement, and breathing has the potential to produce sexual ecstasy. While not all sex of the tantra practitioner may be on this plane, using the ecstatic as the foundation allows us to experience the highest levels of sex while gaining full control of the elements that contribute to its possibility. We can apply our understanding and skill to direct our sexual appetites to include everything from the quickie, to the creatively erotic, to the playful, to the carnal, to the spiritual.

Embodied Consciousness

Embodied consciousness allows us to face fears, embrace uncertainty and discomfort, and build nuanced physical awareness in ourselves. It also fosters our ability to listen to others and direct our attention meaningfully. This skill is fruitful on any number of fronts. Confidence emanates when this skill is possessed. Practicing mindfulness, learning to take in all that is around you without distraction or attachment, practicing dynamic tension exercises, doing visualization, and using empty mind- and movement-based meditations are all examples of embodied consciousness development. So is directing focus and attention wholly to another without losing track of yourself. Learning to include these elements in relation to your partner will allow you to tap into this space within the sexual

257

domain.

For embodied consciousness to emerge as the powerful positive force it can be, the timing of our actions should be examined.

Fantasy, for example, can be a note of caution or deep arousal inclusion. Fantasy is produced by the imagination and allows you to remove yourself from the present. When you first meet someone, the anticipation you feel, the story you create about this person, can leave you operating in spheres other than the *now*. The sexual stress experienced as we seek a partner and the fantasies that stress can inspire can mislead us in this early time. Ill-timed fantasies can replace real connection with your partner. When misled, we may find ourselves in undesirable situations or relationships. We settle for mediocrity, or worse, we miss the yellow and red flags.

Be clear with your fantasies and explore them for their positive influences. Fantasy explored to drive desire, to augment your sexual pursuit and bolster your sexual stress response can be beneficial. Fantasy can also be an incredible tool to exploring creativity, possibilities, newness, spontaneity, adventure, eroticism, sensuality, or any number of positive outcomes. When fantasy is used intentionally, the heights are unknown. Learn to time your fantasies so that they are a positive addition to sex, rather than another distraction.

Embodied consciousness helps you to tap into messages from your body and mind, including what you want and what you don't want. It is a method to help you learn to really listen to your body and mind. It is where you can learn to truly accept yourself.

When directed toward another, embodied consciousness can help you learn to accept your partner. Shifting focus to really listen to your partner, using verbal and non-verbal cues alike, is essential to finding deeper acceptance, fostering trust, and navigating the intricate weave of sexual relationships. Mystery, stability, and spontaneity become simultaneously possible instead of mutually exclusive in the sexual domain. Embodied consciousness is what directs the highest art of sex.

It is through embodied consciousness that we can shore ourselves up as individuals, planting ourselves firmly as a separate entity who can intentionally step forward to willfully engage with another. To possess the skill of embodied consciousness, you must show up whole. It requires that you be empowered to make your own decisions about the messy nature of sex and all of its contradictions.[71] Our wants and desires within the sexual realm can often seem strangely at odds with our other life desires. Learning to reconcile and accept these contradictions is a step toward greater freedom.

The stress involved in finding a partner or connecting with an existing partner can be substantial. As we seek companionship, whether for an evening, a lifetime, or something in between, we are immediately confronted by insecurity, doubts, fear of rejection, and the wholesale discomfort of the entire process. We lie, drink, settle, and cheat to try to get what we want. We are often distracted. We hesitate. We make excuses. We feed resentment and insecurity when we subjugate ourselves to fear, doubts, and insecurities. The sheer distress often provokes us to turn to poor solutions in an attempt to make up for the perceived deficit, or to avoid the process altogether.

Practicing embodied consciousness is a way to confront discomfort and be ok with it. Fear of rejection turns into embracing uncertainty, a survival stress tool staple. Boldly facing the unknown replaces the need to self-medicate the discomfort away and hoping we won't have to face the challenge.

Pursuing a partner, new or long-term, can create a great deal of undesirable tension. This tension can be debilitating—or we can shift our mindset, allowing the risk to cultivate desire, augment creativity, and fuel exhilaration instead of tension. Bringing about awareness in the body and brain alike allows for this shift to occur. It is incredibly liberating.

For some, the sexual experience relies primarily or solely on alcohol, drugs, and porn. The question of whether such methods lubricate good sex is not easy to answer. But if we start as a fully-present individual by embracing uncertainty and discomfort, and if we move past the negative side of fear, then we are free to utilize methods that heighten particular moments and encounters. Whatever substances, visuals, toys, or games you and your partner choose to use is up to you. We simply don't want to turn to such resources for fear of an inability to access the erotic, the intimate, or the sensual. Knowing how to intentionally activate and steer the stress response and manage its flow, arousal level, and direction eliminates the idea that something other than the humans involved in the sexual encounter is necessary.

State Shifts and Mood

Life is full of moments when shifting focus from responsibilities to sexual desire can be a challenge. And I'm not talking about a seven- or eight-hour marathon in the bedroom. That kind of sex simply isn't practical if we want to be intimate with any kind of frequency and still pay the mortgage, raise kids, travel, read, or whatever combination of activities makes up your life. What we need is a way to engage consistently, deeply, and seamlessly, so that the time we do spend in an intimate setting with our partner yields all the mental, emotional, and physical benefits it can.

The time needed to transition from ordinary tasks to intimacy can create difficulties and mismatched timing among couples. However, knowing how to actively and fluidly shift mental and arousal states can greatly alleviate these problems. This is one key situation wherein knowing how to willfully induce a stress response using a combination of the breath and embodied consciousness is extremely useful—especially a stress response that is controlled. To intentionally make this shift, you must have the ability to generate *enough stress* for heightened sexual excitement, as well as learn how to mitigate outside stressors that impair the sexual domain. Making the shift also involves guiding one's hormonal balance, thereby improving the ability to rise to such occasions and limiting physical setbacks like impaired vascular capacity.

Managing Risks

There are many risks involved in sex. I do not wish to suggest that everyone should be out training for sex through sport fucking. Sex can have consequences, including STIs, unwanted pregnancy, and emotional fallout to name but a few. There's also the simple, but sometimes overlooked, hygienic habits we need to observe such as washing our hands and toys. Not washing either can easily lead to infections and health problems. To heighten one's sense of adventure and excitement by pursuing partners in quantity, rather than for quality, tends to substantially elevate risk. Though I am not here to lecture on how many sexual partners you should have, it is always advisable to practice safer sex utilizing condoms and birth control, and to get tested often. Don't be afraid to request that your partner use protection. Don't be afraid to ask to see your partner's test results. If a partner refuses these responsible, proactive, and transparent practices, seriously consider choosing another partner. Don't be afraid to tell your partner exactly what you are looking for. Being upfront and clear with what you want—a relationship or just an evening together—is a good practice to build trust, truthfulness, and clarity in your relationships. Avoid the road of manipulation. Be extremely cautious whenever drugs or alcohol are part of the equation. There is no such thing as implied consent, especially under the influence of substances.

Final Thoughts on Sex

Once you know how to state shift on command, discomfort is replaced with curiosity, fear fades while excitement and intrigue take the helm, mystery is restored for exploration, and you get to unleash your creativity to cultivate desire: to want and to be wanted. The knobs and levers to control all of this are located in the nervous system and your ability to tap into it to master stress.

Preparing our bodies by living a lifestyle that harnesses stress is one precursor to great sex. And make no mistake about it: Even if you are already having good sex, by improving your hormonal balance, vascular strength, and conscious attention, the door to having earth-shattering sex will be opened.

BREATHE

WE HAVE EXPLORED several survival stress tools that can help us combat chronic stress & get closer to optimal. These tools fortify our immune function and strengthen our vascular systems. We have learned to improve physical prowess and refine our sensory perceptions and awareness. We have examined why discomfort is so important to include in training. We have seen how survival stress tool training helps to form bonds between individuals in a variety of arenas. We have seen how these tools help us modulate high stress and allow us to approach life and face fears with calm focus.

The Breathe tool, when used correctly, is the portal that offers direct access to your nervous system so you can use it for maximum benefits and results. Via proper applications, you can induce an acute stress response to harness stress and/or experience rest states as desired. Proper use of the Breathe tool will allow you to establish healthy breathing patterns, improve immune function, optimize hormones, reset your nervous system baseline operations, and refine nervous system messaging. This training will also strengthen your respiratory operation and cardiovascular health, improve blood flow and healing, rapidly clear metabolic waste, and vastly improve recovery times. Mentally and psychologically, breathing techniques help to confront fear of death, resolve traumas, improve focus, and heighten flow state potential. Breath is the physical, mental, and emotional rudder that steers the nervous system for peak human performance. When combined with the other survival stress tools presented in this book, you will unlock ever-growing peak potential.

Take a breath. Let it go. Did you feel that? Pay close attention. Try it again. Take a breath. Let it come in. Let it go. Observe. Do it again. The breath is the doorway to the nervous system. It's your access point to physical, mental, and emotional control.

We can debate when life begins but I'm certain that no matter your beliefs, the first breath a baby takes is evidence of life—awe-inspiring life. I clearly remember my daughter's birth. I can recall the bright fluorescent lights, the smell of the delivery room, the drab pink, blue, and turquoise furniture and paint meant to compliment the brightness and joy of parents-to-be.

When it was time for the pushing to happen, I was front and center, ready to catch my new baby girl. As she came out, her skin was a startling pallor, contrasting with the black hair on top of her head and dusty blonde bangs. She looked like a beach baby who had fallen asleep after a long day of sun, and I was interrupting her nap.

For a moment, her eyes were closed and her body was tense. Then she took her first breath and exploded with a momentous wail. With that cry, her color changed to a purplish-red. The sound reverberated around the whole room. It was her nervous system's signal that all was in proper order. Through my tears, I smiled with the purest joy I've ever known. Hearing the sound of a first breath, my own breath lodged a lump in my throat. How precious life is! This story reminds me that breath is life, something we so often take for granted 20,000 times per day, the average number of breaths a human takes in a twenty-four-hour cycle.

What is breathing? In the simplest of terms, it is the process of using oxygen and expelling carbon dioxide to fulfill energy requirements. In order to breathe, oxygen is taken from the atmosphere and inhaled into the lungs, and carbon dioxide is exhaled from the lungs back into the atmosphere. The primary reasons humans breathe include:

1. **Health**: To provide oxygen to the trillions of cells throughout your body and eliminate carbon dioxide, regulate pH, trap and dissolve blood clots, protect against outside pathogens, and influence chemical messengers (in the arterial pulmonary blood capillaries). The meaning and takeaway of this speaks to foundational health. In order for our bodies to be healthy and function well, every one of our trillions of cycles needs the fundamental element of oxygen. In order to prevent strokes, our lungs must dutifully deal with blood

clots. In order for the system to prioritize action and rest states, our breath acts as a communicator, so that the vascular system widens or restricts our vessels appropriately. To keep us from becoming sick, our respiratory system helps function as an immune defender.

2.   **Energy Production:** To supply the necessary ingredients so that oxygen-dependent processes such as cellular respiration can take place. It is by cellular respiration that the body breaks down glucose into carbon dioxide, thereby releasing energy. Breathing better by getting oxygen to the cells results in energy production that is fifteen to twenty times more efficient. Breathing better by being efficient and intentional with our breathing habits literally equals more energy.

3.   **Better Flow:** To create a respiratory pump to assist with pressure and flow needed throughout the body. The respiratory pump increases the overall pressure difference between the peripheral veins and the heart, a critical component to keep the body's blood moving and flowing. This highlights the need to breathe at different frequencies and to create different pressures. It serves as a reminder that gravity is always exerting its force and necessitates a strong heart and vascular system aided by the life force of oxygen.

Humans are high-oxygen-demand beings, and we live a very short time without an adequate supply of oxygen to our bodies—on the order of minutes. Because of this fact, we have a series of built-in mechanisms to ensure that enough oxygen gets to where it needs to go. Because oxygen is of absolute importance when it comes to survival, when any of these mechanisms fail to work properly, or struggle to maintain efficiency and effectiveness, we compromise our health, our energy production and our blood flow, whether at rest or under high-intensity demand. This has profound implications on our physical, mental and emotional health and performance. The habits and conditioning of the human body are influenced tremendously by what we each choose to do on a given day. Having a consistent breath practice, one that you start each day with upon waking, will produce incredible results. The ideal practice will have a short-term stress component and a rest and recovery component. It can take as little as ten to fifteen minutes of your day. This will help you wake up better and clearer, help keep your bowels regular, and set a tone for the day, to name just a few of the benefits.

Breathing is an autonomic process, meaning it is governed automatically without having to think about it. But breathing can also be influenced voluntarily by the motor cortex of your brain; your conscious attention and direction can build proper breathing habits that will support better health, maximize performance, and give you a deep-seated control of your mind and body. Developing your breath is not just about surviving, it is about learning to use it to thrive.

When approaching breath development, it is helpful to understand the possible variables when it comes to breathing itself, as well as those you may encounter when you begin to explore breathing exercises with specific applications.

I have included many exercises in this book. I discuss breathing mechanics along with a series of applications to offer a clear understanding of how breathing functions, what variables you can practice to develop greater breath control, and how to maximize breathing in every circumstance. With these exercises, you will have a solid foundation on which to build principle-based applications. This means that regardless of the stress-inducing activity, you will have a clear idea of how to manage your breath for optimal results. For a supplemental tutorial, check out the breathing videos and classes I offer at mattsoule.com.

For now, let's explore helpful aspects of breathing so that we can uncover not only what makes it possible, but what parts we can influence to make it ideal under a variety of conditions.

There are three overarching components to breathing: the physical, the neurophysiological, and the mental-emotional.[72] All three have an integral role in how breathing affects the performance of an individual under different circumstances. They all overlap and interrelate. However, from a learning and teaching perspective, this separation provides clearer insight into what variables you can influence so that your training best serves you. Over- or under-emphasizing the influence of any of the components is a grave mistake. Understanding the role of each and how they interrelate is not only illuminating, it is the key to mastering your breath.

Part 1 – The Physicality of Breathing

The physicality of breathing includes your chest, ribs, intercostals (the space in between your ribs), diaphragm, and auxiliary breathing muscles, as well as the coordination of your mouth, nose, and throat. Compliance and elasticity—how easily the lungs stretch and how easily they return to original form after expanding—contributes to the ease or difficulty you experience as you breathe. The volume of air taken in with each breath and how well your heart pumps blood around the body to distribute oxygen are two other factors.

Existing breathing patterns and the tensions that you subconsciously or voluntarily create throughout your body contribute to your breathing success. This includes tensions in the tongue, soft palate, spaces between the soft and hard palate, jaw, mid-section, valves in your venous system, and muscles in your body. The strength of the various muscles involved and different postures assumed while breathing contribute greatly as well. Vocalizations and coordinating them with various tensions and postures also contributes to the physical expression of breathing.

The good news is that with specific training, you can strengthen your breathing muscles, remold your connective tissues, and improve your ability to control tension, include vocalizations, and coordinate multiple variables. In doing so, you will more easily be able to manage the depth, and pace of your breathing. The rhythm and flow of your breath will be smooth and optimally functional.

The primary muscles that contract when you breathe include your diaphragm and intercostal muscles. Your diaphragm is a thick, ribbon-like muscle that wraps completely around your midsection. It separates your lungs from other organs. Muscles in your abdominals relax to make room for the diaphragmatic contraction when you breathe in. This action pulls the diaphragm muscle down to create a larger cavity in which your lungs can expand.

When your abdominals release tension to allow the diaphragm to function, it leaves you potentially vulnerable in certain contexts on an inhalation. Have you ever been hit in the stomach by something and gotten the wind knocked out of you? Now you know why.

The auxiliary muscles used in breathing include your pectoralis minor, the sternocleidomastoid, and the scalene muscles. But also involved are the abdominals and obliques, as well as the tongue, soft palate, jaw muscles, and lips and throat muscles, which foster nuanced control.

When you take a breath, your ribs expand upward and outward and your sternum moves forward. The bigger the breath, the greater the movement. This upward and outward expansion increases the thoracic cavity space to allow the lungs to expand when you inhale.

So upon inhalation, the full action is as follows: the diaphragm pulls itself down, the intercostals move up and out, and the sternum moves forward, creating one continuous, multi-directional expansion, like a balloon being inflated. Upon exhalation, the diaphragm returns to a flat position and the intercostals move back down, all of which serves to decrease thoracic cavity.

We can practice initiating low in the diaphragm when we breathe, work on thoracic breathing by focusing on intercostal expansion, or even fill the clavicular space to maximize breath volume. However, the foundation for an optimal breath is to understand how different depth and rates of breathing will affect the outcomes we pursue. In all cases we need to use good timing while creating proper tension to control speed and air flow.

Exploring Capacity

Let's take a few different breaths to explore volume capacity. Start off breathing easy. In other words, try not to put any effort in either the inhale or the exhale. Just breathe quietly. Let the air flow in and out. You may find this easiest using primarily the nose, or inhaling through the nose and exhaling through the mouth. Notice how small the breath is. This is called tidal volume: the total amount of air coming in and going out during quiet, unforced breathing. Very little tension is present. Relatively few muscles are involved.

For an adult male, tidal volume tends to average approximately 500 ml per breath: 500 ml in and 500 ml out. This is roughly equivalent to a 17-oz travel mug full of air. However, there is dead space in the conducting airways of our anatomy. There is also a little dead space in the alveoli.[73] The total amount of dead space is about 150 ml, which reduces the volume of air inhaled or exhaled in any given breath. *Much of our normal breathing should be around tidal volume or just slightly above. This will help us remain calm and far less stressed throughout the day. In other words, we can and should engage in deliberate short-term stress activities and push our breathing to its full capacity, modulating it as needed. However, once we return to the more restful states post-stress, our goal is to recover quiet, rhythmic inspiration and expiration which will very often resemble tidal volume.*

When you breathe in, oxygen moves from the lungs to the blood. The heart pumps the blood to distribute oxygen to the tissues via the arteries. Then the deoxygenated blood is pumped back to the heart via the venous system, which has valves to ensure that blood does not flow backward. This entire process is commonly referred to as the venous blood return to the heart. Because gravity is always exerting a force on the body and blood, the heart's pumping and the valves' assistance in the veins are vital to keep the flow moving continuously in the same direction. When a person is walking or moving, muscles in the legs assist with this process. This is one reason why sitting all day can negatively impact your heart—it has to work harder without leg muscles to assist it.

During exercise, blood circulation is less affected by gravity because the working muscles in the body, especially the legs, assist the directional blood flow. At rest, this is less so. Bear this fact in mind whenever you practice breathing exercises at rest, especially if the exercises involve a faster pace of breathing. I recommend you sit or lie down when practicing most breathing exercises. The exception, of course, is breath training for specific activities. This is covered in more detail later in the book, as well as in the breath control series I offer on mattsoule.com.

Now let's explore a more active breath. While seated or lying down in a safe area, take some deep breaths. First, we'll focus on inhalation. Breathe slowly as we do this exercise. As we engage our breathing muscles and auxiliary muscles to maximize our breath intake, you should notice just how much more air you can take in during this concerted effort. In fact, the average is approximately 3,100 ml more than when just quietly inhaling. Take two more deep inhales slowly to really feel the difference. Avoid straining or trying to breathe in or out more than you can. Just go to the spot where you have exerted effort to fill your lungs completely. Avoid lifting your shoulders, as that will impair your ability to maximize volume. Go slowly to avoid injury.

With a good, deep breath, you should feel the entire thoracic cavity expand in all directions. The amount of air beyond tidal volume to maximum inhalation is known as the inspiratory reserve volume. If you want to know your total inspiratory capacity, you would need to add tidal volume to inspiratory reserve volume. It is usually around 3,600 ml. *Working on reaching full capacity can help us strengthen the respiratory muscles and remold connective tissue over time. The result is that we are able to take a large breath more easily.*

Next, actively focus on the exhalation. Don't just go back to the tidal volume exhalation—what I often refer to as lung neutral—but push all the air that you can out of your lungs. You'll notice your abs and obliques are hard at work, but make sure you also engage your lips and throat to maximize the full exhalation. The amount of air that you can fully exhale with maximal effort is approximately 1,200 ml and is called the expiratory reserve volume. This does not include the tidal volume. If you want to know your full exhalation capacity, add the tidal volume and the expiratory reserve volume. In this example, it would be around 1,700 ml. *Practicing full exhales can also assist with building stronger respiratory muscles and extend your full range of motion.*

Now, you might think that you have gotten rid of all of the air in your lungs, because it feels like there is nothing left to push out. In fact, there is a fair amount of air left in your lungs, approximately another 1,200 ml. Without this reserve, your lungs would collapse. This leftover air that keeps your lungs inflated is called the residual volume. So, although while quietly breathing we inhale and exhale a volume of around 1000 ml in, our total lung capacity is about six times that amount, around 6,000 ml. *You can work on developing your lung capacity by engaging in these efforts that push and stretch both sides of the inspiratory and expiratory volumes.*

Posture

Let's take a look at ideal posture while performing stationary breathing exercises, so that you have a solid baseline from which to operate. I recommend that you start by lying down on your back. Bend your legs so that your lower back is flat on the ground. Your pelvis should be very slightly tucked while holding a neutral spine. Align your chin position so that your neck is not bent, but flat and neutral. If you need to, you can put a pillow or bolster underneath your knees or neck for support. As you practice different breathing exercises, whether seated, lying down, or even standing, you will often want to refer to this ideal posture.

Take a few easy breaths in this position. Then take three breaths fully in and fully out. Notice if or where any restrictions impede your ability to take a full breath. Adjust your posture in the hips, knees, back, or chin to see if you can find better alignment.

Next, come to a seated position. Feel free to cross your legs if sitting on the floor, or find a comfortable chair. If you need support in the seated position, a floor cushion or pillow can assist you here too. Assuming ideal posture in the pelvis, lower back, spine, neck, and chin, breathe easily in this position. Then take three breaths fully in and fully out. Make sure to avoid slouching or arching, as both will interfere with ideal posture. Notice if or where any restrictions impede your ability to take a full breath. Adjust your posture in the hips, knees, back, or chin to see if you can find better alignment.

Next, come to a standing position. Find the posture that mimics the alignments of ideal posture. Here, you will need slightly bent knees, a neutral pelvis, a natural spine with a gentle curve, and an aligned neck and chin. Take a few easy breaths followed by three large breaths. Notice if you are having trouble getting a full breath or if you need to adjust your posture.

Finally, try one more position. While standing, bend your legs, put your hands on your thighs close to your knees, and find the neutral spine, slightly tucked pelvis, and aligned neck and chin of ideal posture. Take a few easy breaths followed by three large breaths. Repeat the same assessments as above.

Questions to ask yourself:

1. *Did you arch your back, lift your shoulders, cock your chin, or twist or strain in any position in an attempt to take a larger breath?* If so, repeat the exercises above, this time avoiding those problems.

2. *Did you get lightheaded in any of the positions?* Since we only took a few breaths, any lightheadedness should be a signal to slow your breathing pace. Lightheadedness happens for a couple of reasons. One is an autonomic function of your nervous system that constricts or dilates smooth muscles and blood vessels in order to meet perceived demand. In other words, deeper and/or faster breathing can induce a stress response and rapidly shift your blood pressure.

Another possible reason is that you have poor venous blood return to the heart. You may have a relatively weaker vascular system that cannot keep blood flow rate appropriate to breathing pace/volume. The timing is off and therefore, the body's equilibrium is off. Gravity also plays a role here. This is why I typically advise lying or sitting down when performing most breathing exercises, so you don't have the extra burden of gravity.

A third reason is that you are not taking a proper breath and too much air is getting lost to anatomical dead space. Since not enough air and thus oxygen is actually entering your system, you are starving your body of the oxygen it needs and feeling the effects. This typically only becomes an issue when the pace of breathing is rapid and shallow, but nevertheless be aware of this possibility.

Nose and Mouth

For this practice, go ahead and lie down or sit in a comfortable position.

When you breathe, you can do so with the nose, the mouth, or both simultaneously. Let's try that now.[74] Closing your mouth, use just your nose to breathe in and out. If you are a bit stuffed up, just proceed easily and you'll likely find your ability improving. If you are still struggling, keep returning to this idea as you practice more. Eventually you will regain your ability to breathe with only the nose.

For many years, I had chronic sinusitis and therefore struggled greatly to use my nose effectively. However, after building awareness and practicing nose breathing regularly, I vastly improved this ability. Today, I no longer suffer from sinusitis and haven't for many years. So while a few exceptions, such as structural defects or injuries, may take more time to overcome, your improvement with consistent practice is likely to be quite rapid.

Nose breathing accomplishes a number of things. It warms and moistens the air, filters out particles, automatically slows the pace of breathing, and ties you into your surroundings through smells and scents. It offers a natural resistance that helps engage the diaphragm to full capacity. Upon inhalation, the nose pulls in nitric oxide produced in the paranasal cavity located in the sinuses. All of these are great benefits and reasons to practice using the nose.

Next, breathe only through your mouth; this method of breathing has several features as well. You will likely notice that when you breathe through your mouth, you naturally pull in much more air at a much faster rate. This can be adjusted by altering tension in your throat, shifting how you engage the soft palate, and changing the degree to which your jaw is open or closed. Where you place your tongue and your teeth also contributes to mouth breathing. Adjust positions to see how it affects your breathing. The mouth allows for maximized volume, more nuanced control, and more efficient exhalation, especially during higher-demand activities. Breathing through the mouth can also conserve the nitric oxide produced in the sinuses.

Next, breathe in through the nose and out through slightly pursed lips. The advantages of this type of breathing are those of nose breath combined with a faster, less restrictive outflow of carbon dioxide from the mouth. It increases nitric oxide consumption, as you breathe in the nitric oxide via the paranasal cavity.

Finally, let's try breathing through both the nose and mouth simultaneously. If you are struggling to coordinate these actions, be patient. You may find that initiating the breath with the nose and then adding the mouth as you continue to inhale is helpful to build this coordination. Keep practicing; with time, this becomes effortless.

Vocalizations

Vocalizations, such as humming or other short bursts of sound that assist with muscular tension and contractions upon exhalation, are useful for several reasons. When humming, the vibration creates oscillations during nitric oxide production, assisting greater quantity intake and improved flow of nitric oxide to the smooth muscles. This improves oxygen delivery to the heart, among other benefits. Humming can also have a mental effect, as will be discussed in the mental-emotional section of breathing, and it can help with breathing rhythm and reducing tension. I often use the rhythmic advantage of humming while running or mountain climbing. Short-burst vocalizations, on the other hand, assist with contractions prior to a tension load, such as striking or kicking a heavy bag, lifting weights, or exploding through a rock-climbing maneuver.

Pressure

As a very basic function, it is important to understand that breathing relies on a series of pressures that move from greater to lesser. Though there are many pressures, I want to focus on the practical here that we can implement.

During quiet inhalation, the diaphragm and intercostals contract and the volume in the lung cavities increases, while the pressure in the lungs decreases relative to the atmosphere. This allows the air to move from the atmosphere into the lungs. During forced or active inhalation, the muscles create an even larger cavity, thus providing a larger volume that further decreases pressure in the lungs.

No muscles are involved in quiet or passive exhalation. This action relies on elasticity, which reduces the volume of the lung cavity and thereby increases the pressure in the lungs relative to the atmosphere. During forced exhalation, abdominal muscles, external obliques, and internal intercostals are all hard at work further decreasing lung volume, which simultaneously increases the pressure in the lungs relative to the atmosphere.

In all cases (quiet or active inhalation or exhalation), air continues to move in or out of the lungs until atmospheric and alveolar pressures are equal.

Then there are the gases that move from higher concentration to lower concentration. These pressures are expressed as partial pressures, because the gas concentration makes up only a part of the whole. For example, after you exhale, there is a greater pressure of air (and with it, oxygen) in the atmosphere than in your lungs. This allows you to inhale. The oxygen in your blood is at a lesser pressure than in your lungs, so oxygen moves from your lungs to your blood. There is still less oxygen pressure in your tissues (your muscles, organs, your brain), so oxygen then moves to those tissues. Once your body has used the oxygen, it exhales carbon dioxide based on the same set of pressures, just in reverse order. In the body, the greatest pressure of carbon dioxide is in the tissues; it is progressively lower in the blood, the lungs, and finally the atmosphere.

This is the most basic idea of how pressures enable breathing. The essential takeaway is that pressure moves from greater to lesser. When air density shifts, as it does at high altitude, it becomes harder for the gas flow to move as easily.

Putting it All Together

The physical part of breathing, as I define it here, focuses on ventilation, volume of air, certain lung mechanics, muscular tension, muscle strength, and muscular control. The physical ease or difficulty of breathing is based on muscle strength and efficiency; compliance; elasticity; connective tissue around the thoracic cavity; ideal posture; vocalizations; rhythm; use of the nose, the mouth, or both; varying breath volumes and capacities; and the basics of gas pressures moving from greater to lesser. In the mental-emotional section, I will include additional exercises to improve each of these variables. Be mindful that as you practice, it is important to be patient with yourself and go slowly enough to learn each part before integrating the next piece. Finally, you will need to reassess each piece as you integrate more individual parts and develop a clearer understanding of how everything interrelates.

The physical involves the lungs, the diaphragm, and all the auxiliary muscles used to breathe. The auxiliary breathing muscles are the pectoralis minor, the scaleni, and the sternocleidomastoid muscles. Typically, leg muscles are the primary helpers in efficient venous blood return to the heart.

The mouth, nose, and tubes that lead into the lungs—namely the pharynx, larynx, trachea, and bronchi—make up the breathing conduits. There is anatomical dead space that is created with each breath. In other words, not all the air entering through the breathing conduits actually gets into the body for gas exchange to occur. We will go over gas exchange in detail in the next section.

In order to be effective in training the physical aspect of breathing, you should follow five steps:

Step 1
Observe your existing breathing patterns. Do you tend to have difficulty taking a full breath? Do you breathe easily and softly? Do you breathe rhythmically? Where do you feel tightness when you take a breath? Just observe yourself.

Step 2
Work on volume by taking quiet, unforced breaths and full, active breaths in different postures, *starting with the ideal postures* mentioned earlier in this section. Then, try the following postures:

• Lying flat on your back, bend your knees and bring your feet together in a butterfly shape. Extend your arms out wide and as high over your head as you can. The backs of your arms should be flat on the ground.

• Support your hips with your hands and put your feet up in the air.

• Gently let your feet come over your head in a pike position so that your lungs are crunched.

• While lying on your back, bend one leg and tuck that foot behind the straightened leg, draping your knee across. Open your arms wide in a T shape. This will twist you near the waist and restrict the diaphragm. Work to breathe at different volumes and different paces. Start slow and easy.

Step 3

Work on coordinating tensions in your throat and tongue while taking two to ten breaths with your mouth using different volumes of unforced and active breathing.

• Open your throat wide while keeping your teeth close together.

• Open your throat and mouth wide.

• Open your mouth and restrict your throat, moving your tongue back toward your throat.

• Place your top teeth on your bottom lip so that the air entering your mouth is very restricted. Try to open your throat to reduce some of the restriction.

• Clench your jaw and open your lips so you can still breathe through your mouth. Move your tongue backward toward your throat.

Step 4

Work on nose breathing by closing your mouth and adding vocalizations. Take five to ten breaths.

• Breathe in with your nose, and as you breathe out, make a humming noise.

• Breathe in with your nose, and as you breathe out, make a humming noise as above. However, with your mouth closed, place your teeth close together and put your tongue on the roof of your mouth as you do this.

• Breathe in with your nose, and as you breathe out, make a humming noise as above. This time, while keeping your lips closed completely, make an O shape with your mouth. The hum will become more of an "OM" sound.

Step 5

Combine breathing through the nose and the mouth. Take five to ten breaths.

• Breathe in with your nose and out with your mouth. Practice unforced and active breathing volumes.

• Breathe in with your nose and your mouth simultaneously, then breathe out with your mouth.

• Breathe in with your nose and mouth simultaneously, then breathe out with your nose and mouth simultaneously.

• Breathe in with your nose and mouth simultaneously and add a humming noise as you breathe out.

The above exercises are not an exhaustive list, nor do you need to do all in a single session. Working on any and all of the above will help you tie into the different muscles at work as you breathe, allow you to become aware of existing patterns, and help build coordination. Further exploration can include trying new combinations while focusing on the physical elements of breathing.

Be mindful that as you practice, it is important to be patient with yourself and to go slowly enough to learn each part before integrating the next piece. Finally, you will need to reassess each piece as you integrate more individual parts and develop a clearer understanding of how everything interrelates.

As we breathe, life-giving oxygen travels to the lungs. There, the bronchi branch into an increasing number of ever smaller, narrower tubes (termed bronchioles), which become even more numerous tubes (alveolar ducts), which finally lead to clusters of alveolar sacs. It all looks like the beautiful roots of a tree. It is in the alveoli that oxygen is transferred to the blood, its transportation to the tissues.

The conducting airways are surrounded by smooth muscle that, upon relaxation or contraction, can partially open or restrict the airways. These actions are largely an autonomic function. However, they can be influenced by the nose and mouth; the pace, volume, and vocalization of each breath; and a combination of the emotional-mental regulation of smooth muscles and intentional innervation of skeletal muscles.

With that in mind, let's turn to the second part of breathing.

Part 2 – The Neurophysiology of Breathing

In the introduction, I mentioned that breathing is automatic yet capable of being influenced. Breathing is primarily controlled by respiratory centers located in the brainstem. Located there are the pons and the medulla and within each of those exists parts that control different aspects of our breathing. Involved in the autonomic process are also receptors that receive signals from the body and send them to these respiratory centers which results in changing the rate and depth of breathing.

You may have heard that carbon dioxide, not oxygen, is the primary breathing stimulus. This is true until a certain level of oxygen deficit is reached, at which point oxygen becomes the primary driver. In a more typical circumstance, it is carbon dioxide that provides the breathing stimulus. The medulla has central chemoreceptors that detect changes in the pH of the cerebral spinal fluid and inter-

278

stitial brain fluid. These chemoreceptors respond to carbon dioxide buildup; once it reaches a certain threshold, the central chemoreceptors signal a breathing response.

Also in the medulla, there are specialized groups that respond to signals from stretch receptors in the lungs; proprioceptors in tendons, joint capsules, and muscle spindles; juxtacapillary receptors around the interstitial fluid, bronchi, and alveoli; and central and peripheral receptors. Other groups have connections to the C3, C4, C5, and T1-T11 nerves, which are involved in breathing. In other words, there is a lot of information traveling from various receptors to these respiratory groups that will influence breathing in order to meet the needs of the body.

Below the medulla, a somatic nerve called the phrenic nerve begins near the cervical spinal roots at C3, C4, and C5, then travels to the diaphragm, which it innervates. The phrenic nerve can also stimulate the T1-T11 nerves, which contracts the intercostals. Certain parts of the respiratory control centers send stimulatory or inhibitory from the control centers to these nerves to regulate breathing.

Other influences on our breathing come from the limbic area and the hypothalamus as we will explore in the mental-emotional section. For a brief primer, you can think of the limbic area as an emotional contributor and the hypothalamus as the director of homeostasis. As our emotions, anticipations and homeostatic disruptions take place, these can all influence the breathing control centers automatically. An easy example of this was discussed in the Freeze section with the cold shock response we experience upon entering cold water. We often take a large gasp and follow that up with breathing that is rapid until we adapt. The emotions the cold evokes is influenced by the limbic area and the stress response induced triggers activation of hypothalamus. These brain centers and their interfaces with the various receptors located throughout the body contributes not only to our responses but also to our existing patterning.

Voluntary breathing is controlled via the corticospinal tract. This is a motor pathway that sends signals directly from the cerebral cortex directly to stimulate the phrenic and intercostal nerves. It bypasses the respiratory control centers. This pathway is used in volitional breathing and also used in breath-holds. Using this pathway, while practicing controlling emotions and engaging the hypothalamus can help us influence, disrupt and reset some of the autonomic processes of breathing.

We can learn new patterns, thereby setting a new baseline of operations, by inducing an acute stress response, but also by becoming more aware of our breathing throughout the day and learning to slow our breathing and/or change its depth. We can train our systems to temporarily handle more oxygen or more carbon dioxide, i.e. create a short-term stress, that will help our automatic breathing processes re-engage fully and adapt. Our active influence can play a key role in helping our autonomic operation to be optimal. The goal is not to pay constant attention to our breathing; simply setting a time to focus on it—as little as ten to fifteen minutes per day—can set you down the path of creating better patterning.

Gas Exchange

The exchange between oxygen and carbon dioxide happens with each breath. The simplest definition of the process is that oxygen moves from the alveoli sacs *to* the lung's blood, and carbon dioxide moves *from* the lung's blood to the alveoli sacs.

To be more specific, with each inhalation, oxygen is pulled into the lungs before traveling through the bronchi and into smaller bronchioles. The smooth muscles surrounding the bronchioles constrict or dilate to help control oxygen flow. The constriction and dilation are controlled by the autonomic nervous system. However, a change in depth or rate of breathing—whether volitional or not—will influence the outcomes.

As the oxygen travels beyond the bronchioles, it enters the alveoli. There, oxygen crosses the air-liquid membrane to interface with the blood. In our blood, we have a very important protein called hemoglobin. Hemoglobin is like a car that shuttles oxygen from the alveoli to the tissues that need it. In one red blood cell, there are roughly 250 million hemoglobin molecules, each of which has the capacity for four oxygen molecules. That means there is the potential for one billion molecules of oxygen per red blood cell!

The four units in a hemoglobin molecule can be understood as seats in the car. Both oxygen and carbon dioxide compete for these seats, and there is power in numbers. When there is a great deal of oxygen present, like in the lungs, oxygen gets most or all of the seats. When more carbon dioxide is present, like in certain tissues, oxygen gets offloaded and carbon dioxide gets a ride.

Hemoglobin also has other chemistry that helps it determine which molecule, oxygen or carbon dioxide, gets priority. Each hemoglobin is a heme group with four subunits called globin chains.[75] That is where hemoglobin gets its name. The globin chains are proteins made up of amino acids. To keep to our analogy, the globin chains act like automatic seat belts; they are locked or unlocked according to signals from associated chemical components: bi-carbonate, protons, and 2,3 bisphosphoglyceric acid (BPG).

Hemoglobin's state shifts depending on these chemical components. For example, blood returning to the heart contains hemoglobin in the T state, which has little oxygen bound to it. Instead, this hemoglobin has a high affinity for carbon dioxide, protons, and 2,3 BPG. When the blood passes through the lungs and picks up oxygen at the alveoli, its state shifts through a process called positive cooperativity: One oxygen is bound to the hemoglobin, making it easier for the next molecule of oxygen to do likewise, and the next. The end result is that the hemoglobin unloads its carbon dioxide, protons, and 2,3 BPG and changes to the R state, in which it has a very high affinity for oxygen.

This process happens very quickly. However, it is dependent on the blood moving directionally and at a pace that keeps up with the need to expel the carbon dioxide created by breathing and energy output. The three main limitations to ideal gas exchange (although there can be other factors) are the heart/blood flow, hemoglobin concentration, and combating gravity. If you are lacking in any of these three, your peak potential will be hampered. A heart that suffers from lack of exercise, a vascular system that is weak, insufficient hemoglobin, or legs too weak to assist deoxygenated blood in returning to the heart will all be problematic. Training with high-intensity workouts, such as martial arts, using breath holds and altitude training to increase EPO, thus finding more ideal hemoglobin concentrations, and making sure to strengthen the legs will all contribute to a more ideal composition for better gas exchange. Furthermore, rhythmic breathing will help maintain efficient flow.

The two types of respiration, external and internal, have their own complex chemistries and processes. However, there is a simple way to distinguish between the two. External respiration is the process of gas exchange where the blood meets the alveoli. Internal respiration is the process of gas exchange where the blood meets tissue cells. These exchanges result in pressure differences that support a high concentration of oxygen in the lungs; from the lungs, oxygen moves to the alveoli, blood, and tissues, in that order. These exchanges also support the relatively high concentration of carbon dioxide in the tissues; from the tissues, carbon dioxide moves to the blood, alveoli, and finally lungs, where it is breathed out.

Temporarily disrupting gas exchange using hyper and hypo-ventilation techniques are an excellent way to train the body to do *more with more* and *more with less*.

Haldane Effect and the Bohr Effect

When hemoglobin takes on oxygen, it is known as the Haldane Effect. As described, this essentially happens in the lungs. When hemoglobin offloads oxygen and favors carbon dioxide, it is called the Bohr Effect. This generally occurs in the tissues. The strength of the Bohr Effect depends on how much oxygen the tissues need and the temperature of the tissues. Greater oxygen need and higher temperatures mean a stronger Bohr Effect.

There is another molecule in the tissue cells called myoglobin. Myoglobin binds to oxygen very tightly and helps the cell respond to immediate oxygen needs for cellular respiration. A good way to differentiate between hemoglobin and myoglobin is that myoglobin responds to the cell's immediate oxygen needs, while hemoglobin responds to the changing oxygen needs of the cell. Our ability to replenish oxygen requires a fine-tuned balance between the speed and depth of our breathing and our heart and vascular system's ability to carry oxygen to the tissues that need it. Actively using thermogenic training to support this balance is a great addition to becoming more efficient. It is also helpful to push yourself to deplete your oxygen levels; when you do, your body comes back more efficient at the next training.

The essential takeaway regarding the Bohr and Haldane Effects is that they describe hemoglobin's biochemistry's adaptive response to deliver oxygen to tissues on an as-needed basis. Although the details of the biochemistry are unnecessary here, it is important to understand that there are many complex compensatory mechanisms in the human body that shift rapidly to ensure metabolic stability in the system.

The best time to influence these mechanisms is in the training preparation phase of performance. For example, I train in extreme temperatures to assist with thermogenesis, to train my body to do more with less (e.g., hypoventilation and breath holds), and to train my body to handle more (e.g, overloading oxygen through high-metabolic breathing and temporarily influencing blood chemistry). Integrating a breath practice with hypoventilation, hyperventilation and breath holds, temperature, and (if available) altitude training can create an incredibly adaptive system. My personal routine involves daily practice of hypo- and hyperventilation and breath holds. I also use temperature training daily, as noted. Altitude training is more of a rare occurrence due to where I live, but I try to include it when I can.

This training allows me to run for miles at pace, even though I rarely run. It allows me to breathe easily under a number of physical demands. When I do show up to altitude, even extreme altitude like Mt. Kilimanjaro, my body adapts extremely fast. This advantage in performance can hardly be overstated. Perhaps the best benefit overall, though, is my daily experience during periods of rest, relaxation, and sleep. The ease and speed with which my body can shift to these peaceful recovery phases is remarkable.

The Heart and Cardiovascular System

The highway for oxygen and carbon dioxide in the body is the thousands of miles of blood vessels that form a network of distribution. That is a lot of vessels.

To successfully navigate that highway, the blood needs the heart to be an effective pump, and it needs enough hemoglobin to distribute oxygen effectively to the tissues throughout the body. Without good blood flow and hemoglobin, this process is significantly hampered.

The protein EPO can increase hemoglobin. And hypoxic exercises and altitude have been shown to boost EPO.[76] The heart muscle is the primary pump to circulate blood in the body. When you're at rest, your entire blood supply, approximately six quarts, is pumped through your whole body every 60 seconds. During exercise, it is even faster.

The right blood pressure will support the demands of the body and route blood where it needs to go. In order for this to happen, vessels need to constrict and dilate appropriately, muscles need to be replenished by oxygenated blood in a timely manner, and oxygen needs to be used efficiently. Your nervous system monitors the demands of your body, whether at rest or active, and adjusts these factors appropriately.

Blood Flow and Oxygen

Your body naturally seeks balance between how much blood is needed by the body and how much oxygen is present. This relationship is referred to as the V/Q ratio. V refers to ventilation, specifically the alveolar ventilation rate, and Q refers to perfusion, or cardiac output. Cardiac output is a combination of stroke volume, or how much blood is pushed with each heart contraction, and heart rate. The V/Q relationship likes to stabilize at roughly 0.8, when the alveolar ventilation rate is approximately 4,200 ml/minute and cardiac output is approximately 5,000 ml/minute. The ratio is never quite perfect, but it describes the relationship your body seeks.

As a rule, breathing faster and more deeply (i.e., increasing ventilation) triggers the heart rate to increase so that blood flow can match the ventilation. Typically, high ventilation produces nitric oxide in the smooth muscle cells of the lungs, and as a result, increased blood flow occurs. On the other side, decreasing ventilation simultaneously lessens nitric oxide, leading to vasoconstriction in the vessels and decreased blood flow.78 These mechanisms support the body's desire for a balanced V/Q ratio.

The body does not like to waste blood or oxygen. The key takeaway is that autonomic regulation of vasoconstriction and dilation is ever-present and working to balance the available oxygen and blood.

Inadequate oxygen distribution is generally driven by a failing blood supply when oxygen is needed. Therefore, the strength and efficiency of the heart, the available hemoglobin, and the strength and adaptability of the vascular system are paramount as demand increases. To maximize your physical capabilities, you must be efficient in your tension, creating rhythm and controlling perception. You must harness your emotional intensity and learn to increase or decrease it to fit your needs. Unintentionally creating greater tension in your musculoskeletal system, breathing arrhythmically, or giving into fear, which spikes your heart rate in anticipation of perceived demand, all lead to suboptimal performance. Training under difficult conditions and working to refine and control rhythm is the most important consideration here.

Part 3 – The Mental-Emotional Side of Breathing

The mental-emotional side of breathing speaks to how the brain interprets sensory information and makes adjustments based on perceived demand. There are constant bi-directional exchanges among the physical, the mental, and the emotional during any activity. Because we can breathe both automatically and voluntarily, these exchanges can occur automatically or, with developed awareness and practice, be steered voluntarily. If we are intentional about what and how we practice, we can build consistency into habits that will help us experience peak performance results.

In pursuing peak performance, recall that on a micro-curve, every breath in stimulates the action-oriented sympathetic nerves, and every breath out stimulates the rest-oriented parasympathetic nerves, and that the heart experiences the same innervation pattern. The difference between a sympathetic and a parasympathetic heart beat is known as heart rate variability, or HRV. A relatively significant HRV tends to be a positive measure of health. For example, HRV tends to be low in those who have anxiety and PTSD. Furthermore, decision-making abilities have been shown to be negatively affected by a low HRV. Learning how to foster balance between the sympathetic and parasympathetic systems, utilize the breath, and pursue high-threshold activities that promote balance and therefore a greater HRV is of great consequence for positive health outcomes and empowered decision-making skills.

Engaging the brain and body through voluntary breathing exercises is a powerful mechanism when done correctly. Matching blood flow with oxygen intake relative to demand is a process essential to remaining efficient and effective in your breathing. We can, for example, train the body to do more with less by using breath holds to create short-term stress through intentional hypoxia (reduced oxygen in the tissues) and hypoxemia (reduced oxygen in the blood). We can also train the body to handle more oxygen, and the hormonal spike that goes with it, through stress breathing while simultaneously steering the mind to calm, peace, focus, and rapid recovery. This exercise fosters plasticity and adaptability in the system. These exercises also build muscle strength in the respiratory and cardiovascular systems while tapping into the mindful intention.

The premotor and motor cortex are used during volitional breathing and intentional breath holds. When you intentionally breathe, the signal generated in these regions bypass the respiratory centers in the pons and medulla, traveling directly to the C3, C4, C5, and T1- T11 nerves to stimulate the diaphragm and intercostals.

But there is another nerve that is involved in breathing: the vagus nerve. It is the master nerve of the parasympathetic nervous system. Learning to add to extra stimulation to the vagus nerve using larger breaths and longer exhales is one key ingredient to modulating stress in high-demand situations. However, these breaths must be balanced with appropriate tension and a focused mind.

Keep in mind that larger breaths, such as those taken during exercise or intentional breathing practices, also greatly involve the sympathetic nervous system. These breaths, especially those with a focus on the inhale, can produce large amounts of adrenaline and increase the heart rate. Done intentionally for specific goals or under guidance, this is good. However, overdo large breaths emphasizing the speed and depth of an inhale in a pressure situation and you are likely to spin off track at a critical moment when physical, mental, and emotional intensity needs moderation for high-level performance.

Many regions of the brain are affected by breathing. During movement or high-demand exercise, proprioceptors send signals through the spinal cord to an area called the primary somatosensory cortex. This cortex gives us conscious awareness in space while we move and increases the rate and depth of breathing. Having efficiency in this process can be greatly bolstered by experience so that the information being sent increases in its accuracy.

Other areas of the brain affected by breathing are the hypothalamus, the master regulator of hormones, and the limbic system, which receives emotional information. The hypothalamus and the limbic nuclei interface a great deal. Learning how your nervous system responds as you engage in a variety of breathing exercises can teach you to increase or decrease emotional intensity while remaining in control. When you experience a rush of adrenaline or fear, you can show up with courage and resolve through your breath and mindset. The breath and the mindset can also be steered to increase sensory information, whether for pleasure, in the case of sex and intimacy, or to reduce and reinterpret pain, emotional, psychological, or physical.

The meta-knowledge of our bodies to do their own work is

quite remarkable. Our misguided interference, our doubts, our tendency to under- or overthink, our mismanaged timing, our broken rhythms, our distractions, our poor postures, and many other human flaws contribute to inefficiency and ineffectiveness.

One thing we must learn is how to get out of our own way. In other words, learn to recognize when to *consciously* make alterations in our breathing—this should mostly be done in the training regimen. Learn how and when to let go and exist in a space of emptiness and the now—this should be the primary driver in the midst of performance. We must learn how to foster awareness without narrowing our minds too much. Think too much about the shape, color, and size of the pebbles that you walk past, and you'll trip over every one of them.

Variables to Develop Breath Control

The variables in mental-emotional breathing include: conscious attention foci, visualizations, mantras, vocalizations, different speeds of breathing, the depth and placement of each breath, emphasized inhales or exhales (or both), intentional breath holds, unintentional breath holds (and learning to eliminate them), over-breathing (hyperventilation), under-breathing (hypoventilation), intentional contortions, and physical pressure contractions and dynamic tensions throughout the body. In addition, the time an exercise lasts or the number of breaths or breath holds it includes often contributes to different outcomes. Finally, breath training in the light can be a significantly different experience from training in the dark or while blindfolded. All of these variables can be explored solo in a resting posture or with movement, as well as with a partner or in a group.

As you train these variables, be mindful that each new aspect will initially require your attention, leaving you less likely to continue the others. I used a piano analogy earlier that still applies. Learning to play first the right hand and then the left has its own process, but as soon as you combine the two, you must all but start over until the new skill is consistent. Try to be patient as you practice each of these skills individually and together.

Mind, Mantras, Visualizations, and Vocalizations

While seated or lying down, begin to focus your mind on your breath. Feel it go in and out. If a thought comes, let it go and return your focus to your breath. This is the most basic teaching for any number of meditative disciplines.

Once you have learned to do this, the next step is to try linking your breath to a visualization or mantra. For example, visualize a ball of light that gets brighter as you breathe in and dimmer as you breathe out. Another exercise I like is to visualize myself doing a perfect action sequence in slow motion. Yet another option is to breathe in all that is good and breathe out all that is bad. It is often helpful to close your eyes with this exercise.

If you wish to use a mantra, choose a word that is meaningless and repeat it over and over as you breathe. This exercise can be done with open or closed eyes. Another way to use a mantra-like chant is to choose a word that does have meaning, such as "now," and to repeat it as you ready yourself. Sometimes I instruct my intermediate martial arts students to repeat this word when they are sparring.[77]

Once you have learned to focus the mind in these ways, try another: Focus on a space two inches in front of the bridge of your nose. This location is known as the third eye. You can breathe into and out of this space. The third eye is a powerful mind-focusing tool. Color will often shift and morph as you become accustomed to using the third eye.

Yet another exercise is to focus on one specific thing, either in your body or your environs. It could be your heart, your big toe, your blood flow, the sounds in the air, the smells of your surroundings, a partner, and so on. Once you have accomplished this, try focusing on everything, the sounds, the smells, the temperature, the hard or soft seat, the tension in your body—everything at once. As soon as your mind tries to focus on one aspect, immediately let go and re-broaden the scope.

A final exercise I will offer here is to focus on nothing at all. Each time your mind grabs onto something, immediately let it go and return to nothing. This is empty mind meditation, and it is extremely challenging for most people, even after many years of practice. The best way to start is to place yourself in environs where your focus is demanded. A pool of 33°F water should do the trick, as should standing in front of a formidable opponent in martial arts. These situations will allow you to practice being fully here and now with an empty mind. Remember, this will take practice. Your mind's desire to interfere is substantial.

Vocalizations can be used separately or in combination with virtually any of the above methods. One vocalization that most have heard of is an *om*. Take a deep breath and with your exhale, make a round shape with your mouth and hum using your vocal chords. End with an "m" sound. The result is a resonant *om*.

Trying humming with both a closed and open mouth as you breathe. The more humming, the slower the exhale. Try to vary your breath to hum with both long and short breaths as you exhale. As you increase the airflow, you will feel the vibration higher in the back of your sinuses.

In WHM, we commonly use the sounds *hoo* and *ha* as we prepare for cold immersion or recover from getting out of the cold water. *Hoo* and *ha* are also healing sounds used in both Qigong and traditional Chinese medicine. A *tsst* sound on the exhale can be useful when striking a heavy bag, as it can assist with controlling tension. I recommend practicing vocalizations and timing seated, standing, and while practicing different activities.

Speed, Depth, Placement, and Emphasis

There are many ways to practice speed, but without also controlling depth and placement, you can quickly lose control of the breath. Your ability to functionally breathe faster over time will improve, but don't rush it. If you are practicing speed, I recommend starting off with four: a natural speed that does not break the flow of a full breath in and out, a slightly faster speed, an even faster speed, and a rapid speed.

Do these exercises seated or lying down to avoid injury in case you get dizzy. If you are getting lightheaded at any speed don't go faster. Practice the speeds until you have sufficient control to move on without getting dizzy or lightheaded. Explore different positions and be mindful of earlier statements regarding dead space, venous blood return to the heart, and other autonomic functions that will attempt to balance your oxygen and blood.

This exercise will also let you work on depth and placement of the breath. Try breathing first mostly in the diaphragm, then in the chest to experience the contrast. Then try different speeds, expanding fully to maximal capacity. See how fast you can go before you begin to lose focus. If you become dizzy, no matter how few breaths you have taken, STOP. That is your current limit. Work with your body to always remain in control. If you ignore limits here, it will often end with injury. Take your time—there is no rush.

The last component here is to work with all of the above and focus on taking a strong inhale and letting it go without forcing the exhale. Then, try a forced exhale and a no-effort inhale. Finally, try a forced inhale and forced exhale. Again, if you become dizzy, STOP. Notice how forced inhalations and forced exhalations are vastly different experiences. Both are useful.

Hyperventilation/Hypoventilation

All of the speeds described above, with the exception of a natural speed, will lead to hyperventilation if performed while at rest. Practicing managing more oxygen and the accompanying adrenaline and other hormones, along with strengthening muscular contractions while at rest, can help your body become more adaptable.

Hypoventilation, by contrast, lets you practice managing with less oxygen. My favorite exercise that I suggest for my students is a 5/5, 10/10, 15/15, 30/30, 1/1. Those numbers represent breathing in and out for particular amounts of time. For example, the 5/5 is five seconds in and five seconds out, 10/10 is ten seconds in and ten seconds out, and so on. The 1/1 refers to a one-minute inhale and a one-minute exhale. If you are just starting off, I recommend practicing up to thirty seconds a couple of times per week and for at least a few weeks before moving to the one-minute round.

This is a wonderful exercise to develop excellent breath control. Be sure that regardless of timeframe, you fully exhale and fully inhale with each breath. This will require that you control tension, flow, speed, focus, breath placement, and posture. It will also require that you manage your stress, as you will go for a period of time without much oxygen flowing in. For fun variation and practice in my breath training work, I like to practice the 5/5, 10/10, 15/15, 30/30, 1/1 exercise after doing rounds of fast-paced breathing combined with breath-holds.

Breath Holds–Intentional and Unintentional

Breath holds are an excellent practice to train the body to become more efficient at doing more with less. Breath holds can also expand both the top and bottom breathing thresholds, as well as restabilize blood chemistry if combined with high-metabolic breathing (faster-paced breathing).

Breath holds can be performed on the inhale, at lung neutral (tidal volume exhale), or on a large exhale. I recommend including all three in your practice. If the breath hold is preceded by high-metabolic breathing, then it should typically be done seated or lying down.[78] If a breath hold is not preceded by high-metabolic breathing, then practicing while standing or walking can usually be done safely.

Breath holds and contractions are a powerful combination that can elicit highly emotional responses. This combination also increases nitric oxide production. Make sure to practice these seated or lying down to reduce the chance of passing out, and make sure you are in a safe environment. Remember, the goal is to always remain in control. Go easy as you practice contractions with breath holds. Control the tension where you can manage it. Go slowly enough with the contraction that if you start to get lightheaded, you can back off the tension.

Breath holds and contractions are also a great way to produce heat. Five to thirty high-metabolic breaths followed by a breath hold and contraction can quickly generate a great deal of heat. This is especially useful after you have done a longer cold immersion In contrast to the positive effects of intentional breath holds, unintentional breath holds can be deleterious. Therefore, it is very important to train yourself to become aware of these moments and release the breath hold as soon as you catch it. Done at the wrong times, such as in the midst of high intensity performance or other times unaware, they can rapidly de-regulate the blood-flow-oxygen balance in the body leaving you breathless.

Dynamic Tension and Breathing While Intentionally Contorted

Dynamic tension and intentional contortions are ways to combine the practices of breath flow and muscular contraction while varying tension. An example of dynamic tension is squeezing your arm muscles and pressing your hand through space while exhaling slowly. You can also use your leg muscles or abdominals doing the same thing.

Breathing while intentionally contorted is found in many disciplines, such as yoga and martial arts. Practice the following exercise. While lying down on your side with both legs straight, bend one knee and bring the foot of that leg behind your opposite knee. Then open your shoulders so that they are flat on the ground. This will create a gentle twist at your diaphragm. Breathe into the lungs, working for effortless expansion and a full breath.

Another contortion exercise is to lie flat on your back and push your feet into the air so that all of your weight is on your shoulders. You can use your hands to support your hips. Practice breathing full breaths. Then, try putting your feet behind you so that your hips and legs are stacked over your body. Again, try breathing full breaths.

All of these exercises take mental acuity and focus.

Partner and Group Breathing

Partner and group breathing varies depending on the context. For example, you may have a sparring partner who practices crushing you in a submission wrestling session. In that situation, you would practice even breaths while in awkward and contorted positions. You would try to find rhythm, manage cardiac output, and modulate tension so that you can explode into movement when the time comes to escape or attack.

Breathing for intimacy is quite different. Try holding your partner in various positions, such as sitting upright while holding your partner's head in your lap; he or she should be lying down, face up. This places both of you in a good posture to breathe together. Or try a breathing session where both of you lie down and just hold hands while you breathe. Doing this using high-metabolic breathing rhythms along with periodic breath holds and mid-section contractions can produce wild effects.

Group breathing is perhaps one of the most emotional and bonding experiences we can have as humans. It is nothing short of incredible to feel, hear, and see tens, hundreds, or thousands of people united in simultaneous breathwork. Such sessions usually involve high-metabolic breathing exercises, such as WHM, holotropic breathwork, *Kundalini*, and other styles of over-breathing techniques.

When done well, your partner or group experiences can be transformative, emotionally therapeutic, or downright psychedelic. Tread slowly for safety, but don't fear engaging and letting go to experience some of these heights. The potential of breath-guided consciousness development is an unknown.

Back to Breath

When I returned to Seattle from Mt. Kilimanjaro in March of 2019, I wanted to try to glean all I could from my quest for breath. Unfortunately, I had little time to spare for nearly three months. As soon as I got back from Africa, I was immediately thrown into my typical routine of work and home life responsibilities. Then I was back on the road for work, traveling to New York in April and Iceland and the Netherlands in May. On my way back from that trip, I got a call from a friend—a fellow trainer and breath work instructor who was studying shamanic practices in Peru—who told me he was coming to Seattle in a few days' time. He ended up staying with me.

During that visit, he told me about the new psychedelic practices and guidance he was learning. In return, I told him about my experiences on Mt. Kilimanjaro and the various experiments I had done on the mountain. I also told him I wanted to complete similar experiments, using a combination of high-metabolic breathing protocols, breath-holds, and muscular contractions. I would use the same oximeters—the HH and the standard blood oximeter—to read my oxygen saturation levels while I performed the breathing exercises at rest, at sea level. This immediately piqued his interest and he asked if he could join in. I gladly said yes and after I strapped on my oximeters, we laid down on my living room carpet. I filmed the experiment.

Over the course of fifty minutes, using high-metabolic breathing and breath-holds—some of which included muscular contractions—I climbed a virtual mountain without leaving my living room floor. Focusing my mind, I went through multiple speeds of high-volume breath using my mouth and nose. The results were highly similar to those that I had experienced on the mountain, at altitude. When I breathed rapidly and deeply, my blood oximeter quickly showed 99 percent and my HH indicated a tissue saturation level in the mid-seventies. When I held my breath, my blood oxygen dropped into the eighties and my tissue saturation decreased into the sixties.

On and on this went, round after round. I controlled speed, depth, tension, posture, vocalizations: all effortlessly and with a clarity of mind. I did not experience lightheadedness; rather, I was fully present as I continually sent my body into a stress response only to reset it. Finally, I went into an extended breath-hold, making my blood oxygen (56 percent SpO2) dip below my tissue oxygen (60 percent SmO2). After several minutes, I restored my breathing to normal and meditated, satisfied and elated in my knowledge that the same results could be produced at sea level and more or less at rest. I had gotten the answers to my questions. A master of breath can be in full control of the symphonic creation, regardless of circumstances.

If we can understand breath as a multi-dimensional tool, we will be on our way to understanding its intricacies.

At first, this viewpoint can appear overwhelming. If you are new to the world of the breath, simply start by building awareness of your breath. Overemphasizing too many details early in the process of developing any skill derails progress. Gross motions should be learned first, then refined as you build the neural and muscular pathways that reinforce good habits. **Establishing the habit of a breath practice is the most important priority.**

Once you have a handle on the fundamentals and equally important, the habit of intentionally breathing regularly, maintain curiosity and growth; refine your breathing and play with variations. Your body will adapt and re-engage focus as you add new input. This is the necessary part of development. Keeping your practice exactly the same, day in and day out, usually leads to complacency.

Your natural ability and potential both become greater as you engage regularly in a practice. Investigate how you can incorporate changes in potential. Find the balance between breadth and depth. Our reward system can be reinforced multidimensionally. Just remember that enough repetition of the fundamentals is required to go deeper.

Become the Artist, Use Science as a Guide

The best practice is a careful blend of science and art. Science became a changing force roughly 500 years ago. Once a clear, simple method to investigate questions and uncover answers was established, knowledge and technology soared in response. I am referring, of course, to the scientific method: a process by which we can establish clear boundaries for questions and answers and isolate or reduce variables to the extent that the answer has validity. The likelihood of any given result yielding meaning is increased by using such methodology. The scientific method offers a way that results can be repeated and independently verified; this verification is demanded in order for the results to be accepted as scientific canon. These checks and balances are why the scientific method is held in such high esteem and the reason that we put so much faith in the processes.

The goal of science is to deepen understanding of what actually is: an ever-reaching, ever-closer approximation of observable truth. Science does not prove things so much as create an accumulation of evidence around a given question so that the answer has the greatest probability of accuracy.

As laypeople, we often misunderstand this very nature of science and instead focus on narrow results as *proof*—only to have that proof overturned by new results, and on and on. Some of us grasp at each new proof in an increasingly chaotic fashion, tethered to the changes without really understanding the question asked, the results yielded, or the interpretation offered. Others have begun to reject science or scientific evidence due the very fact that it does change. Having both a 10,000-foot view and an up close perspective is hard for a scientist, never mind a layperson. And there are other challenges in the scientific community: keeping up with the more than 100,000 scientific studies published monthly, and dealing with various self-serving agendas that bend the rules of the scientific method to foster results that only appear to have meaning.

All of this has produced is an ever-increasing requirement that methodologies in all aspects of life be validated by scientific "proof." We are being conditioned not to trust our own observations without outside, scientific verification, and this has produced deeply mixed results. There is no doubt that we need to be aware of the good that science can offer: an independent review of data, tested by experts and free from our own internal biases. Unfortunately, not all science meets these criteria. Furthermore, it would be virtually impossible to scientifically qualify or quantify every possible question and get immediately usable answers. These are significant challenges. And, though I believe the *vast majority* of scientists are attempting to seek the truth, not all questions get to be asked or funded, and not all research conducted is published, because the answers to certain questions have greater monetary implications. It is just the way it is. We can work to improve the system, but not by denying its current truth.

For starters, we can make some headway by utilizing a variety of experts and not just accepting findings that garner headlines. Understand that humans, experts included, frequently get things wrong. This is especially true when the variables are extensive and/ or the data are limited. Listen to opposing points of view. Do a little research into each of their backgrounds to look for potential biases you should be aware of. Try to use the Internet less to prove your pre-existing idea and more to come to an informed understanding of a topic. Treat this thing we call life like a grand experiment, because it is.

Stay humble. You might know just enough to be dangerous or terribly wrong. Trust in your ability to listen and discern. And finally, especially when it comes to the health, performance, and capability of the human body, with all its complexity and variation, *use science as a guide and guardrail.* In point of fact, it is very difficult to perform a tightly controlled experiment with large groups of humans; therefore, few actually occur. So respect the forthcoming data, but also go beyond the headlines and take responsibility to investigate and experiment. Learn to optimize risk—you can't eliminate it anyway. Learn to listen to your body. And pay attention to the changes that you see. Take action and be grateful for the next scientific breakthrough.

If science pushes the boundaries of knowledge through its methodical quest to disrupt, reveal, innovate, and define, then art pushes the boundaries of life through its mission to upset, create, and imagine. Art accepts ambiguity where science does not. It allows for a range of possibilities that encompass the totality of the human experience, yet in order to *be art,* it exists as the pinnacle of expression. There is a great deal of power in art, and each field has its giants: the De Vincis of the world, the Issac Newtons, the Marie Curies, the Richard Feynmans, and the Carl Jungs. When someone displays an expression of his or her field that reaches the zenith, it is art, whether the person is a scientist, a mathematician, a painter, or a plumber.

Don't undermine the value and power of science. It has long provided humans with incredible insights and contributed greatly to our lives. Honor it and use it. Good science is disciplined and allows us to move ever closer to the truth. It can serve as a useful guide for decision making. Where you find relatively definitive evidence, act accordingly. Where there is much debate, investigate and ask why. Where there is guidance, be grateful and incorporate it. Use science.

Don't underestimate the power and value of art. Let your pursuance of art be your willingness to explore the outer reaches of every boundary. Unleash the creative power of your human spirit to unlock the potential of possibility itself. Learn to make the impossible possible. Use art. By becoming the person who reaches for the highest expression of your practice, mastery will be available to you.

Master stress, optimize your performance.
Master stress, own your health.
Master stress, elevate your relationships.
Master stress, expand your consciousness.
Master your stress response, master your life.

To master stress response is the single most important thing we can do to optimize our human potential. The key to mastering stress lies in the ability to access and guide the nervous system in highly specific ways. Survival stress tools stand at the peak of training modalities to consistently penetrate all levels and areas of the nervous system so that we can steer the stress response for intentional and positive outcomes.

The key to steering the nervous system begins and ends with mastering your breath. Know that you have the control levers within you. Practice to become adept at knowing how they operate within you as an individual.

There are many approaches that help build quality practices over a long arc. They all require discipline. Personally, I've found that curiosity drives discipline far better than virtually anything else. I've also found that for best results, curiosity should be tempered with focus. Set clear goals and remain mindful of what you are really seeking. Build a routine that you will stick with; consistency is more important than intensity.

An intentional walk, however slow, will lead you in a purposeful direction. Get curious about the path of your intentional walk. You are likely to happen upon wild discoveries and happy accidents.

FINAL THOUGHTS

Many of us struggle to either get started training, or to keep up with a training regimen once we finally get started. This can be especially true for regimens that require discomfort and the need to face our deepest fears. If you are totally unaccustomed to these types of practices and are struggling to get started or stay committed, I highly suggest listening to the spoken word album "Mastering Discomfort" (masteringdiscomfort.com).

There are things we learn over a lifetime of training that can get lost. As we begin to slow our momentum and plateau in our learning, we often lose motivation to keep practicing. Without practice, over time, we forget what we have learned. As a result, the value of what we spent our time doing decreases.

I once had a teacher who told me that motivation is a result of action. In other words, action comes first and motivation comes second. This was an odd concept when I heard it the first time, but as I look at all the practices and habits in my life, the statement resonates as true: Action often does precede motivation, and I would add, especially as practice continues.

While there may be many reasons for this truth, here is one simple neurochemical explanation. As we move toward a goal—in other words, when we take action—we are encouraged by our brain's chemical reward circuitry, most notably dopamine. However, the initial excitement of learning something new eventually subsides. Learning to stay curious about a subject and taking action to investigate and experiment allows us to stay engaged and deepen a practice.

The other side of the coin is to recognize the progress you have made and learn to find enjoyment in repeating the same thing over and over, so that you experience peace as well as depth along the way. This taps into the serotonergic circuitry, which affects personal satisfaction. Reflecting on progress and experiencing bouts of satisfaction helps to ensure that we are not constantly chasing more and losing sight of what contributes to a full practice. Finding balance between the drive circuitry and the satisfaction circuitry is really what the art of a practice is based on.

Combining the five survival stress tools offers a cohesive training platform with the necessary breadth and depth to master the stress response. Independently, the survival stress tools and breath training presented in this book are of tremendous value when fully engaged and practiced. But because each tool or practice trains nuances of our physical, mental, emotional, and chemical systems, there are limitations to what each can do on its own. They can and should serve as tools to support each other. **To master the stress response, you must stack all the tools together.** The key is to keep your training simple and consistent while respecting the rest, sleep, and recovery that will allow you to train with longevity in mind.

To those who are willing to take the time to engage with the potential of the practice and to cultivate it, it can offer benefits beyond anything you might imagine. The new you that you see in the mirror days, weeks, months, and years from now will continue to astonish you.

Book III Endnotes

1 Josh Waitzkin is author of *The Art of Learning*, a world champion chess prodigy, tai chi push hands world champion, and Brazilian jiu-jitsu blackbelt under famed Marclo Garcia.

2. Such students include those who train using only solo drills such as bag work, shield work, strikes and kicks in the air, tracking a tennis ball, or any number of other exercises, even if those exercises require some level of adaptation or reaction.

3. If you have past trauma that has not been dealt with, the body and brain can quickly default to rapid escalation, overwhelming the nervous system . It is therefore wise to tread slowly and retrain this your system in smaller increments than may be presented here. However, in principle, you can still follow these steps.

4. There are many reasons in martial arts to intentionally shift your weight in particular directions. My point is not that we should always be in a fifty-fifty weight distribution, simply what that type of balance does to the emotional space in which we operate.

5. Dr. Roger Clark, scientist and photographer, has some interesting calculations to describe the human eye: Clark R. 2018. Notes on the Resolution and Other Details of the Human Eye [online]. ClarkVision. com. Updated December 28, 2018. Available from: https://clarkvision. com/articles/eye-resolution.html.

6. Mattsoule.com covers conditions such as martial arts training, recovery, and competition, as well as confrontations ranging from verbal de-escalation attempts to the need for survival fighting.

7 The power pocket describes the space where full speed and power are supported, rather than closer to an opponent or further away. This type of training is not exclusive to muay thai; many martial arts that comprise sparring include this feature.

8. Rao V, Rosenberg P, Bertrand M, Salehinia S, Spiro J, Vaishnavi S, Rastogi P, Noll K, Schretlen DJ, Brandt J, Cornwell E, Makley M, Miles QS. 2009. Aggression after Traumatic Brain Injury: Prevalence & Cor-

relates. J Neuropsychiatry Clin Ceurosci 21(4):420-429.

9. Tsun Jo® practitioners retrain the flinch reaction and learn how to position our heads for maximum safety.

10. In this context, sticking refers to maintaining physical contact against another individual while also exerting high pressure.

11. Combat jiu-jitsu, which does include intentional head contact, is on the rise. There are also other styles that include both submission grappling and intentional head contact. My comments do not represent all individual styles or schools.

12. Tapping is the method by which you or your partner knows to stop when a submission attempt has succeeded in placing you or your opponent in a position that cannot be escaped. This is considered a submission hold. Before the joint is broken or someone is rendered unconscious, tapping signals that the person submits to the other.

13. Laukkanen T, Khan H, Zaccardi F, Laukkanen JA. 2015. Association Between Sauna Bathing and Fatal Cardiovascular and All-Cause Mortality Event. JAMA Intern Med 175(4):542-548.

14. Exceptions are extended heat exposures, such as being in a desert or participating in certain heat ceremonies that tend to last for hours.

15. Kox M, Stoffels M, Smeekens SP, van Alfen N, Gomes M, Eijsvogels TMH, Hopman MTE, van der Hoeven JG, Netea MG, Pickkers P. 2012. The influence of concentration/meditation on autonomic nervous system activity and the innate immune response: a case study. Psychosom Med 74(5):489-494.

16. Bosma-den Boer MM, van Wetten M-L, Pruimboom L. 2012. Chronic inflammatory diseases are stimulated by current lifestyle: how diet, stress levels and medication prevent our body from recovering. Nutr Metab (Lond) 9(32):https://nutritionandmetabolism.biomedcentral.com/articles/10.1186/1743-7075-9-32.

17. The trigeminal nerve is the largest and most complex of the twelve cranial nerves.

18. VICE. 2015. The Superhuman World of Wim Hof: The Iceman. https://www.youtube.com/watch?v=VaMjhwFE1Zw. 39:43.

19. For an introductory tutorial, the WHM organization offers a free app available on IOS and Android.

20. At the advanced module, we dug into Wim Hof's 2012 published case study (Kox et al. 2012), wherein a two-minute ice bath at around 32°F enabled him to shift his inflammatory markers for six days. I learned *why* the breathing itself was affecting (i.e., reducing) my inflammation and the speed at which I was healing physically.

Next we looked at the 2014 WHM endotoxin study (Kox et al. 2014), during which Wim demonstrated substantial reductions in pro-inflammatory cytokines while increasing anti-inflammatory markers through breathing techniques. The study concluded that this could have important implications for addressing a number of conditions associated with "excessive or persistent inflammation." It went on to note that the implications could be highly relevant to autoimmune disorders by which the body's immune and inflammatory response is highly overactive and thus counterproductive.

21. One of the primary health principles in the Russian martial art systema is to strengthen the body by dousing it with cold water. There are many cultures, Nordic, Turkish, and others, that regularly and ritualistically engage in cold water ceremonies of one kind or another. There are also Yogic practices, such as *Kundalini*, that tout cold as a beneficial practice exercise.

22. For more about *Shugendō*, check out "Initiation in the Shugendō: the Passage Through the Ten States of Existence: Blacker C. 1965. Initiation in the Shugendo: The Passage through the Ten States of Existence. In: Initiation. Vol 10. Numen Book Series. pp 96-111. Available from: https://doi.org/10.1163/9789004378018_013.

23. *Furitama*, or "spirit shaking" is practiced while standing with the legs shoulder-width apart. The hands are placed together with the left hand over the right. A small space is left between the hands. The hands

are placed in front of the abdomen and shaken vigorously up and down. The practitioner inhales to the top of the head rising up naturally, then exhales to the bottom of the feet, continuing to shake your hands up and down.

24. In some rare cases, jumping into extremely cold water can cause a heart attack, due in part to the rapid vasoconstriction that occurs and the simultaneous sympathetic and parasympathetic inverse responses to cold water. Such a response is typically associated with underlying heart conditions.

25. NWSC. 2020. 1-10-1 Principle [online]. National Water Safety Congress. Available from: https://nationalwatersafetycongress.wildapricot.org/1-10-1.

26. NWSC. 2020. Cold Water Immersion: A Hands-on Approach. Instructor manual [online]. National Water Safety Congress. Available from: https://nationalwatersafetycongress.wildapricot.org/resources/Documents/Instructor_Manual_ColdWaterImmersion_Final.pdf.

27. USSARTF. 2020. Cold Water Survival [online]. US Search and Rescue Task Force. Available from: http://www.ussartf.org/cold_water_survival.htm.

28. The HPT axis (the T standing for thyroid in this case) is also indirectly involved in cold exposure. For more on this, see: Rondeel JMM, de Greef WJ, Hop WCJ, Rowland DL, Visser TJ. 1991. Effect of Cold Exposure on the Hypothalamic Release of Thyrotropin-Releasing Hormone and Catecholamines. Neuroendocrinology 54:477-481.

29. Certain types of fasting have been shown to also contribute to the beiging of white fat through non-shivering thermogenesis. For more information, see:

Thyagarajan B, Foster MT. 2017. Beiging of white adipose tissue as a therapeutic strategy for weight loss in humans. Horm Mol Biol Clin Investig 31(2):/j/hmbci.2017.31.issue-2/hmbci-2017-0016/hmbci-2017-0016.xml. doi: 10.1515/hmbci-2017-0016. PMID: 28672737.

Finlin BS, Memetimin H, Confides AL, Kasza I, Zhu B, Vekaria HJ, Harfmann B, Jones KA, Johnson ZR, Westgate PM, Alexander CM, Sullivan PG, Dupont-Versteegden EE, Kern PA. 2018. Human adipose beiging in response to cold and mirabegron. JCI Insight 3(15):e121510. https://doi.org/10.1172/jci.insight.121510.

30. Leppaluoto J, Westerlund T, Huttunen P, Oksa J, Smolander J, Dugue B, Mikkelsson M. 2008. Effects of long-term whole-body cold exposures on plasma concentrations of ACTH, beta-endorphin, cortisol, catecholamines and cytokines in healthy females. Scandinavian Journal of Clinical and Laboratory Investigation 68(2):145-153.

31. Keep in mind, Wim is one of the most seasoned practitioners.

32. Roberts LA, Raastad T, Markworth JF, Figueiredo VC, Egner IM, Shield A, Cameron-Smith D, Coombes JS, Peake JM. 2015. Post-exercise cold water immersion attenuates acute anabolic signalling and long-term adaptations in muscle to strength training. J Physiology 593(18):https://doi.org/10.1113/JP270570.

33. Ouellet V, Labbe SM, Blondin DP, Phoenix S, Guerin B, Haman F, Turcotte EE, Richard D, Carpentier AC. 2012. Brown adipose tissue oxidative metabolism contributes to energy expenditure during acute cold exposure in humans. J Clin Invest 122(2):545-552.

34. Lee P, Linderman JD, Smith S, Brychta RJ, Wang J, Idelson C, Perron RM, Werner CD, Phan GQ, Kammula US, Kebebew E, Pacak K, Chen KY, Celi F. 2014. Irisin and FGF21 Are Cold-Induced Endocrine Activators of Brown Fat Function in Humans. Cell Metabolism 19(2):302-309.

Dana-Farber Cancer Institute. 2015. New study confirms presence of exercise-induced hormone in humans [online]. Updated August 13, 2015. Available from: https://www.dana-farber.org/newsroom/news-releases/2015/new-study-confirms-presence-of-exercise-induced-hormone-in-humans/.

35. Although extremely rare, there have been incidents of users inhaling

excessive nitrogen in cryochambers. Because these devices cool air using nitrogen, if the surrounding area is not sufficiently ventilated, it can pose a serious risk.

36. Freezers cost around $300 to $500 at most big box stores, and they cost about $1 per day to run.

37. To convert a freezer, you line the corners with marine-grade silicone and fill it with enough water that you can submerse yourself but not so much that it will overflow once you are in. To keep the water clean, a little bromine goes a long way. Magnesium salt will also help keep it clean and allow you to get temperatures lower than 32°F without having a freezer full of block ice. Of course, you will need to change the water from time to time.

38. You can buy a laser temperature reader for as little as $15 on Amazon.

39. Definitions of fasting vary throughout literature, experiments, and expert advice. I have chosen the definition of more than twenty-four hours for this book because it is supported by research as being associated with specific benefits.

40. Grigg D. 1981. The Historiography of Hunger: Changing Views on the World Food Problem 1945-1980. Transactions of the Institute of British Geographers 6(3):279-292.

41. Work done by Amartya Kumar Sen and others has shown that limits in food production are now secondary to problems arising from food distribution. In other words, we have enough food to feed the global population, but challenges around food distribution account for a significant percentage of the approximately 815 million hungry/chronically undernourished people worldwide: WHES. 2020. 2018 world hunger and poverty facts and statistics [online]. World Hunger Education Service. Available from: https://www.worldhunger.org/world-hunger-%20 and-poverty-facts-and-statistics/.

42. CDC. 2020. Adult obesity facts [online]. Centers for Disease Control

and Prevention. Updated June 29, 2020. Available from: https://www. cdc.gov/obesity/data/adult.html.

CDC. 2019. Childhood obesity facts [online]. Centers for Disease Control and Prevention. Updated June 24, 2019. Available from: https:// www.cdc.gov/obesity/data/childhood.html.

43. For a useful review of different types of fasting and time-restricted eating, please see: Patterson RE, Laughlin GA, Sears DD, LaCroix AZ, Marinac C, Gallo LC, Hartman SJ, Natarajan L, Senger CM, Martinez ME, Villasenor A. 2015. Intermittent fasting and human metabolic health. J Acad Nutr Diet 115(8):1203-1212.

44. Browning KN, Travagli RA. 2014. Central Nervous System Control of Gastrointestinal Motility and Secretion and Modulation of Gastrointestinal Functions. Compr Physiol 4(4):1339-1368.

Um SH, D'Alessio D, Thomas GL. 2006. Nutrient overload, insulin resistance, and ribosomal protein S6 kinase 1, S6K1. Cell Metabolism 3(6):393-402.

45. Melatonin is largely produced and found in the gastrointestinal tract. However, that melatonin appears to have different functionality than melatonin in the brain. See: Chen C-Q, Fichna J, Bashashati M, Li Y-Y, Storr M. 2006. Distribution, function and physiological role of melatonin in the lower gut. World J Gastroenterol 17(34):3888-3898.

46. For a full treatise on sleep, read Matthew Walker's *Why We Sleep.* See also: Schmidt MH, Swang TW, Hamilton IM, Best JA. 2017. State-dependent metabolic partitioning and energy conservation: A theoretical framework for understanding the function of sleep. PLoS ONE 12(10):10.1371/journal.pone.0185746.

47. This assumes a diet that includes carbohydrates. If you eat an exclusively carnivore diet or a very low-carbohydrate diet, you already operate on a primarily gluconeogenesis platform.

48. Widmaier EP, Raff H, Strang KT. 2003. Vander, Sherman, Luciano's Human Physiology: The Mechanisms of Body Function. 9th ed.

Mcgraw-Hill (Tx).

49. This assumes no underlying health conditions and sufficient water available to drink.

50. Any number of doctors are putting forth large amounts of evidence to support the benefits of fasting. For example, see: Longo VD, Panda S. 2016. Fasting, circadian rhythms, and time restricted feeding in healthy lifespan. Cell Metabolism 23(6):1048-1059.

You might also want to look at Dr. Rhonda Patrick's interviews with other experts on fasting: Patrick R. 2020. Fasting [online]. FoundMyFitness. Available from: https://www.foundmyfitness.com/topics/fasting.

51. Mihaylova MM, Cheng C-W, Cao AQ, Tripathi S, Mana MD, Bauer-Rowe KE, Abu-Remaileh M, Clavain L, Erdemir A, Lewis CA, Freinkman E, Dickey AS, La Spada AR, Huang Y, Bell GW, Deshpande V, Carmeliet P, Katajisto P, Sabatini DM, Yilmaz OH. 2018. Fasting Activates Fatty Acid Oxidation to Enhance Intestinal Stem Cell Function during Homeostasis and Aging. Cell Stem Cell 3(22):469-778.

52. DMT stands for dimethyltryptamine.

53. I set my alarm as an "oh shit" back up in case I don't wake naturally.

54. E and X are the initials of my daughter and the woman who was then my partner.

55. Henning SM, Yang J, Shao P, Lee R-P, Huang J, Ly A, Hsu M-H, Lu Q-L, Thames G, Heber D, Li Z. 2017. Health benefit of vegetable/fruit juice-based diet: Role of microbiome. Sci Rep 7(1):2167.

56. High metabolic breathing methods include WHM and certain Yogic practices.

57. The previously described HPT circuit also indirectly influences many sex hormones.

58. There are other important sex hormones besides testosterone. However, this discussion of hormones is simplified in an effort to focus the topic at hand.

59. Straftis A, Gray PB. 2019. Sex, Energy, Well-Being and Low Testosterone: An Exploratory Survey of U.S. Men's Experiences on Prescription Testosterone. J Environ Res Public Health 16(18):3261.

60. Travison TG, Araujo AB, O'Donnell AB, Kupelian V, McKinlay JB. 2007. A Population-Level Decline in Serum Testosterone Levels in American Men. JCEM 92(1):196-202.

Nordal E. 2010. Testosterone levels decreasing in Danish men [online]. Icenews. Updated May 17, 2010. Available from: https://www.icenews.is/2010/05/17/testosterone-levels-decreasing-in-danish-men/?cookie-state-change=1606706422706.

61. I include this discussion of vasopressin with regard to males because it has a larger overall effect on that gender, due to naturally higher testosterone production. However, these same functions occur in females as well.

62. For example, men with abnormally high testosterone have been shown to be at increased risk of strokes, heart attacks, blood clots, hardened arteries, and heart failure: Luo S, Yeung SLA, Zhao JV, Burgess S, Schooling CM. 2019. Association of genetically predicted testosterone with thromboembolism, heart failure, and myocardial infarction: mendelian randomisation study in UK Biobank. BMJ 364:https://doi.org/10.1136/bmj.l476

63. Missmer SA, Eliassen AH, Barbieri RL, Hankinson SE. 2004. Endogenous Estrogen, Androgen, and Progesterone Concentrations and Breast Cancer Risk Among Postmenopausal Women. Journal of the National Cancer Institue 96(24):1856-1865.

Wharton W, Gleason CE, Olson SRMS, Carlsson CM, Asthana S. 2012. Neurobiological Underpinnings of the Estrogen-Mood Relationship. Curr Psychiatry Rev 8(3):247-256.

Stefanick ML. 2005. Estrogens and progestins: background and history, trends in use, and guidelines and regimens approved by the US Food and Drug Administration. The American Journal of Medicine 118(12):64-73.

64. Veale D, Miles S, Bramley S, Muir G, Hodsoll J. 2014. Am I normal? A systematic review and construction of nomograms for flaccid and erect penis length and circumference in up to 15 521 men. BJUI 115(6):https://doi.org/10.1111/bju.13010.

BUMC. 2020. Female genital anatomy [online]. Boston University School of Medicine. Available from: https://www.bumc.bu.edu/sexual-medicine/physicianinformation/female-genital-anatomy/.

65. Note that this does not include the whole vagina. Except in certain places, there are fewer nerves inside the vagina and for good reason, most notably childbirth. Nature is cruel but not entirely crazy.

66. Achieving orgasm via stimulation of the pubis alone is thought to be possible because the clitoris is situated at the lower edge of the pubis. When the pubis is stimulated, it can generate an indirect stretching of the vulva and clitoris, making the entire zone more sensitive.

67. Due to the location of the G-spot relative to the urethral gland, it may also be related to female ejaculation during orgasm.

68. In women, the Skene's glands are sometimes referred to as the female prostate, but anatomically they have many differences.

69. Be mindful that anal intercourse may also produce pain due to the involuntary contractions after stimulation of the muscles that surround the anus.

70. De-binding is a method that allows you to engage the nervous system to release protective tension. This is done using a combination of specific body positions, gravity, breathing, and mindfulness. For videos and a full tutorial, please visit mattsoule.com.

71. Read works by Esther Perel for a full meditation on this subject.

72. Although significant overlap often exists, because these three components are by my own definition, they likely will not be wholly interchangeable with others' definitions and descriptions.

73. The alveoli are small, air-containing compartments of the lungs in

which the bronchioles terminate and from which respiratory gases are exchanged with the pulmonary capillaries.

74. Be sure to breathe slowly enough to avoid lightheadedness. This will vary from person to person and also change with time and practice.

75. Heme is a substance precursive to hemoglobin; heme is biosynthesized in both the bone marrow and the liver.

76. EPO is like any other component of the body in that too little or too much over an extended period of time is often detrimental.

77. Mantra-like chants can also be used when shooting a bow or practicing precision shooting. Expert Joel Turner, for example, instructs his students to use a rhythmic mantra, such as *here I go*, as they slowly move through the final action of releasing the arrow or pressing the trigger.

78. The exception could be during exercises at altitude for highly experienced practitioners or for other specific applications.

ACKNOWLEDGEMENTS

I have to start by thanking my daughter, Evie, who has been remarkably supportive, allowing me extended periods of time to write, deep think, and push forward. Completing this book has been perhaps one of the most difficult things I have ever done in my life. The time, sacrifices, setbacks, and barriers to overcome to accomplish this project were far more numerous than I had imagined. *Thank you, Evie.*

To my teachers...

John Beall, aka Brother John, you have been one of the most influential figures in my life. Thank you for your friendship, with its countless hours spent exploring every health topic, consciousness development strategies, practical advice, emotional support, and more, but thank you most of all for your teaching. Thank you for your dedication to creating the Tsun Jo® system, and for helping me reach thousands of students to share this beautifully engineered system. You have shaped my way of thinking and it has bled into every area of my life: principle-based understandings, stacking advantages, how to determine high-percentage outcomes, improved decision-making skills, expansion of consciousness…the list could go on and on. I have grown so much because of you.

Wim Hof (and Isabelle, Laura, Enahm and Michael), I'm grateful for all the insights and inspiration and for giving me the key to unlock one of life's mysteries. I am eternally appreciative. Thank you for allowing me to help teach your incredible method, and for opportunities to travel around the world sharing powerful transformational work with so many people.

Thank you to these teachers and others who have pushed me to think differently.

To my book team...

Without all of you, this book would be a fraction of what it is.

I want to thank the beta readers—Brad LaMar, Alex MacLeod, Fiona Morgan, Jake Levine, Dr. Ariadna Uriarte, and John Beall—for your invaluable support and feedback in making this book the best it could be.

Thank you Jenny MacLeod for your hours of consulting, organized checklists, design, feedback, emotional support and encouragement, and thoughtfulness at every turn. You have been truly fantastic to work with these many months. Thank you for believing in this project and pushing it ever forward. I couldn't have done it without you.

Thank you Yakup Trana of Seattle Creative Works for your beautiful designs, logos, branding choices; thank you for the book cover, the artwork, and the graphs and charts, all which were elegant and clear.

Thank you to my editor, Shana Schorsch, with whom it has been an absolute pleasure to work. Thank you for making my ideas clear and concise, and for helping me to express each concept with precision. Thank you for elevating my voice. I'm forever grateful.

To Dr. Ariadna Uriarte, thank you for your foreword and your answers to the hundreds of medical, conceptual, and scientific questions I have asked you. Thank you for setting up conversations with your colleagues Drs. Enrique Santillan Aguayo and Alicia Miranda Vargas, who were instrumental in clarifying concepts around vascular physiology and breathing. Thank you for reading and giving early feedback, challenging my concepts, and offering insight. Thank you for teaching me so much. I am so grateful for all you have done.

To my colleagues, friends and students...

I want to thank Jake Levine for the countless hours, experiments, conversations, support, and challenges in investigating root connections among so many seemingly disparate subjects. Jake has supported me emotionally and challenged me physically and mentally to be better; his clear and timely feedback on each part and concept of this book has been irreplaceable. Thank you for always reaching to break down complex concepts into simple, actionable parts. I'm grateful for more than I could ever list, brother.

I want to thank Kelly Peters for personal advice and help through many of my life's most stressful moments. The hours you spent challenging me on a wide range of topics with level-headed clarity contributed to this book. And I want to thank Scott Kim for his support and help in pushing through life's obstacles. Our searches helped lead me here. Thank you, brothers.

I want to thank Dr. Trisha Smith (aka Doc Trish) for all of her insights into cold training, breathing, teaching, and performance. Your friendship and career support have been so valuable. I want to thank Kasper van der Meulen for his teaching and lectures in the Wim Hof Method.

I want to thank Jay Sachdev for helping me run various experiments with breathing protocols and sparring. The results proved to be so helpful in validating or calling into question many concepts that contributed to this book.

I want to thank Cliff Gomes for his assistance with leading people into the cold waters of the Pacific Northwest during so many of my workshops. He has been an anchor I've known I could count on. I also want to thank him for his incredibly adept mind and insights in helping me expand my own consciousness, working to solidify ideas around teaching meditative practices, and ensuring that I've held fast to my center while keeping my feet firmly on the ground.

I want to thank Dr. Nicholas Andrews for answering questions on physiology and putting me in contact with his colleague, vascular specialist Dr. Tom Resta. And thank you, Dr. Resta, for taking time out of your schedule to answer my questions on the vascular system.

I want to thank my students Geneva Neubauer, Jacob Greenleaf, Fernando Martinez, Chris Carsley, Zavere Weeks, Scott Sanchez, Fiona Morgan, Jef Faulkner, Gaelle Sabben, Jason Thams, Marc Amsberry, Brian Biladeau, and so many others. Thank you to all of you for your questions, feedback, dedication, and insights; you each have challenged me to become a better teacher and a forever student. Your contributions have significantly shaped this book.

I want to thank the Kili Crew—Pi, Marcin, Rafa, Steven, Dustin, Sergio, Mark, Raul H., Raul R., Natalie, Bart, and Jozef—for inviting me to participate in one of the most challenging and rewarding experiences of my life. Thank you for your planning, insights, willingness to experiment, grit, determination, interviews, and power of the human spirit. I want to thank Salim for his willingness to take a large risk on the mountain to help us summit in incredible time, as well as all of our team support from Climbing Kilimanjaro tour company. You guys were amazing, to say the least.

To my family...

I want to thank my mother for being a forever optimist and encourager of my pursuits; I am thankful for the thousands of sacrifices she has made to help me accomplish my goals and aspirations.

Thank you to my late father, Andrew, who always demanded the most from me, taught me to hold myself to the highest standard, and taught me to search for calm in the chaos of life.

I want to thank my brother, Joey, who helped out at a moment's notice so that I could work to meet deadlines.

I want to thank my uncle Duncan for sending me information on cold exposure and warrior-tribe living, and for his instruction in hunting and other critical tutelage.

I want to thank my cousin Evan for his help in creating website content, clarifying my messaging, and challenging me to be succinct in my own writing.

I want to thank my uncle Don for his business advice and for his support during a pivotal point in my career allowing this book to be possible.

I want to thank my aunt Suzanne for her help with my daughter, as well as her keen advice through many of the most stressful moments of my life.

I want to thank my uncle Carson for inspiring me to take a scientific approach to problems and showing me early on how fun conducting experiments can be.

I want to thank my sister, Lady, for always encouraging and believing in me. I am grateful for how she has inspired me to look at the world through the artist's eye. I also want to thank her and her partner, Michael, who have helped with my daughter and assisted me as I labored over this book.

I want to thank my step-father, Ed, one of my strongest and earliest influences to examine life from a principle-based approach, and to determine why certain concepts have advantages over others. Our hours of conversation applying this concept to financial markets, products, and services have had a profound impact on my thinking and ability to select appropriate criteria for evaluation. Ed's guidance has stirred me to search for root connections everywhere.

This book would not have been possible without all of you.

With gratitude,
Matt

Table of Figures

Book Credits and Information

Foreword | Dr. Ariadna Uriarte

Cover and Graphic Designer | Yakup Trana

Interior Book Design | Jenny MacLeod

Editor | Shana Schorsch

Typography

Body text was set in Times New Roman, size 10.5
Headings are in Euclid Circular B, with punctuation
and numerals borrowed from Futura

MATT SOULE

MATT SOULE IS an entrepreneur, writer, speaker, and professional instructor focusing on *survival stress tools*™ that develop peak individual potential. He is a black sash and certified instructor of Tsun Jo® under system founder, John N. Beall. Matt was certified in the Wim Hof Method with the first group of U.S. instructors learning directly from Wim. Matt lives with his daughter in Seattle, Washington, and takes a cold shower every day.

Workshops and more resources can be found at:

@soulemd | mattsoule.com

Made in the USA
Coppell, TX
30 January 2021

49167831R00204